SPAG

SPAG

An American Business Legend

Elsa B. Tivnan
and
Catherine I. Nickerson

CHANDLER HOUSE PRESS

WORCESTER, MA

SPAG: AN AMERICAN BUSINESS LEGEND
Copyright © 1999 by ELSA B. TIVNAN and CATHERINE I. NICKERSON

ISBN 1-886284-54-7
Library of Congress Catalog Card Number 99-067103
First Edition
ABCDEFGHIJK

Published by
Chandler House Press
335 Chandler Street
Worcester, MA 01602
USA

President
Lawrence J. Abramoff

Editorial/Production Manager
James A. Karis II

Book and Jacket Design
Michele Italiano-Perla

Map Illustrations
Kathleen Hughes Sumpter

Cover Photo
B.A. King

Chandler House Press books are available at special discounts for bulk purchases. For more information about how to arrange such purchases, please contact Chandler House Press, 335 Chandler Street, Worcester, MA 01602, or call (800) 642-6657, or fax (508) 756-9425, or find us on the World Wide Web at www.chandlerhousepress.com.

Chandler House Press books are distributed to the trade by
National Book Network, Inc.
4720 Boston Way
Lanham, MD 20706
(800) 462-6420

—Tom Keegan

In loving memory of my mother, Brigida, whose serenity, courage, and understanding of human nature inspired those who knew her. Her gentle influence has left a continuing legacy.

CONTENTS

Acknowledgments

First and foremost, I wish to thank Catherine Nickerson. I am mindful that her abounding enthusiasm and unstinting assistance were paramount in bringing Anthony's biography to fruition.

Working with Elin Woodger, my editor, was a pleasure. I appreciated her warmth, sensitivity, and expertise as she patiently helped Cathie and me to refine the manuscript for publication.

I am very grateful to Peggy McNary and Linda Miller, who spent many long hours editing the manuscript while it was in progress—and also to Clif Nickerson for his computer expertise and the digitizing of the photos.

My gratitude also goes to my brother, Anthony, for entrusting the writing of his story to me. Further gratitude for their thoughtful insights goes to Mary Borgatti, Joseph E. Sullivan and Steve Tankinow, Anthony's close friends and business colleagues; and to Nora Hakim, my life-long friend.

Many thanks to my brother Bobbie and my nieces, Carol, Jean, and Sandy for their encouragement. I also appreciated the assistance of John Cullen, Bob Lutz, and Mary Donovan. Whenever I needed to check out some facts, all I had to do was pick up the phone and call Vinnie Mastro. Thank you, Vinnie. And thank you Judy Pickett and Marie Wolik for so cheerfully finding answers to my frequent inquiries. My thanks also go to Dale Fair, Lucy Ward, and Arthur Dobson for taking the time to write their interesting accounts, portions of which have been included to provide colorful detail.

Special thanks go to Kathy Bocon, my neighbor, for transcribing audiotapes and countless pages of my scribbled notes. My gratitude goes also to the SPAG'S store family, customers, salespeople, friends, and acquaintances who generously shared their experiences and recollections. Due to space constraints, they are not acknowledged individually.

In conclusion, I wish to thank Jim, my fine husband, for his patience and understanding. He was behind me all the way, and he's the one who made it possible for me to maintain my focus on this project.

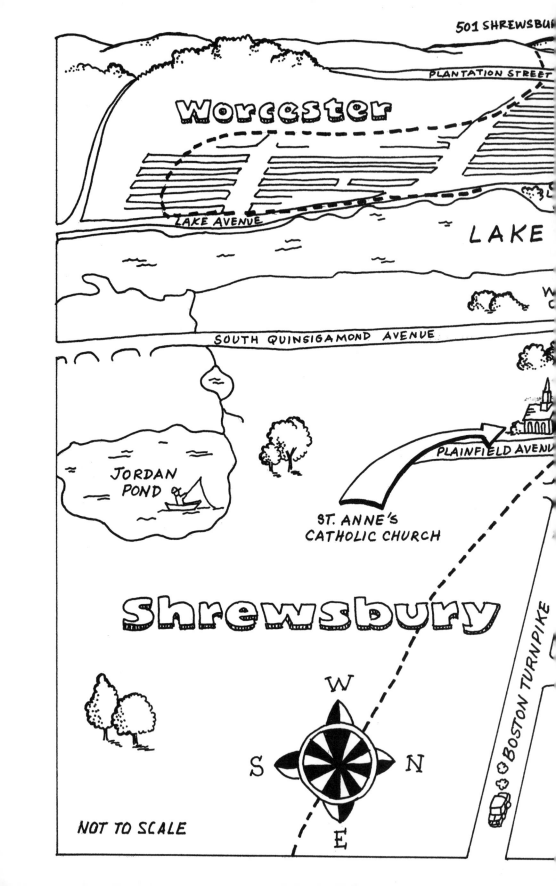

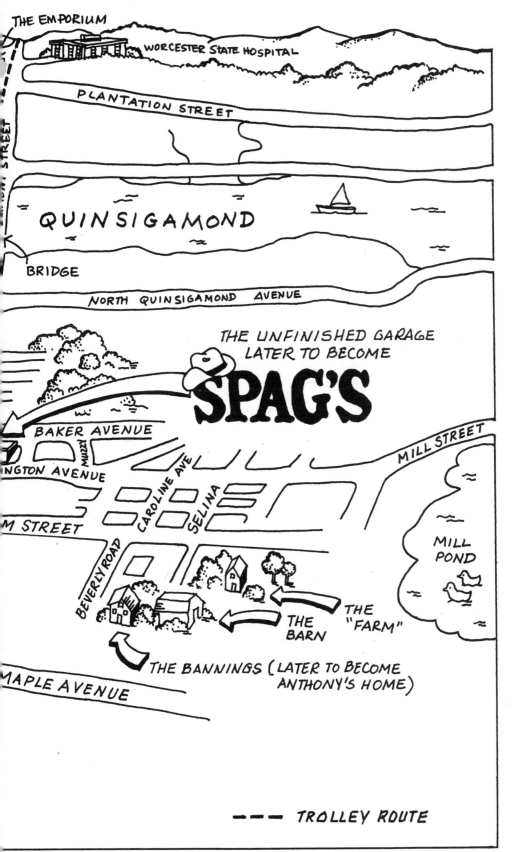

THE EMPORIUM

WORCESTER STATE HOSPITAL

PLANTATION STREET

QUINSIGAMOND

BRIDGE

NORTH QUINSIGAMOND AVENUE

THE UNFINISHED GARAGE
LATER TO BECOME

SPAG'S

BAKER AVENUE

MILL STREET

NGTON AVENUE

MUZZY

CAROLINE AVE

SELINA

M STREET

BEVERLY ROAD

MILL
POND

THE
"FARM"

THE
BARN

THE BANNINGS (LATER TO BECOME
ANTHONY'S HOME)

MAPLE AVENUE

--- TROLLEY ROUTE

—The source was a map from the collections of Worcester Historical Museum, Worcester, Massachusetts.

Preface

In his later years, my brother Anthony ("Spag") frequently mentioned that he intended to write a book about his store, SPAG'S Supply, Inc., and all the wonderful people in his life. But since he preferred talking to writing, he never began the project.

I prodded him several times about getting started with his book, because I thought that he had an interesting story to tell. When his health began to deteriorate, I could see that he simply did not have the energy. Consequently, I suggested that we work on the book together. The idea pleased him, but due to his failing health, he rarely thought about it.

One day, I asked him, "Would you like me to try to write your story?" I sensed his relief when he replied, "Well, that will be very nice, Elsa. I have a folder called 'Book' and a carton with things in it that I want to include."

In the folder and carton, I found letters, greeting cards, printed programs, notes Anthony had written on paper scraps, newspaper clippings, magazine articles, and photographs. I drew upon these, along with my personal recollections and the many stories I learned from others to begin what would become a true labor of love.

Shortly after I embarked on this project, Anthony became seriously ill and died, leaving me with the task of writing his story without his input. Encouraged by family and friends, I resumed work on the book with a determined effort. I have found that writing about my brother's life has been a challenge full of pleasant experiences and several surprises. It seems as though just about everyone who has ever known Anthony has a "Spag" story to tell. On reading or hearing these stories, I learned that my brother's legacy was more than that of generosity and business acumen; to many he had become, even with his shortcomings, a role model, a mentor, and a legend.

I should not have been surprised, however. When Anthony and I were in our teens, Mother, in one of those many precious moments when we shared our deepest thoughts, had said, "Anthony is going to accomplish great things, and always his purity is going to radiate from within." She paused and then continued, "You will be able to watch his accomplishments as they unfold over the years, and you will be proud of him."

If Anthony knew about Mother's prediction, he would have answered modestly, "Oh, I don't know about that. All mothers think their kids are great."

Years later, when reporters and friends asked Anthony about his secret to success, he usually replied, "We worked hard, and we were lucky. But you can turn negatives into positives. It's how you respond to life's challenges that makes the difference."

My challenge has been to fully convey Anthony's multi-faceted personality. Not everything came up roses for him; he had his trials and tribulations, and he had his flaws. One of Anthony's shortcomings was his liberal use of earthy and sometimes startling expletives. In fairness to Anthony and to preserve the integrity of the book, I reluctantly have set aside my personal objections and have told it the way it was.

Since I found that Anthony's relationships with others (his employees, customers, salespeople, and friends) were best described by them, in many cases I have allowed these people to speak for themselves. From their many letters and stories, a strong portrait of Anthony emerges. Regrettably, the material included represents but a mere sampling of what has been received, and as we go to press, additional stories continue to arrive. I only wish we could publish them all.

—*Elsa B. Twnan*

Guilty As Charged!

I fought against the unjust Fair Trade law always.
—Spag

My husband, Jim, was stocking shelves next to the checkout counter at SPAG'S Supply, Inc., when Anthony, my brother and the store's owner, came to take over one of the three cash registers. Standing there in his usual working garb of khaki shirt and pants, and topped by a ten-gallon hat that made him look taller than his 5'5", Anthony's blue eyes twinkled behind his rimless spectacles as he smiled and greeted Jim.

"Filling in for Joe," he said. Jim smiled back. He knew that Anthony liked "filling in" at the checkout counter; it gave him a chance to visit with his employees and customers.

"Anthony and I were chatting," Jim later recalled, "when a deputy sheriff, an acquaintance of ours, entered and greeted us. After his breezy 'hello,' he handed Anthony a court summons and quickly disappeared." Jim waited while my brother read the summons.

"Looks like I gotta go to court in Boston on the fair trade baloney," Anthony said casually as he folded the summons and placed it in his shirt pocket, behind his spiral pad and pencils.

"That's the law that requires you to sell products at the prices set by the manufacturer, isn't it?" Jim asked.

"Yeah! What right do they have telling me at what price I have to sell my stuff? I paid them the price they asked. I should be able to set my own prices."

"Who filed the complaint, Anthony? That sports supplier?"

"Yeah, you know I've been expecting this. Their salesman told me that someone from the sporting goods store in the city has been complaining to their supplier. They don't like competing with our prices."

"So they're taking you to court?" Jim asked.

"The hell with them! Let 'em take me to court. I'll go, and I'll fight it!" Anthony replied vehemently as he turned to wait on a customer who was approaching his checkout counter.

I learned about Anthony's court summons later that afternoon. I had taken my mother and sister Olga for a ride through the country, and we had just returned to Mother's for a cup of tea. We were sitting in the den when we heard Anthony's familiar whistle. He was dropping in on one of his daily visits to Mother. As he plunked himself into a comfortable chair, he was his usual chatty self, filling us in on what had been going on in his day—the salesmen he had seen, the pace of the business at the store, and so on. Then he pushed his ten-gallon hat back off his forehead, revealing a tuft of honey-colored hair, and nonchalantly mentioned, "Just got a summons to appear in court."

The thought of Anthony going to court was unsettling. I blurted out, "What for?"

"I've been selling stuff at reduced prices! That's what's for! But I knew this was coming. Various stores in the area have been sending in their 'shoppers' to check our prices, and we've been getting their complaints."

Listening intently, Olga leaned forward in her wheelchair, wide-eyed. "What will they do to you, Anthony?" she asked anxiously.

"I don't know yet, but they're not gonna stop me!"

Mother sat serenely in her rocking chair, listening quietly as the conversation continued.

Still perturbed by the news, I asked, "Will you have to raise your prices on all those items?"

"Hell, no!" Anthony's response was quick. "The prices will stay just as they are marked!" Shaking his forefinger to emphasize his point, he added, "Let 'em take me to court. I'll go, and I'll fight that Fair Trade law. The working man needs a break. I sell at prices he can afford. And I'm gonna fight it all the way!"

Then Mother spoke, saying, "You do what you think is right, Anthony."

Anthony's Way

For my brother, Anthony Borgatti, Jr.—known as "Spag" to everyone
outside his family—doing what was right invariably translated into
doing things his way, whether or not it was the conventionally accepted way. This was true in how he approached both his business and his
personal life. He dared to be different, and he didn't care what others
thought or said, as long as he thought it was right. As a result, thousands of people benefited from his unique way of thinking—the customers who shopped at his store, the employees and vendors who
worked with him, the friends and strangers on whom he bestowed acts
of generosity, and the family members who were gifted by his presence
in their lives. He found pleasure in doing for others.

For instance, there was the quiet joy he took in giving, whether it
was providing "spagtacular" bargains for his customers, helping people
in need, or simply being there for others—such as the patients at the
Shrewsbury Nursing Home, where he was a regular visitor. I didn't
realize how popular he had become at the nursing home until one day,
when I was visiting there. As I was walking down the corridor on my
way to see a resident friend, I heard music; it was a Viennese waltz. I
paused at the door of the lounge, as one might do, to see what was
going on.

The music was coming from a television set; Lawrence Welk's
orchestra was performing. A capacity audience filled the room.
Around the perimeter of the room, some residents were in wheelchairs; those who were ambulatory (mostly ladies) were in chairs that
formed a semi-circle in front of the wheelchairs. In the center of the
room, there was an open area, and who do you suppose was on the
floor dancing? None other than my big brother, waltzing to his heart's
content with one of the resident ladies.

Their "mini-dance" was in progress. Everyone was beaming.
Judging from the big smile on Anthony's face, he was in his glory. His
partner's smile told me that she was having a great time, too. The
other ladies, graciously waiting their turn to dance with Anthony,
were swaying and waving their hands to the music.

I continued on toward my friend's room. As I passed the staff's
desk, I stopped to tell the nurse about my pleasant surprise.

"Oh," she replied, "Spag comes here every Saturday afternoon for

Lawrence Welk. We know if he isn't here, it's because he just couldn't make it. It's the highlight of their week. They listen for his whistle as he steps off the elevator. When they hear it, they smile; they know then that he's heading for the lounge where they're waiting for him."

Anthony had many ways of making people smile. Take the way he approached the game of golf. Playing with Anthony was a riot. He played, but he never kept score. When he hit a ball out of bounds, which he was prone to do, he would say, "Oh, the hell with it!" Then, as he reached into his pocket for another ball and dropped it on the fairway, he would add, "They make golf balls every day." When playing a game with Anthony, no one could take it seriously.

Doing things his way meant injecting elements of fun and surprise into everything Anthony did, whether it was wearing an unusual hat or tie, giving away tomato plants, thrusting chocolates and flowers on strangers, or making unusual purchases for the store—like the suit of armor he once put on display. Looking at it, one skeptical employee asked, "Who will buy that?"

Anthony replied, "There are so many customers that come through this store. Someone is bound to like it."

"If no one does buy it, then what?" asked the clerk.

"If it doesn't sell, I'll be throwing my own money away," Anthony replied.

Amazingly, it sold! But that probably didn't surprise my brother too much. He had a gift when it came to buying items for the store, from basic staples to the unique; his customers snapped them up. And he had a gift for delighting not just his customers but also his vendors. One of my favorite stories about Anthony was told to me by my sister-in-law, Mary Borgatti:

> The phone rang; it was Anthony. "Mary, come down to the house," he said, "I think I have something here you'll be interested in." Knowing Anthony well, I put aside my work in the real estate office and hurried down to the office in his house.
>
> When I arrived, Middle Eastern music was blaring forth from the Hi-Fi set in the family room. Someone had pushed aside the furniture to make room for a pile of rolled-up Oriental rugs. Mr. Aram

of the Brookline Oriental Rug Company was standing while his two assistants unrolled the rugs, one at a time.

There, in the middle of the room, was Anthony wearing a turban—a Turkish towel wrapped around his head—singing and dancing to the exotic music. Waving his arms as he whirled and twirled, he performed his version of an Arabian belly dance. It was hysterically funny. He was having the best time!

Mr. Aram and his assistants were laughing—thoroughly amused by what was going on. This was their first meeting with "Mr. Spag," as they called Anthony, and their first invitation to his house. As Anthony danced, the assistants chuckled and continued to methodically unroll the rugs, one at a time, and pile them on top of each other. The mound of displayed rugs grew.

I looked at Anthony, but he did not stop to speak; he just continued his dancing, seemingly oblivious to anyone else in the room. Mr. Aram, no doubt, figured that Anthony was too busy having fun to notice the rugs as the men displayed each one. When the assistants unrolled the last rug, however, Anthony danced over to the Hi-Fi set and turned it off.

Bowing low to Mr. Aram and his assistants, he waved his arms, pointed toward the pile of rugs, and said, "I'll take 'em all."

That was Anthony's way. He had fun, and he also made quick decisions, which, with rare exceptions, were right for his vendors, for his customers, and for himself. He stuck faithfully to his own unique way of running SPAG'S. While others might have disagreed with his methods, they certainly worked for him. Lee Zolla, his secretary, remembered:

Employees would call from the store when they wanted to put something on sale at a reduced price.

Spag would check what he paid for it, and off the top
of his head, give them a selling price—no complicated pricing formulas for Spag. He seemed to know
what would be a good price to sell the item.

He did what he thought was right for his customers; he made no
special deals for anyone. Everybody who shopped at his store benefited
from the bargains he provided.

In the beginning, many people simply couldn't believe that his
rock-bottom prices were for real. "I had the hardest time convincing
people that I sold quality goods!" he said repeatedly. Because other discount houses at that time were selling seconds, damaged goods, and
items made of shoddy material, customers going to SPAG'S found it
hard to believe that there were no defects in the merchandise.
However, they soon learned that Anthony sold only high-quality items.

"My customers know that if they buy anything that is not right, they
get their money back without a hassle," Anthony used to state firmly.

That, too, was his way.

Acknowledging the success of Anthony's enterprise, some competitors asked, "How can you run a store on such a narrow margin?
How do you cover your overhead costs?"

"I'd rather have a fast nickel than a slow dime," he would reply.
This meant that contrary to the prevalent "supply and demand" theory,
which proposes selling at the highest price to make the best profit,
Anthony, dedicated to serving the working man, depended on a large
sales volume to provide a modest profit. As his friend, Joseph E.
Sullivan[1] noted, "Anthony revolutionized retail merchandising in his
own way—he introduced the human factor and added a new dimen-
sion to retailing."

In a nutshell, Anthony knew what people could afford, and his
low prices attracted customers by the thousands. As his customer base
expanded, sales increased, allowing him to buy in larger volume at
lower prices per item. This allowed Anthony to reduce his prices further and pass on even more savings—and it had the effect of drawing
customers away from department stores, hardware stores, and specialty
shops in Worcester. When their suppliers began to file legal complaints, that was when Anthony received the first of many summons to
appear in court.

[1] Retired chairman of Vigoro Corporation and former president of Swift & Co.

Fighting the Fair Trade Law

To learn more about the summonses and court appearances, I queried
several SPAG'S employees, as well as Jim, who remembered talking
with Anthony on occasion about "the fair-trade baloney" during that
time in the early 1950s.

According to Jim, Anthony was determined to make his position
understood. So, he dressed in his working clothes and ten-gallon hat,
and accompanied by his wife Olive and the SPAG'S attorney, he
drove to the Suffolk County Court House in Boston, the first of many
such trips he would make. He never discussed the details of what happened in court—nor did he ever plead guilty to the charges against
him.

"Anthony? Plead guilty? Never!" said Jim emphatically. "He
never admitted that he was breaking the law. He didn't plead guilty
because he believed that he hadn't done anything wrong. Remember,
Elsa, what he used to say? 'You're never wrong when you do the right
thing.'"

"But what did he say when the judge asked him if he were selling
fishing reels at less than the list price?" I asked.

"The truth! He told the truth, of course. He said 'yes.'"

"Did he have a chance to say why he cut prices?"

"Oh, yes, you can bet on that!" replied Jim with a smile. "He told
the judge the same thing he'd been saying to everybody all along. You
know what he would say: 'I believe that when I buy something, I have
the right to sell that product for a price I think is right. I think that
the prices set by the manufacturers are too high for the average person. By selling quality items at affordable prices, I'm helping him to
make ends meet. Someone needs to speak for the working man.'"

But the working man was not being considered when "fair-trade"
laws were enacted by a number of states, including Massachusetts.
They came about as a result of a loophole in the Miller-Tydings
Amendment to the Sherman Antitrust Act, a federal law enacted on
July 2, 1890, which declares:

> Every contract, combination in the form of
> trust or otherwise, or conspiracy, in restraint of trade
> or commerce among the several States, or with for-

eign nations, is declared to be illegal. Every person
who shall make any contract or engage in any combination or conspiracy hereby declared to be illegal
shall be deemed guilty of a felony, and, on conviction
thereof, shall be punished by fine not exceeding
$10,000 if a corporation, or, if any other person,
$350,000, or by imprisonment not exceeding three
years, or by both said punishments, in the discretion
of the court.[2]

The Miller-Tydings Amendment, which exempted commodities
resold in states where price maintenance contracts were legal, was
passed in 1937. Forty-two states took advantage of this loophole to pass
their own "fair-trade" laws, many of which contained a "non-signer
clause" that permitted manufacturers to restrict retailers to agreed-upon
prices. Massachusetts was one of them. In May 1951, the United States
Supreme Court determined that the Miller-Tydings Act did not grant
such power to the states. But in 1952 Congress passed a new bill that
granted manufacturers the right to impose minimum prices on all
retailers—in essence, price fixing.[3]

Many people objected to the Fair Trade law; Anthony was one of
its most vociferous opponents. When reminded by a judge that "anyone who purchases branded or trademarked products must obey the
law," he would be quick to respond that "the Fair Trade law is not fair
and should be changed." But his arguments fell on deaf ears, and they
certainly didn't help him when the judge imposed a fine. When Jim
asked Anthony what happened in the sporting goods case, my brother
replied, "The son of a bitch! I got stuck for fifteen hundred dollars!"

"Fifteen hundred dollars!" Jim said incredulously. "I couldn't
believe it when he told me! Those were the days when people were
working for fifty cents an hour! That fifteen hundred dollars would be
the equivalent of about $25,000 today. And that was only the first
summons he received!"

It was, indeed. For the next several years, Anthony was slapped
with "cease and desist" orders and summonses to appear in court as a
result of complaints from several suppliers. And each time he went to
court, he voiced his objections to the law and was fined. The total
amount he paid in fines was staggering.

[2] Sherman Antitrust Act—15 U.S.IC., sec.1.
[3] *Encyclopedia Americana*, 1956, Vol. 2, "Anti-Trust Laws," page 43.

"And so it continued into the 1960s," recalled John Cullen, the store's current general manager. "Spag challenged the legitimacy of the law, and each time he was summoned to Boston, he defended his right to sell at reduced prices."

As Jim and I speculated on the reasons Anthony was taken to court so often, we realized that it began at a time when SPAG'S Supply, Inc. was really taking off and becoming popular, which undoubtedly resulted in sales losses for full-price stores.

"The suppliers' salesmen were not complaining," Jim noted. "Many of them would say, 'Don't tell me what you sell your merchandise for; just give me the order.' They were working on commissions."

After the first court hearing, Anthony switched to buying his sports equipment from another supplier. "Changing suppliers was to become a normal course of action for him," as Jim recalled. "Sometimes when a supplier filed a complaint, Anthony would either return all the items he had in stock to the provider or he would hold a sale and sell off the items at a real low price. That's what happened when a popular maker of wristwatches filed a complaint. Anthony sold off several thousand self-winding watches he had in stock—for five dollars apiece! Then he found another supplier of watches."

"Finding another supplier was easy," said Gordon Prosser, Sr., one of the store's managers (now retired). "When a supplier filed a complaint about our low prices on insecticides, we had no trouble finding another source. It's a cinch when you order by the boxcar load and pay cash."

"Some providers did give Spag a hard time," added John Cullen. "They would continue to ship, but they would be late, or they would lose the order, or ship only part of it. Sometimes they shipped tools with parts missing. But that didn't stop Spag; he continued to cut prices on the merchandise that he was able to buy. He wasn't about to give in to them, even if it was taking up a lot of his time and costing him a fortune in legal fees."

"Spag had his method for pricing, and he stuck to it," added Vinnie Mastro, SPAG'S retired general store manager. "They tried to make him raise his prices, but he was thinking about our customers. Most of the complaints were from manufacturers of tools and appliances."

"Anthony did make one exception with a certain maker of glass bakeware," said Jim, who continued:

They threatened to withhold all future orders of their products unless Anthony sold every item at list price. They were adamant. They could afford to be adamant. They happened to be the sole manufacturer of glass bakeware, and their cake and loaf baking dishes were much in demand. Anthony agreed to sell all the glassware at list price to accommodate his customers, but as one might expect, he found a way around this restriction. He knew he couldn't sell the merchandise for less than full list price, but he also knew that he could give it away free. And he did— he gave away glass bowls and measuring cups by the thousands! He also used the additional profits from the list price mark-up on the glassware to further reduce his other prices.

Gordon Prosser remembers telling Anthony about the complaints he received from a company selling appliances. "Spag's reply was, 'Sell 'em for what they're worth!' So I cut their list prices for toasters and steam irons in half."

"And that's the way it went," Jim remembered. "Each time one of our competitors complained to a supplier about allowing SPAG'S to sell at a lower price, the supplier would file a complaint, and Anthony was hauled back into court again."

"Being a pioneer in discount merchandising was not entirely a joyride [for Spag]," wrote reporter Pat Corwin. "The Fair Trade law, designed to protect the full-price stores, kept him in court frequently as news of his bargains began to spread." [4]

The court sessions were an aggravation to Anthony, but he continued to act on the strength of his convictions. He defended his viewpoint at Rotary Club and other service club meetings, in addition to speaking up at hearings held to discuss the legitimacy of the Fair Trade law. In Anthony's files, I found a note expressing his objections to the law. He had written it on the back of a get-well card sent to him by a customer. Inside the card, the customer wished Anthony a quick recovery and thanked him for a low-priced fishing rod, as well as for his kindness in allowing payment for the rod in monthly installments. On the back of the card, Anthony had jotted down the following:

[4] Pat Corwin, "Everybody Has a Niche." *Discount Merchandiser*, July 1992, page 61.

Back in 1937-1938, I bought these [fishing] rods. I was the only store that discounted them. We sold all fishing tackle at 40% off the list (price). The suggested list price was:

$40 – we sold for $24.
$30 – "   "   " $21.
$20 – "   "   " $12.

Almost everything was fair-traded at [that] time. I figured that if I sold the items for less than the suggested list price, that was my choice. I had lots of court citations for cutting prices.

I also found a scrap of paper in Anthony's files on which he had written, "I attended [hearings and spoke up] against [the Fair Trade law]. My contemporaries in business loved it. I fought against the unjust law always."

"In the middle 1960s," recalled John Cullen, "when a popular producer of cooking ware filed a complaint, we won! We won that one!"

"The case was probably dismissed because the courts had received a glut of complaints and could not process them all," Jim speculated.

When the Massachusetts courts repealed the Fair Trade law in 1969, due in part to the difficulty in enforcing the law, Anthony wrote, "This is what makes it all worthwhile. The working man never got a break. I hope I can always continue to serve my friends and customers and help them enjoy [life]."

In 1975, Congress repealed all state fair-trade laws.

A "People Person"

Anthony often said, "Business is not just a matter of dollars and cents; it's about people." This attitude would endear him to hundreds of thousands of customers, employees, friends, neighbors, and family members. And it would turn him into a business legend.

But he was more than just a businessman. Over the years,

"The working man needs a break!" Anthony (Spag).

Anthony became known as much for his generosity, integrity, and jovial nature as for his success in turning a $35.00 investment into a multimillion-dollar enterprise. While his unique business concepts would be copied worldwide, his ten-gallon hat and infectious smile would turn out to be just as well known as symbols of fun, humility, and compassion.

As I set to work on this book, I began to wonder how Anthony had become this free-thinking, caring person who, driven by his dedication to serving working men and their families, challenged the unfair trade law. The reasons became increasingly apparent to me as I journeyed back into our childhood and delved into memories of our family's beginnings as the children of two Italian immigrants...

Brigida Minelli and Antonio Borgatti, on their wedding day. March 15, 1912.

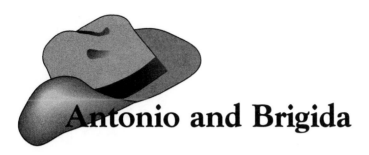

Antonio and Brigida

This is everybody's world. There is enough for
everyone with a little sharing and caring.
—Spag

In 1909, Antonio A. Borgatti packed up and left his family farm in a country village near Bologna, Italy, supposedly for a short sightseeing trip to Venice. Instead of returning home, however, this strong, handsome young man sailed to America. He was bright, fired with ambition, and confident that the culinary arts training he had received in Switzerland would make it easy for him to find a waitering job in the States. Upon landing at Ellis Island, he headed for Wellesley, Massachusetts, where his cousins were already well established.

Arriving in Wellesley about that same time was petite Brigida Minelli, who had come to the States to comfort and care for her ailing sister, Ceserina Minelli Simoni. Ceserina, an attractive, brown-eyed, well-proportioned brunette, had come to Wellesley as a bride in 1907. Her husband, Enrico, had joined his brothers in their thriving contracting business, but she had become homesick for her brother, sisters, and parents in Italy. When she became seriously ill, her doctor, recognizing the symptoms of homesickness, wrote to her parents and said that Ceserina really needed to have someone from her family at her side.

When the letter arrived in Italy, Ceserina's six sisters excitedly gathered around their mother while she read it aloud. As she grasped the seriousness of the situation, she immediately looked up at her daughters.

"Who," she asked, "would like to go to America to be with Ceserina?" Then without hesitation she turned to the sibling next in age to Ceserina, and said, "Brigida, would you like to do this?"

Brigida's almond-shaped, soft brown eyes brightened. "Of course, Mother," she replied quickly, "if that is what you would like me to do."

Upon Brigida's arrival in America, the two sisters reunited with tears streaming down their happy faces. Ceserina soon began to recuperate. The two devoted sisters were to support each other through many joys and heartaches in the following years.

Even though Brigida and Antonio had come from villages only a few miles apart in Cento in the province of Ferrara, northern Italy— he from Rennazo and she from Buona

Mother's sister, Ceserina Simoni.

Compra—they were destined to meet in Wellesley. Upon meeting Brigida through family members, Antonio was immediately smitten by her beauty and genteel nature. Shortly thereafter, he obtained a waitering position in the prestigious Massasoit Hotel in Springfield.

To visit Brigida on weekends, Antonio took a train to Worcester, then traveled on to Wellesley. Occasionally on his return trip to Springfield, he would stop off in Worcester to visit with friends who had migrated from the same region in Italy.

Antonio was impressed with Worcester. The thriving industrial community included such companies as American Steel & Wire Company (U.S. Steel), Norton Company (abrasives), Pullman Standard (railroad passenger cars), Heald Machine, Whittall Carpet Company, and Morgan Construction, all leaders in the industrial revolution. Antonio was quick to recognize the city's promising future and the opportunities it would offer. At Plunkett's, an upscale private club in Worcester, he secured a waiter's position that provided a more-than-adequate income to support a family. He was a dashing waiter with his black, wavy hair, his broad smile, and strong physique.

With his engaging personality, Antonio won Brigida's heart. After their wedding in 1912, they moved to an apartment on the east side of

Worcester, where most Italian immigrants had settled. The areas on both sides of the Boston–Worcester railroad tracks offered low-rent apartments to the new immigrants.

The Emporium

Antonio's income from waitering and tips was phenomenal for those days. When other workers were happy to be making $8.00 per week, he was bringing home $50-$100. He returned late each evening, his pockets bulging with money. Within a short time, Antonio had saved enough to purchase a three-decker at 501 Shrewsbury Street. He and Brigida moved into the second floor apartment of this house, the first of Antonio's many investments in property.

Shrewsbury Street joins Belmont Street at the top of Belmont Hill, near the entrance to Worcester State Hospital. During those days, people traveled from afar by trolley to visit patients at the hospital, which was soon to be recognized for its pioneering in the field of psychiatry. The hospital had become a major stop for the Boston–Worcester trolleys, which paused at the entrance of the hospital to pick up and discharge passengers.

As Antonio watched the hustle and bustle of passengers coming and going to and from the hospital, he saw the need for a combination luncheonette-convenience store, commonly called a "spa" in those days. Next to his three-decker was a vacant lot situated on the intersection of Belmont, Warden, and Shrewsbury Streets. Like most Italians, Antonio had a strong desire to acquire property. He lost no time in buying the lot and having a one-story brick building constructed on it. A wall running lengthwise through the building provided space for two stores. He rented one to a pharmacy; in the other, he established his spa.

Antonio placed a soda fountain lengthwise down the middle of his store. There he could stand and scoop ice cream from the tubs in the freezer to make banana splits and college ices (now known as sundaes in New England) for customers seated on the ten stools. Parallel to the soda fountain, he built a smaller counter to take care of customers who wanted to buy fruit, candy, gum, tobacco, or magazines. On one end of this counter, near the door, he placed a cash register.

ONCE AN HOUR LIMITED

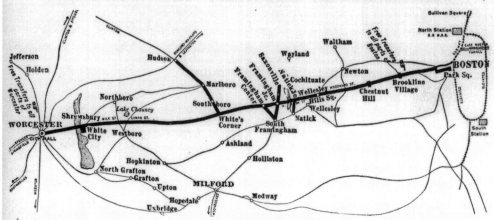

Limited Cars leave Worcester, City Hall and Union Station (daily except Sundays), at 7.05 A. M. and every 60 minutes until 5.05 P. M.

Leave Boston, Park Square, at 9.00 A. M. and every 60 minutes until 6.00 P. M.

Running time, one hour and fifty minutes, regular fares.

Round trip rates, One Dollar.

One way rates, Fifty-five cents.

Local cars every thirty minutes.

Try the Clean, Comfortable, Fast Line.   Lowest Fares.

BOSTON & WORCESTER STREET RAILWAY CO.

Trolley stop at the Worcester State Hospital entrance, June 1911.

He also purchased five smooth, dark brown vitreous tables with ice-cream chairs and placed them at the rear of the store near the kitchen. A black ceiling fan provided necessary relief during sweltering summer days.

Antonio envisioned his store as a miniature Venice Emporium, a train terminal in Venice that he had visited before shipping out to the States. He loved to talk about his visit to the city of canals, a seaport built on several small islands in Italy. Customers sat enthralled as he regaled them with stories about the bustle of activity in the terminal through which people passed as they arrived at and departed from the mainland. Antonio also described the teeming throngs of people who queued up at the stands and counters of the Venice Emporium, some of whom were waiting their turn to buy tickets or to receive accommodations of one kind or another.

Consequently, Antonio named his own spa the Venice Emporium, and true to its namesake, it did teem with travelers. His successful investment became even more profitable when the trolley company established a ticket agency in Antonio's Emporium. Passengers came into the spa to buy tickets, and while they were there they also bought fruit, candy, or magazines to bring to the patients. Neighbors and customers also came into the Emporium to make telephone calls in the mahogany-stained telephone booth tucked into the rear corner of the store, from which they could watch for the trolley through the folding glass doors.

Some customers would hoist themselves onto the stools at the soda fountain to cool off with ice cream or a drink. Others were drawn toward the kitchen at the back of the store, from where the aroma of homemade soups and freshly baked bread wafted forward. Soup, sandwiches, and pies were the order of the day. The buxom cooks in neat white chef's aprons, their hair drawn back tightly and netted, stirred the soups and removed the custard and apple pies from the hot oven of the oversized, black stove. Almost giddy from the delightful aromas of baked pastry, eager patrons watched while the cooks cut the pies. Custard and apple pies were always on the bill of fare, as were rhubarb and squash when in season.

Just as it is today, the perennial favorite was apple pie served with a wedge of cheese—an old English tradition. Occasionally a patron would decline the cheese and opt for a scoop of ice cream instead.

When this happened, someone would remind him that "a piece of apple pie without cheese is like a kiss without a squeeze."

On the floor along the wall near the crates of fruit, Antonio placed barrels of basic goods, such as beans, peanuts, raisins, sugar, flour, legumes, prunes, tea leaves, coffee beans, crackers, and cookies. Neighbors used the three-cornered scoop on the hanging scales to measure their purchases. In those days, this was the way that all grocery stores and convenience stores like the Emporium carried such staples and stocked their shelves.

As with most businesses, advertising signs adorned the walls of the Emporium inside and out. Signs advertising Pepsinic Seltzer and Moxie were on the wall above the staples. On the opposite wall to the left of the soda fountain, Antonio hung a painted tin sign advertising RIVAL TWIST, a chewing tobacco. It included a picture of the dark-blue, tin tobacco box and the message: "THE BEST CHEW." Next to that was a sign that advertised AUSTIN'S DOG BREAD. It depicted an attractive young matron holding up a biscuit in front of a litter of puppies. The caption read: "DON'T ALL SPEAK AT ONCE!" (That particular piece of history, now a collector's item, commanded $900 at a recent auction.)

Before the era of cement and asphalt, mud and dust were underfoot everywhere. To control the dirt tracked in from the street and sidewalk, most store owners laid down a covering of sawdust on the floor. Sweeping up the old sawdust and spreading a clean layer frequently was essential.

For Antonio, there was another "must." He loved to dance and sing, and dance and sing he did—much to the delight of his customers. An electric player-piano to the left of the kitchen at the rear of the store provided the music. The piano played automatically when a customer deposited a nickel; a pneumatic device controlled by a piano roll activated the keys. More often than not, the invisible pianist filled the Emporium with lively tunes, either classical or popular. The music was for everyone to enjoy, and tables at the back of the store were quickly moved aside for a spontaneous dance or two. Customers could grab a partner and twirl around to the music until the piano roll reached the end of its slotted scroll. Rarely did Antonio forego the opportunity to dance with a friend or stranger, even at the busiest of times. He also had a penchant for kissing the ladies, and he took advantage of every opportunity to do so. Brigida saw it as just lighthearted fun, and the ladies evidently understood that, as well. A few minutes of dancing and merriment were a welcome relief to the nurses, doctors, and attendants on lunch break from the Worcester State Hospital (who, like many people in the 1920s, often worked twelve hours a day, six days a week—a total of 72 exhausting hours!).

Antonio also entertained all with his singing. Accompanied by the player piano, he put his whole heart into singing such popular songs of the day as "Ramona," "Always," and "O Sole Mio." Antonio must have inherited his melodious tenor voice from his Uncle Giuseppe, an opera tenor of renown in Cento, Italy, in the late 1800s.[1]

Like Giuseppe (and all the Borgattis, for that matter), Antonio loved a good time. Wherever he was, there was gaiety. Due to the Emporium's cheerful atmosphere, its good food, and its prime location at the trolley stop, it soon became a great success.

Anthony A. Borgatti, Jr. is Born

During these happy years at the Emporium, Brigida helped at the store—until February 29, 1916 (Leap Year), when she gave birth to their first child. The baby was light-complexioned, with fair hair, blue eyes, and dimples. Antonio proudly named his son Anthony A. Borgatti, Jr.—the fifth descendent in the Borgatti family to receive the name.

Antonio purchased a handsome St. Bernard dog, named "Barnie," to herald the expected new arrival. As Anthony Jr. grew, he became endearingly fond of his Barnie; but Mrs. Pauline DiNoie, a tenant in their three-decker, clearly remembers that "Anthony was even more fond of spaghetti. When he was just a few years old, he would ask, 'Mamma, are we having "skettie" today?'

"If Brigida answered, 'No, not today; we had it yesterday,' he would cry. Oh, how he cried!" How apropos that people would some day call him "Spag."

Anthony was the first of four children to arrive on the scene. I was born four years later; Olga in 1924; and Robert in 1930. As the oldest, Anthony blazed the trail for us at home and in school.

---

[1] The opera house Il Teatro Borgatti in Cento, which still holds performances, houses within it a small museum of Giuseppe's artifacts.

Above, Anthony at six months.
Right, Anthony at four years old.

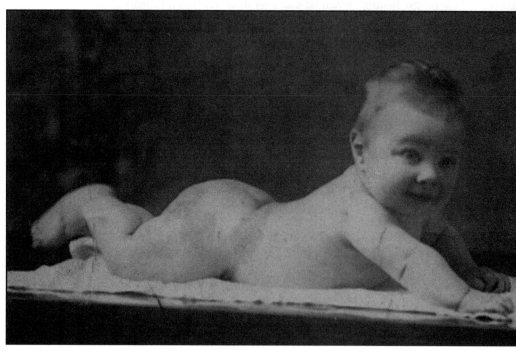

Anthony (Spag) at three months old.

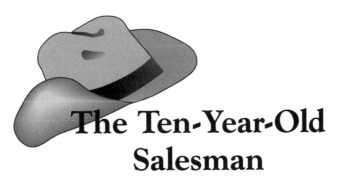

The Ten-Year-Old Salesman

Father was a taskmaster.
—Anthony

"Anthony was a happy, inquisitive chatterbox," said Mrs. Borgatti.
"Always smiling. When he was only three years old, he helped me in the kitchen. He was short for his age, but he went behind the counter to wait on customers when he was six. I was always sure he would do well. Even then, he waited on customers like an old man. He was a born salesman."[1]

Anthony liked to talk about his childhood and the way it used to be when we were both very young and living in Worcester at 501 Shrewsbury Street, next to the Emporium. He was highly sentimental.

"We didn't have much time for playing in those days," he said, recalling the formative years when he assumed his responsibilities at the Emporium. "Father was a taskmaster. It was my job to open the store in the morning as he stood behind me. After school, I was expected to work. It didn't do me any harm. It was good for me."

Immediately after school each day, Anthony went directly to the Emporium and promptly donned a chef's white apron. The apron was much too long, but quickly made to size by virtue of the ties that secured the slack when wrapped about his waist. Then he started to

[1] Jack Tubert, "The Man Called Spag." Feature Parade Section, *Worcester Sunday Telegram*, 8 March 1964.

work on any number of chores that were waiting for him. There in the Emporium, starting at age six, Anthony learned the value of hard work and the pleasure in serving others.

He began his chores by cleaning the glass case that held an assortment of nickel and penny candies. Wiping off finger prints from all four sides of the candy case was fun for Anthony, especially since the routine started and finished at the sliding door of the case. Anthony had a sweet tooth; peppermint patties and the "old fashions" (chocolate-covered creams) were his all-time favorites. Other candies, such as Necco wafers, caramels, Tootsie rolls, licorice, gumballs, corn cakes, and the pièce de resistance—the 1-inch bull's eyes with creamy white centers surrounded with chocolate—were enough to make any child ecstatic. "Yup," said Anthony, "I tried 'em all."

I especially recall how he regularly stuffed his pockets with Necco wafers, squirrel bars, and peppermint patties to share with kids at school. I did not dare tell on him because he had caught me doing the same thing. I was four years younger than Anthony, but in a sense we grew up together. We spent most of our childhood days in the Emporium.

Anthony did not stop with candy though; he also had a passion for ice cream, especially the ice cream made by the Leofanti family nearby on Franklin Street. In a workroom at the back of their house, they filled a tub with cream, sugar, and flavorings, fastened the lid and paddle, and placed the tub of cream in a bucket of ice. Then they rigged up the back wheel of a bicycle with bevel gears and a belt which they attached to the lid of the tub. As someone pedaled the bicycle, the paddles rotated, churning the cream, which gradually thickened. They placed the tubs of churned cream in their icebox "freezer." The Leofantis did not have elaborate mechanized equipment or electric freezers, but at least the bicycle made the job a little easier.

Johnny Leofanti delivered ice cream three times a week, and more often when the demand exceeded the supply. Responding to a request made from the Emporium's pay telephone station, the Leofanti truck would rumble over the cobblestone streets to restock the Emporium's freezer.

Ice cream "to go" was hand-packed in quart, pint, and half-pint containers; no prepacked quarts and gallons were available in the 1920s. Customers could request a mix of flavors. Anthony told me that

Elsa, two years, Anthony, six years, and Mother, 1922.

"scooping and packing the ice cream could be tough work when the ice cream was frozen hard."

When our parents left Anthony in charge of the soda fountain, he and I would have an ice cream bonanza. Anthony would hurriedly take out a deep dish, scoop ice cream onto it until it could hold no more, and then place the dish between us. Together we would gobble it down. If time allowed, he would scoop up an encore.

"Boy," he said years later, smacking his lips in fond retrospect, "I can still taste that strawberry-vanilla-chocolate mix I made, like it was yesterday. It was so delicious!" Then he would often add, "It's a good thing I filled up on it then, usually a pint at a time, because I can't do it now." For some reason, Anthony was a chubby little boy.

Emporium patrons asked for double scoops of ice cream, college ices, and the ever-popular banana splits. Just think, 35 cents would buy the biggest banana split! "At the Emporium," recalled Anthony, "our banana splits started with a whole sliced banana and four generous scoops of ice cream. On top of that, we put three more scoops of either vanilla or maple walnut to build it up, and then the sauce, nuts, and real honest-to-goodness whipped cream to top it off."

As Anthony grew, Pa gave him more jobs to do, all the while encouraging him by saying approvingly, "That's the way to do it!" Mother also expressed her appreciation often for the help he gave her by saying "That's a good boy, Anthony!"

Another task waiting for Anthony was taking care of the fruit, which was a big selling item in those days. A stalk of bananas hung from the ceiling, close to a counter piled high with pyramids of apples and oranges. Anthony's job was to go through the neat piles of fruit and remove the bruised ones. From the box of apples and an orange crate under the counter, he then rebuilt the pyramids. In reflecting about this chore, he noted, "You'd just finish piling when invariably a piece at the bottom looked damaged and had to be removed. It seemed as if we sorted fruit all day long."

One of Anthony's other tasks was much more rewarding: the saw-dust detail. He swept the sawdust into a pile and then, with dust pan and brush, checked it carefully for coins. Occasionally, patrons in a hurry (to catch a trolley, perhaps) would drop a coin, mostly pennies, but sometimes a nickel or a dime. Once in a great while, someone would drop a 25-cent piece. That was a lot of money in those days.

Mother told Anthony that he could keep any coins that he found.

"The first time I found a nickel with a few pennies in the saw-dust, I showed them to Father, who promptly reached over and took the nickel," Anthony recalled. "Yup, after that I hid them [the occasional nickel or dime] fast. He only fooled me once. From then on, I made good and sure I only showed him the pennies." That was Anthony's way of dealing with what he saw as an unfairness. He needed the coins; he was saving them to buy a birthday present for Mother. When he had collected enough, he proudly presented her with a ten-dollar gold piece.

Another of Anthony's duties was tending the magazine racks at the Emporium. At first, he just straightened the stacks of magazines and kept the area clean. Later he learned how to restock the piles with newly-delivered publications. When he started to sell magazines, they ranged in price from five to 25 cents.

At an early age, Anthony made a significant discovery which affected his business decisions for the rest of his life.

"One day I noticed that the more magazines there were in a pile, the more that sold," he recalled. "I tested my observation. There was no mistaking it. When the racks were scant, people barely glanced at the magazines, but when the racks were neatly arranged and piled high, people always paused and, more often than not, reached for one or two." That was when Anthony discovered that "If you pile 'em high, they will buy."

When Anthony was nine years old, Father put him in charge of ordering the publications. Magazine sales zoomed, and Anthony whistled a happy tune. He had just learned how to whistle. A boy at school had shown him how to curl his tongue behind his lower teeth, pucker his lips, and blow. From that time on, he whistled while straightening out the magazines, polishing the glass candy case, sweeping up the sawdust, and even while he was doing his homework. He whistled the same unidentifiable tune when he was walking, working, or just sitting and thinking. There was not much time for "fooling around" when he was working at the Emporium, but whistling while he worked did help pass the time away.

When he was about ten years old, Anthony took on a job that became his favorite. On Saturdays and Sundays, laden with a large tray of sandwiches, drinks, and magazines, he boarded the trolley heading to Park Square, Boston. Passengers returning to Boston from Worcester reached happily for the boiled ham, chicken, and cheese sandwiches, Hershey bars, Teaberry and Beechnut gum, magazines, and bottles of Moxie, a popular carbonated beverage.

"It made me feel good that they liked what I was selling," said Anthony. By the time the trolley reached White's Corner in Southboro, Anthony's tray would be empty, and his pockets would be jingling. There he would switch to a trolley returning to Worcester, whistling—happy and proud that he had served his customers by selling them what they wanted or needed.

On occasion, my parents allowed me to go with Anthony on his trolley trips. I boarded the trolley with my brother, carrying a small tray of Life Savers, Necco wafers, Canadian peppermints, and nonpareils (chocolate patties sprinkled with white jimmies). I, too, returned with an empty tray, jingling pockets, and a big smile.

My brother's greatest pleasure was seeing how happy he was making his customers. To Anthony —even at the ripe old age of ten— every customer was a friend for life.

The "born salesman." Anthony's First Communion photo, 1926.

Childhood

At least we know now...
—Anthony

The Emporium was our second home; Anthony spent every spare minute he had in the store cleaning and restocking, as well as preparing and serving food. I helped by cleaning counters, wiping off chairs, and picking up papers. On occasion, Anthony allowed me to clean the candy case; I was always happy to oblige.

Father worked long hours at the store when he was not taking care of the numerous properties that he continued to buy. The Emporium's great success and the care of his properties kept him busier than ever. He rarely took a day off to relax with Mother or friends, or with any of us in the family, for that matter—except when he took Anthony to the Barnum & Bailey Circus at the County Fairgrounds, a 60-acre tract of land in Worcester where the Norton Company is now situated.

Anthony looked forward to those two full days with Father, and we looked forward to their return from the circus, when we would hear all about the exciting events of the day. Anthony would tell us about the sulky races he had watched. He went into great detail describing the popcorn and the extra-large ice cream cones Pa had bought for him.

To keep the record straight, I, too, had special times with Pa. According to Mother, when I was a baby, Pa would hold me and turn on the player-piano we had in our home. As he danced around the room with me in his arms, I would squeal with delight. Later, when I had learned to walk, I would place my stocking feet securely on his polished, black shoes, and then we would sway to the music. Mother, sitting on the sidelines, would smile happily as she watched us. I loved to dance with Pa, especially at weddings. As soon as the orchestra began to play, he would give me a knowing glance that meant, "Let's dance." He continued to enjoy dancing well into his 70s.

We were so proud of Pa. He could be so much fun, but he was also a mystery to us. He reminded us, almost on a daily basis, that he had "gone only as far as the fourth grade," yet he had beautiful handwriting, could speak five languages, and continually amazed us with his wide knowledge of the world's history and geography.

Sometimes, however, I wished that Father were not so smart and that he would not embarrass me by asking questions I could not answer. For instance, he would ask me a question about a place that I had never heard of, like "What is the capital of Persia?" When I would answer, "I don't know, Pa," he would throw his arms up in the air and exclaim, "How come you don't know that Teheran is the capital of Persia? I know, and I only went as far as the fourth grade!"

I was crushed! I could not understand how I was supposed to know or why I did not know the answers to his questions. I used to believe that he stayed awake nights gloating over his sport at my expense and making up new questions to ask me.

Later, I came to realize that Pa meant no harm by his teasing and that he truly was a doting father in all other respects. As I look back, I can see that he was always eager to please me. I don't think he ever balked at giving me anything I asked for.

Father did, however, begin to act in ways that puzzled and worried us. At times, without any provocation that we could discern, he would become irritable. These frightening episodes became even more pronounced in 1924, when Olga was born. She had beautiful dark hair and large brown eyes, and she was perfect from the waist up. However, Olga was born with an incomplete backbone, known as spina bifida. Her deformity was more than Father could bear. When Olga cried out in pain, Father would hold his hands to his ears and leave the room, extremely distressed.

Mother, on the other hand, patiently tended to Olga's needs, and as she did so, Anthony and I learned how to help our little sister. In her younger years, I passed many hours taking her for rides in Anthony's wagon. When she was older, we played games and made dolls' dresses. We giggled and laughed a lot; Olga had a wonderful sense of humor. As a teenager, she was stunning. She had clear, olive skin, a blush in her cheeks, flowing black hair, and pencil-thin eyebrows framing her almond-shaped eyes. She remained at home for all but the last seven months of her 39 years. That was 11 years beyond the life expectancy for someone with her condition at that time. Doctors marveled at her survival and they attributed her extended years to the loving care she had received and her strong will to live. Before her long, lingering death, Olga bequeathed her eyes to the eye bank.

The Farm

Olga was only a year old in 1925, when Father purchased a small cottage and apple orchard on Elm Street in Shrewsbury. The "farm," as Father called it, was no doubt "too good a buy to pass up." We suspected that the six-room cottage, the barn, and the chicken coops reminded Pa of his family farm in Italy.

On those rare occasions when Mother could convince Father that he should take time off for a day's rest, going to the farm was a happy time for Anthony and me. But getting there was another matter. Mother would pack a picnic lunch and get Olga ready for the ride in the Hupmobile. That ride was an experience in itself. Even though Father was one of the first men in our neighborhood to buy a car, we were never eager to ride in the Hupmobile unless someone other than Father was behind the wheel. I don't know if it was Pa's nervousness as a new driver or if he did not have enough lessons, but his foot did not always find the right pedal, especially when he needed to stop. Driving uphill and on level terrain was not much of a problem, but the ride to Shrewsbury began with a slope down Belmont Hill toward Lake Quinsigamond. We knew, from a few previous close calls, that braking was not a certainty, so we held our breath as we headed down Belmont Street to the Lake Avenue intersection at the foot of the hill.

There was one saving grace, however. Before the era of traffic lights, policemen manned the raised traffic box in the middle of the Lake Avenue and Belmont Street intersection. Fortunately, they knew Father and recognized his car. Whenever the policeman on duty spotted the Hupmobile coming down the hill toward him, he would blow his whistle vehemently, hold up his white-gloved hands, and stop all other cars from entering the intersection; they would come to a screeching halt, and we would go sailing through the intersection.

As we crossed the lake all in one piece, Anthony and I would breath a sigh of relief, thankful that we had made it. Anthony would whisper, "Wow, we were lucky again! The rest of the way is easy." Our hearts, which had been in our mouths, would slip back to where they belonged. The ordeal was over quickly, and soon we were turning into the long driveway to the little farmhouse.

When we pulled to a stop, Father would say, "Well, we're here!" Then he would take a walk through the apple orchard, checking out the dozen or so apple trees. With the glee of young children, Anthony and I would head for the barn. Together, we would pull the sliding door back, run across the barn floor, past the three empty stalls on the left, and up the steep stairs to the hayloft. (The hayloft was Anthony's favorite reading place; he could often be found there, curled up in the hay with a book in hand, oblivious to the world around him.)

After checking out the barn, we would run around to the back of the barn to open the squeaky doors to the two empty chicken coops. These coops were great hiding places to keep in mind when we played

The "farm" cottage and barn, 86 Elm St., Shrewsbury.

"hide-and-seek" with our friends. To the left of the chicken coops stood the "one holer" [1] where last year's mail order catalog, usually *Sears Roebuck*, hung with a rope from a nail. A few pages from the catalog also served as an effective bee swatter when the need arose.

In the meantime, Mother would carry Olga to the back porch, then take the picnic basket into the kitchen and return with a chair. From the back porch, she, with Olga on her lap, would look out to the field behind the house where Anthony and I were scampering about.

At lunch time, Mother would call Anthony to come in and pump water at the black slate sink in the pantry. Anthony was adept at priming the pump and bringing forth the clear, sparkling water for drinking and washing our hands. The well, while not deep, provided enough water for our visits.

In the fall, Anthony also helped Father pick apples and lug the heavy baskets to the house—not that Father needed help. With his broad shoulders and bulging biceps, he could lift just about anything.

Our days at the farm were fun. Mother was grateful to see Father unwind and relax while we were there. She, too, enjoyed the quiet and the opportunity to sit for a few hours in the sunshine. All of us looked forward to those days at the farm, even if it did require a life-threatening ride to get there.

As if riding with Pa was not exciting enough, he also went out of his way to make life exciting. On one occasion, however, he planned a surprise for Mother that did not bring the response he expected. He knew how much Ma loved her sister, Zia[2] Ceserina, and how they enjoyed being together whenever they could manage it.

The two sisters had supported each other through many ups and downs. For instance, when Zia's husband died suddenly in 1920, Mother helped her through the difficult adjustments of widowhood. Zia had five children to clothe and feed. With Mother's support, she established a small grocery store on the first floor of her three-decker in Newton Upper Falls. This small business grew and enabled Zia Ceserina both to provide for the children and remain financially independent. Throughout the years, the two sisters continued to keep in close touch, visiting often and supporting each other in many ways.

Father's plan would make it possible for Mother and Zia Ceserina to be together every day as neighbors. He had contracted to have two houses built next door to one another on Agate Avenue, a new resi-

[1] An outhouse.
[2] Aunt.

dential area near the Emporium. The idea seemed logical to Father; he figured that Mother would be thrilled. However, the thought of consulting beforehand with her or Zia Ceserina evidently had not occurred to him. Consequently, he did not reveal his plan to anyone in the family until workers were giving the two houses on Agate Avenue their final coats of paint.

One mid-afternoon in 1929, Mother and I were in the sun room enjoying the warmth of spring, when Father burst into the room.

He exclaimed proudly, "My dear Brigitina, I have a surprise for you. On Agate Avenue, I have had two houses built next to each other—one for you and one for Ceserina. Now you can be together every day. The houses are just about finished. You and Ceserina will be able to move in very soon."

Mother looked up in amazement. She paused for a moment as thoughts raced through her head. Then she said, "But Tony, that is not where I want to live!"

He looked at her, dumbfounded. "You *don't!*" he blurted out. "Then where *do* you want to live?"

"On the farm," she replied calmly. She had decided in her wisdom that Father needed the quiet, country atmosphere far more than she needed a new house with all the fixings.

"The *farm?*" he replied in disbelief.

"We can make it possible," she murmured softly. "It will be easy."

Father stood there staring at Mother as she continued, "We'll need more water than what the old well can give us. We'll have an artesian well dug and a pump put in for running water, and we'll need a bathroom. We had better put in steam heat. It will be too cold for the children with only the coal stove in the kitchen." Folding her hands together and dropping them into her lap, she smiled and said, "That's all we need to do."

Father's frown faded away as he began to understand what Mother was saying. Father loved the farm; he loved the fragrances of early morning, the stillness of early evening, the chirping of the crickets and the songs of the tree toads. Mother knew the farm was the only place where he could relax.

"Brigitina, you are right!" he exclaimed. "Nothing would make me happier than moving to the farm."

"Good! Then it's settled, isn't it?" said Mother.

Father was elated. He could envision the farm with all the improvements Mother had suggested.

"And I'll find out if we can have a telephone put in," he said as he left the room.

Mother breathed a sigh of relief. Father had gone along so willingly with her idea. Her choice turned out to be a wise one.

Changes

When the stock market crashed in October, 1929, and the Great Depression followed, neither event affected Pa directly. He had not invested in stocks, not even the new Coca Cola stock at four cents a share, which a broker had begged him to buy. Instead, he continued to buy properties. In addition to his usual business concerns, he was busy winterizing the house on the farm. By fall, the artesian well-diggers had found an ample supply of water at a depth of 90' and had installed a pump that fed running water to the kitchen and the bathroom (which Father had created by closing off part of a bedroom).

The move to the farm in the spring of 1930 was a happy occasion. Mother settled us in comfortably. In the one and only clothes closet, she stored our Sunday best, our school clothes, and after-school clothes. She stocked the pantry with all the basics. The black, cast-iron Glenwood coal stove kept the kitchen warmer and cozier than the other rooms, which were heated by inefficient steam radiators. So the kitchen became the natural center of activity, as it was in most homes then.

Each evening, we gathered around the kitchen table, where we did our homework while Mother knitted or sewed. Olga would be tucked into bed in her room off to the left. Father sat in the corner of the kitchen by the stove, reading the *Evening Gazette*.[2]

The kitchen had seven doors in all, five of which opened into the den, the cellar, two bedrooms, and a bathroom (complete with indoor plumbing and bathtub). Another door led to a partially-finished bedroom upstairs, where Anthony slept. There was also a pantry, which differed from other pantries in that it was not a separate room; it was the part of the kitchen furthest from the back door. A door at the end of the pantry opened into the living room; off to the right of the living

---

[2] The two main newspapers at that time were the *Worcester Telegram* and the *Worcester Gazette*. In 1988, they merged to become the *Worcester Telegram and Gazette*. In 1989 the owners shortened the name to *Telegram & Gazette*.

room was a bedroom with the only closet.

The artesian well provided an abundant supply of crystal clear water, so much so that during a drought, when other wells in the area went dry, people came to our house to fill their buckets with water. We were happy to share it with others. Everything worked out just as Ma had said it would.

Then, in the early 1930s, the country began to slide deeper into the Great Depression. Several of Father's tenants lost their jobs and had to move themselves and their families in with relatives. One by one, Father's properties were becoming vacant. He wanted to complete the cement-block "garage" at 193 Boston Turnpike that he had recently purchased, but he had no funds. The garage was his prized possession, primarily because it was located on the Boston Turnpike. He had predicted that "fifty years from now, there will be businesses all the way along Route 9, from Worcester to Boston, like one big city." He kept telling us that "any property on Route 9, the Boston Turnpike, will be good." Pa really wanted to buy more property on the Turnpike, but the situation was bleak—with one exception: the Emporium was still highly profitable. In fact, it had become our main source of income.

Then my father did something that would puzzle us for many years to come. Upon arriving home from work one day, he announced, "I sold the Emporium!" Mother was aghast! She knew how much Father loved his Emporium. It was his pride and joy, and business had been thriving.

"You've sold the store!" she exclaimed.

"Just the business, not the building."

"But, why?" Mother asked incredulously.

"Because I *wanted to!*" was his emphatic reply. Mother knew by the tone of his voice that she was not to question further. She did not want to aggravate him and cause him to act up. He could not tell her why he "wanted to" sell the Emporium; he kept his reasons to himself.

Mother had to accept Pa's decision. She knew that the lack of income from the Emporium would increase the pressure on him, so she did what she could to make the best of the situation.

As the Great Depression continued, and as most of Father's properties became vacant, he became more tense and belligerent. When Pa drove into the driveway, Anthony and I, then fourteen and ten years old respectively, would scoot to our bedrooms. Olga, six years old, had also learned that it was better to be out of sight when Father walked in the door. As Mother spoke calmly with Father, his anger would subside a little.

Afterward, she would explain to us, "Your father is exhausted from working such long hours. Three hours sleep is not enough. Too much work! Too much!"

Shortly after Father sold the business, a fire of unknown origin damaged the interior of the Emporium building. Pa was devastated; consequently, his behavior become increasingly irrational, and he made threats that were frightening. At those times, Mother would take hold of our hands and, facing Father, she would speak softly. Usually her voice was enough to quiet him, but as the situation became more life threatening, she became concerned about Father's well-being and our safety, so she went to see our doctor. After consulting with other doctors, Dr. Benaglia called on Mother.

"Mrs. Borgatti, Antonio needs help," he said.

"Yes, I know that something isn't right," Mother replied.

"He needs treatment," Dr. Benaglia continued. "It will be necessary to hospitalize him as soon as possible. It's going to take a long time."

Knowing that the doctor was right, Mother agreed with a heavy heart to Pa's confinement at Worcester State Hospital on Belmont Hill. Father knew many of the hospital staff members, especially those who had crossed the street to buy their lunches and enjoy a moment of relaxation from their long hours of duty. They knew Father well and admired him. He had served them; now they would be serving him.

The day Father's cousin came to take him to the hospital was a day of sadness for us; it was also one of great relief. Pa went willingly. He knew he needed help. We stood in the driveway until the car turned the corner.

As we were walking back to the house, Anthony said, "It's better this way, Ma. It's better for Pa: better for us, and better for you, too."

Mother turned to him and nodded. "Yes, Anthony."

I remember glancing up at Anthony as he spoke. He had no tears, but he swallowed the hard lump in his throat as he tried to console our mother. At that moment, whether or not he was aware of it, Anthony became the "father of the family." He comforted Mother, who turned to him for support and reassurance. For us, his siblings, he assumed the role of protector; we revered him. In retrospect, he took on an awesome responsibility for a fourteen-year-old.

Today, the medical profession knows a lot more about mental illness. In 1930, however, psychiatry was in its infancy. Fortunately for Father, the Worcester State Hospital was on the forefront of research in the diagnosis and treatment of mental illnesses.

As far as I can remember, Anthony's classmates did not bother him about Pa being in the state hospital. At least I do not remember ever hearing him talk about it. My experience was different, however. On the playground at school, the other children would taunt me about Father. On reaching home, I would bolt through the doorway, and run sobbing into my mother's arms.

"The kids say that Pa is crazy, Ma," I stammered between sobs.

In her gentle voice she would say, "It's because they just don't understand, Elsa. There is no reason for them to speak to you like that."

Most of our friends and neighbors were understanding and helpful. Mr. Holmes used to come over and ask, "Anything I can do for you today, Mrs. Borgatti? Fix something? Move something?" It seemed as if there always was something for him to do. I do not know how we would have survived without his help.

—Jim Tivnan

The home of Mr. and Mrs. Banning,
later to become the home of Olive and Anthony.

We loved the chocolate cupcakes that Mrs. Warren used to send over to us, and the loaves of homemade bread that other neighbors shared with us. Our neighbors were thoughtful in many ways. I felt special when Mrs. Banning, who lived around the corner, gave me pretty colored ribbons for my sewing basket, and it was during that time that Mr. Banning taught Anthony how to play chess. Anthony became an avid chess player and "an opponent to be reckoned with," according to Mr. Banning.

A few of our neighbors distanced themselves from us at first, but later they too began to understand and extend their friendship. We were so fortunate to have them during this difficult time.

A month after Pa went into the hospital, Mother gave birth at home to a baby boy, whom we named Robert and nicknamed Bobbie. Anthony, fourteen years older, served as a father figure to Bobbie while he was growing up. (The two of them drew closer later on as their business and social activities brought them together.)

Anthony, the Brother

Up until the family's move to the farm, Anthony and I were pals. Then I discovered that the last person a teenager wants to have at his heels is a kid sister, especially one who was a pest, like I was. One day, I was more obnoxious than usual and I went too far. Anthony and his friend, Eric Holm, were about to leave for a hike in the woods.

I called after him, "Anthony, wait for me. I want to go with you."

"No, you're not! This is just for us guys. Now scram!" he said. I followed anyway as they started down the path to the woods.

"Go on home!" he yelled at me. I continued to follow close at his heels. His face was getting red; his patience became frayed. "I told you to scram!" With that he delivered the medicine that I am sure I had coming to me; he gave me a glancing blow and a shove. I felt the sting from a slap as it glanced off my cheek. No harm done, except to my pride.

"I'm going to tell Ma on you!" I cried as I ran back to the house.

Mother was brushing Olga's hair as I rushed in, hollering my head off. Of course, I played it to the hilt, sobbing, "Anthony socked me! Anthony socked me!"

"Elsa, you shouldn't bother Anthony when he is with his friends, but he should never have hit you. I will take care of him when he comes home," she said as she took Father's razor strap from its hook behind the stove and placed it nearby.

When Anthony returned home a little later, he scooted like a rabbit into the nearest bedroom with my mother in pursuit. He dove under the bed and out of reach. This did not faze Mother. She promptly placed a chair in the doorway to the bedroom and sat down. With the strap lying across her lap, she calmly announced, "I can wait. I have all day and no place to go."

As far as I can remember, that was the first and only time the strap was ever used. It was more a symbol of authority than an instrument of discipline. Mother made it clear to Anthony: "Always treat a girl with respect and no other way!"

As a rule, Mother, who did most of the disciplining, taught by example; we knew what was expected of us, and we did it as a matter of course. She seldom had to scold us; her firm but loving ways were generally effective. Anthony learned his lesson; he never had to be told again.

Nevertheless, we still regarded each other as a real pain during our teen years. Then, when Anthony discovered girls, I found that I had a green monster of envy in me. I remember a particular incident that happened shortly after he had learned to drive a car.

Pa's Hupmobile was long gone. A family friend had kindly offered us the use of his car so that Anthony could run errands for Ma. I thought this was great. But I soon found out that my dear brother did not find it convenient to have me accompany him on any of these errands.

One stormy winter day, he told Mother that he had to be somewhere, and before I could say anything about the errand I had to do, he was off in a big hurry. A few minutes later, I left the house to do my errand in Worcester. Trudging through the snow to the bus stop down the street, I bucked the bitterly cold wind. I could feel more snow in the air as I waited for the bus to come along. It seemed like forever. As I waited, I watched the cars go by. Cars in those days did not travel very fast, and there were not that many on the road, so it was easy to spot Anthony as he drove toward me. Expecting him to stop, and happy at the thought of getting a ride, I stepped closer to the curbing as he approached. With a barely visible wave of his left hand on the wheel, and a smirk on his face, he went sailing past me. I could see that his right arm was cozily wrapped around a perky blond snuggled alongside him. Who needed me? Unquestionably, I was excess baggage. Can you imagine my indignation? My chagrin?

He did it more than once! Mother had to speak with him several times before he changed his ways and permitted me to sit in the back seat when one of his many girlfriends happened to be in the car. We remained at odds until I accepted the fact that he was going to have girls in his life, and he accepted that there would be times when he would have to put up with having his sister in the car. Then we became friends again.

Incidents like these aside, Anthony was a good and thoughtful brother. For instance, he went out of his way to spend time with Olga. If she were in her room, he would whistle a few notes at her bedroom door and then go in and chat with her. Usually, from his bulging pockets, he pulled out a book on birds, crafts, or whatever he thought she would like. After noticing her delight in receiving a souvenir letter opener he had brought her, he began to collect them for her. (Years later, whenever he returned from a trip, he would present her with one or several new openers. On his travels, he must have searched extensively to find various shapes and kinds of openers that would please her. Olga kept her collection of over two hundred in a decorative cedar chest, and she spent endless hours admiring them or showing them to friends. Anthony looked for ways to make Olga happy.)

It was not surprising that the happiness of others was uppermost in Anthony's mind when I asked Mother for a bicycle. Anthony's friends had bicycles, but he did not have one himself, nor had he asked for one. Mother turned to him and asked, "Anthony, do you think we should get a bicycle for Elsa?"

Without hesitating a moment, he replied, "Oh, yes, Ma! I'll go into Worcester and buy the best one they have!" Most brothers in that situation would have said, "How about me?" Not Anthony. His greatest pleasure lay in making someone else happy—except for the teasing, of course. In that regard, Anthony was a "chip off the old block." He loved to tease, and after watching Father, he probably learned that I was fair game. There was a difference, however. Whereas Father teased me to prove that he was more knowledgeable, Anthony teased me for the fun of it; moreover, he continued to tease me well into our adult years. Otherwise, he was the best big brother that any one could ever want. Olga, Bobbie, and I idolized him.

Learning the Truth

Mother never learned the reason Pa sold the Emporium, but Anthony did. However, he didn't tell me about it until Memorial Day shortly after Mother died, when we had gone to the cemetery together to place fresh flowers on our parents' grave. As we trimmed the grass around the headstone, Anthony looked at me and said, "You know what, Elsa, Pa told me why he sold the Emporium."

"He did!" I replied, wide-eyed.

"Yeah, one day we were working on the stone walls, and the subject of the Emporium came up. That's when he told me that he was *forced* to sell the business."

"He what?" I asked, puzzled.

Anthony lowered his voice and continued with a pained expression. "He told me that two men tried several times to force Pa into selling the business. Then Pa remembered that a few years back, the owner of a grocery had refused to sell his store, and soon after, his 16-year-old daughter disappeared. She was never seen again, Elsa. That's why Pa decided to give in and sell. He was afraid for Ma and us."

"Oh, Anthony! How awful!" I responded, barely above a whisper. "Ma never knew about that, did she?"

"No," he replied as he shook his head.

"But you know, Anthony, this doesn't answer the other questions we have about Pa."

"What do you mean?"

"You know. How come Pa knew so much? How come he was so smart when he only went as far as the fourth grade?"

"I don't know. Just smart, I guess," replied Anthony. We accepted the fact that we probably would never know.

However, a few years later, in 1976, Father's younger brother, Zio[3] Pietro Borgatti, made his first trip to the States to "visit my brother's children in America." Zio Pietro was a retired farmer living on the family homestead in Renazzo, Italy. He stayed with my husband Jim and me, and he was a delight to have as a guest. During his three

---

[3] Uncle.

weeks in this country, Zio visited with Anthony as well as other members of the family. He enjoyed our joking and bantering in our broken Italian, but during the last few days before he was to return to Italy, he preferred to sit quietly and chat about his younger years on his farm.

On one of those warm August days, he was telling me something about the value of the family farm land in Italy when he suddenly stopped, turned to me, and asked, "Elsa, did your mother ever tell you that your father studied to be a priest?"

I could not speak; I was confused. Did I understand correctly or were my ears deceiving me? He repeated his startling question. I shook my head in disbelief.

Pietro continued, "On finishing his studies prior to his ordination into the priesthood that was to take place on the next Saturday, your father went for a few days on a sightseeing trip. Mother had laid out his vestments on his bed upstairs awaiting his return. For fifty years they lay there until they fell apart due to the sun and age."

Astonished, I gasped in my broken Italian, "Zio Pietro, would you please repeat that?"

He did repeat it, but even on the second telling, I found it hard to comprehend.

"My *father?*" I asked, still not able to believe what I was hearing.

"Yes, *your* father," Zio said. "Three months later, a letter from Antonio arrived by steamship. Enclosed was a sum of money with a note. In the note, Antonio told us to give the money to the church. That money was the first of many installments he sent to the church to honor his obligation. It was payment for the education he had received."

My head began to swim. A thousand thoughts came to mind as memories of Pa swirled around in my head. I recalled hearing Pa speaking in different languages to customers in the Emporium, and how amazed we were by his extensive knowledge of history and geography. I could see his beautiful handwritten letters, and I could hear his litany, "I only went to the fourth grade in school."

Zio Pietro continued, unaware of my bewildered state of mind, "We were poor farmers when your father was growing up. Public education in rural Italy was limited. Church subsidized education was available only to aspiring priests. Antonio sent money to pay for his education."

I tried to listen to Zio, but my thoughts kept running back to those days when Pa was extremely agitated, remembering how this happened especially when Olga was in pain.

"Why, Zio Pietro?" I stammered. "Why didn't he tell us?"

Realizing that I knew nothing about my father's training for the priesthood, he asked, "Why do you suppose your mother did not tell you that your father was supposed to be a priest?"

I recall answering simply and without any doubt in my mind, "Because she didn't know, Zio Pietro."

Lunch seemed to take forever. When it was finally over, I left Zio Pietro to have his siesta, and wasted no time in driving over to Anthony's office. He was sitting at his desk when I burst in and blurted out, "I have something unbelievable to tell you! Zio Pietro just told me that Pa studied to be a priest, and...."

Anthony gasped, "What!"

Breathlessly, I related Zio's story.

"No wonder that Pa knew so much!" Anthony said as he leaned back in his chair and cupped his chin, a habit of his.

"That's where he learned to speak English, German, French, and Latin," I added.

"His handwriting!"

I nodded, knowing that Anthony was referring to Pa's beautiful script.

"You know, Anthony, in those days, leaving the priesthood was like forsaking God, and a disgrace to the family, too. Pa must have felt terribly guilty."

"Yes, and Olga… He must have felt that God had punished him by making her an invalid."

"That's probably why he couldn't bear to hear her cry," I added. "It all begins to add up and make sense, doesn't it?"

"Yeah," agreed Anthony. "His guilty conscience must have plagued him, making him miserable. It could have been the reason for his illness."

"Oh, Anthony," I said as I sat down in the chair across from him, "Zio Pietro's story explains so much about Pa: those long hours he worked, possibly to crowd out the guilt, the lack of sleep, the exhaustion, the stress..."

"The hollering that scared us silly!" Anthony added.

"Pa must have been under this terrible stress long before he had been forced to sell the store."

"Right! But today, it's not like it was then, Elsa. Seminary students today may change their minds about the priesthood. It doesn't have any dishonor attached to it, not any more than any other change of vocation."

"I know, Anthony, but wasn't it unfortunate that Pa locked that secret burden within him and suffered such untold anguish all those years? He could have shared his burden, at least with Ma, the pillar of understanding who was always there right at his side."

"It is sad," replied Anthony, heaving a sigh, "That's what it is, sad!"

We agreed that this was probably the saddest thing that had ever happened to our family.

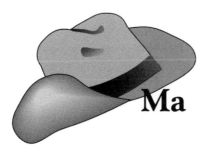

Ma

"How did Ma do it?"
—Anthony

While Pa was in the hospital, Anthony seemed to be fully aware of how much Mother was going through, and he tried to help whenever he could. He went on errands, did the grocery shopping, kept the coal hod full, fed the dog, cut the grass, and shoveled snow. He couldn't do enough for her.

He also learned a great deal by observing how Ma handled difficult situations. Goodness knows she had her hands full after Pa went into the hospital. In addition to the cooking and cleaning, the care of our new baby brother and of six-year-old Olga, who still required a great deal of attention, she also had the responsibility of the already precarious business finances.

With Father's hospitalization, all of his business affairs had come to a standstill, and unfortunately for Mother, he carried many of his real estate records in his head. She found very few papers or files. Men sealed most agreements with a handshake, not an unusual practice then.

To add to Mother's difficulties, very few of Pa's financial affairs and investments in real estate were known to her. She was aware that the two new houses on Agate Avenue, the building that had previously housed Father's Emporium, the three-decker next to the Emporium, and the unfinished garage at 193 Boston Turnpike were all standing vacant. The existence of other properties became known as tenants reported a problem with plumbing or some such thing. By asking the tenant about the location of the property, Ma gradually learned about some of Father's other holdings. She often became aware of others when mortgage payments came due and real estate tax bills arrived. Father's lawyer and good friend, Mr. Nicholas Fusaro, helped Mother as much as he could by advising her on property matters and finances. Like many others who had invested in real estate, we had become property poor.

Mother's situation could have been overwhelming, but she was a realist and a positive thinker. She accepted what could not be changed and focused her efforts on what had to be done. Optimistic by nature, she spoke often of the time when Father would be released from the hospital.

"I have to hold onto Father's property for him," she explained. "I have to keep it for the time when he comes home. If I lose his property, it could cause him to have a relapse from which he may never recover."

Almost daily, Anthony used to say, "Ma can make it happen."

Fortunately, Ma's sister, Zia Ceserina, helped us during these trying times. Ceserina's small grocery store was thriving. So she was able to lend us money so Mother could meet some of her business obligations, such as real estate taxes. Consequently, Ma was able to hold onto some of Pa's properties and managed to pay for the completion of the garage on the Boston Turnpike, Pa's favorite piece of property.

Ceserina also sent her oldest daughter, Angelina, to help Mother. Angelina was like a big sister to us. She had Mother's even features and her black wavy hair, but her eyes were blue. She used to spend her weekends and summer vacations with us. Now, at sixteen, she was a tremendous help to Mother, caring for Olga and the baby. Anthony also helped on weekends and after school, returning by trolley from Grafton Street Junior High in Worcester, where he was completing the eighth grade.

Through it all, Mother kept a spotless home. On Sundays, when Zia Ceserina and our cousins came, we had dinner in the dining room. For our other meals in the kitchen, Mother spread a white linen table cloth. She was always cheerful; I remember her big smile and twinkling eyes. She loved to laugh and had a warm welcome for all. Never did she make a fuss about the burden she was carrying or ask, "Why me?" She simply and gracefully accepted her lot, and in doing so set an example for us all. Unquestionably, Mother was Anthony's inspiration throughout his life—and with good reason.

Father's Return

Mother's faith was rewarded as Father responded to the fine care and treatments at the hospital. Three years later, the time arrived when the doctors allowed him to come home for a few hours, and later they extended his visits to overnight. We were happy to have Father home, but memories of his frightening rages were still vivid in our minds. I was worried about what he might do; Anthony was also deeply concerned. Later, he said, "I slept with one eye open. If I heard Pa get up in the middle of the night, I'd come downstairs to the kitchen and ask, 'What are you doing, Pa?' He would usually answer, 'Getting a drink of water.' Once Father was back in bed, I would return to my room upstairs." Mother slept soundly through all of this.

Eventually, we became more comfortable with Pa being at home, especially after he took over the care of the chickens and started working in the garden. He began to rebuild the stone walls around the property; this activity seemed to be good for him. We learned, however, that when we discussed any business matters in his presence, he would become agitated and volatile. It probably reminded him of his limitations and frustrated him.

At long last the hospital discharged him permanently. Pa was never his old self again, but he did gradually relax and become happily involved with the farm, especially so, when a neighboring farmer gave Pa a three-teated Jersey cow named Patsy. Patsy did not meet specifications for the farmer's newly-installed milking machine. Pa, who knew how to care for a cow and how to milk her by hand, was delighted. Later on, a Morgan mare joined Patsy in the barn.

Pa looked forward to the fall, when the ritual in practically every Italian household was the making of wine and the restocking of the wine cellar—a ritual in which my father took part with great energy. The grapes from California arrived in New England in early October. Mr. Adams, one of the distributors, parked his Reo truck laden with grapes on Shrewsbury Street. As he unloaded some of the wooden crates of fruit and stacked them in a pile on the sidewalk next to his truck, a pungent fragrance of grapes enveloped the area.

With Anthony in tow, Father joined the dozens of other wine-makers, usually the men of the families, as they gathered around Mr. Adams and his truck and began bargaining for the grapes. It was a bee-hive of activity; business was lively and noisy. At times customers' voices became louder and more vociferous as they aggressively tried to apply their negotiating skills. Anthony loved to listen as Pa bargained, a carry-over custom from his native land, where it was not only an accepted procedure in transacting business but an expected one. This was true in most foreign lands, and it exists even today, especially in rural areas. But Mr. Adams, the grape merchant, did not care to bargain. He would shout, "This is America, not back home [in Italy]. The price on the box is the price you pay." Anthony remembered Mr. Adams' simplified pricing method. At SPAG'S, he made sure the price was the same for everyone.

Mr. Adams offered two varieties of grapes: white Muscato grapes for making Muscatel wine and red Zinfandel grapes for making Zinfandel wine. Pa bought mostly red grapes and a few crates of white to make his own blend. At family meals, he served his Zinfandel, first pouring a sampling of a half inch or so, which he then offered to one of us kids to test for approval. Pa said, "This is to make you discerning." Then he served the wine to everyone, children included. Our parents wanted us to realize that wine was for enjoyment and aided digestion. They wanted us to learn respect for it there at our own table. As Father reminded family and friends, "Always remember, wine is to drink; water is to wash your feet."

Although Father was not completely well, there were situations in which he exerted his authority firmly. I remember it well. On one occasion, I was the recipient of his tongue lashing after I had made a negative comment about a garbage collector. In a loud voice, Pa said, "Any person who carries out his responsibilities to the best of his ability is to be honored and respected! Do you understand that, Elsa?" I hung my head in shame and never forgot that lesson. Neither did Anthony, who heard it all.

Mother calmly went about her business, taking each day as it came with full trust that everything was just as God had intended it to be. Her love and compassion for her family extended to everyone who came to the door. Her generosity and respect for others was exemplified in her dealings with Mr. Horseradish.

"Horseradish! Horseradish! Need any horseradish today?" he would call out. His voice was gentle; his words were unclear, probably due to his hair-lip impediment. When we heard his familiar voice, we made a bee-line to the back door to let him in—it was our friend, Mr. Horseradish. That was the only name we knew, even though he came once a month during the horseradish season for many years.

He was a kindly old gentleman, tall, but slightly stooped, and rough shaven. Carrying the horseradish in a covered wooden bucket, his tattered clothes, although clean, made him look shabby.

Mother, a steady customer, took an empty canning jar from the pantry to make her purchase. When Mr. Horseradish lifted the cover, a pungent whiff of freshly-ground "stuff," as he called it, filled the kitchen. Using the wooden cup that hung inside the bucket, he doled out his product. I do not know what Mother did with the horseradish she bought. It was neither a condiment nor medicine for us; we just never saw it again.

Anthony later recalled those days: "Ma didn't pay him the few cents that he asked; instead, she always gave him what he could use, 50 cents. Every visitor received a warm welcome at our house." Throughout his life, Anthony continued to welcome everyone who came to his door. I can remember him saying, "The day my friends can't come to my house is the day I go out of business."

"How?"

All through his adult life, whenever he received any awards or praise, Anthony always passed on the credit to others—his wife, his employees, the customers, vendors, his friends, and his community. But seldom a day passed that he didn't in some way mention our mother, Brigida, and express his admiration for her. She had been his mentor and his guide. Consequently, whether in an interview or in a talk, he would speak of her. Anthony once said, "Whenever I was faced with what seemed to be an unsolvable problem, I just asked myself, 'How would Ma handle this?'" The answer would come, he would act accordingly, and somehow things seemed to work out.

Mother's capacity for coping—always with grace and calmness—

was a source of wonderment and inspiration to us all. Anthony would shake his head and ask, "How did she do it, Elsa? Not only did she care for Olga and Bobbie, a newborn, but she also visited Father in the hospital and consulted with the doctors regularly. She also was faced with handling Father's business matters for the first time. How did she handle it all?"

"I don't know," I replied, but I decided that I would ask her.

Mother and I were enjoying a pleasant drive ride through the countryside one Sunday afternoon when I made my inquiry.

"Brigie [the name by which I affectionately addressed her], how did you ever manage to bring us through those difficult times when Pa was in the hospital?"

I had only to look into her beautiful Madonna-like face for the answer. Her serene radiance was even more pronounced in her twilight years. She had learned the art of living.

"God," she responded without hesitating, "God gave me the strength to live one day at a time. Besides, I knew He wouldn't give me anything I could not carry."

"But, Brigie," I asked, "how could you sleep at night?"

Matter-of-factly, she responded, "Every morning was a new day. With God's help, I did the best I knew how. At night, I said my prayers, then went to bed. I never thought of the tomorrows nor what was yesterday." As she said this, I recalled seeing Mother in the bedroom on bended knees, her head bowed in fervent prayer. Her life was built on an unwavering faith that gave her the strength to meet the challenges of each day.

"Never look back. Take each day as it comes," was her philosophy.

"But," I pressed further, "how could you not worry about Olga's future, Ma?"

"Elsa, I could not have endured it if I had worried about the many years that Olga would suffer. Instead I took each day and appreciated the joy that Olga brought us." After a pause, she continued, "Yes, Elsa, some of the best laughs I ever had were moments when Olga and I were alone."

As she spoke of Olga, Mother's face glowed. She radiated an inner peace. Small wonder that so many friends—some close, some not so close, of all ages and in varied walks of life—sought her out. They came for advice, or consolation, or a solution to what seemed to be an insurmountable problem. Some came to draw upon her deep under-standing of life, or just to hear her comforting voice. She must have been helpful to many, for I easily recall the words of gratitude expressed by visitors as they took their leave. She was greatly missed when she died in 1972.[2]

[2] Father passed away in 1968; Olga died in 1964.

Anthony "Spag" Borgatti, Jr. High school graduation, 1934.

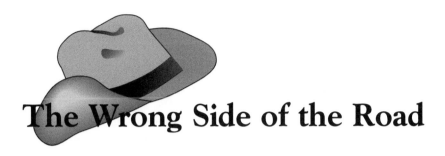

The Wrong Side of the Road

I like to talk, and I like to sell.
—Spag

"Anthony's fame started in high school," said Ernie Tosi, a teacher at Major Howard Beal Memorial High School. Well, Anthony did, at least, acquire the nickname "Spag" in high school due to his well-known fondness for spaghetti and to a slip of the tongue.

When James Cooke, the principal, called the daily class roll, he usually pronounced Borgatti as "Borgetti." But one morning he inadvertently called out, "Spaghetti." Gales of laughter filled the hall.

From that time on, Anthony's pals called him "Spaghetti;" they rarely ever used his given name. The die was cast. It was inevitable that his classmates would shorten "Spaghetti" to "Spag," a name he carried for the rest of his life.

High School

From the time he served his first customer at the Emporium, selling was Anthony's strength. While in high school, he had enjoyed his after-school job selling Fuller brushes door-to-door. At that time, he was the star salesman of the New England area.

"How could I miss?" he would say with a grin. "I was always quick to put my foot in the door the minute it opened. And I liked Fuller brushes. I believed that every household should have them, so I gave my full spiel explaining why they should own one of my brushes. Boy! Was I lucky! Almost everyone bought at least one. The best part was that I became their friend, and was welcomed the next time I came to call."

During his high school years, Anthony also sold Watkins baking products, such as vanilla, cream of tartar, baking powder, and soft soaps. "They were good products," he said, "but money was scarce. The Great Depression was in full swing. I sold about eight dollars' worth in a week; that probably netted me about $2.25." Everything he made he gave to Ma.

Anthony traveled his route by bus and foot to reach the friends and neighbors he called on regularly. Norina Costa, whose family was on his route, told me that "Anthony whistled his way to the back door; his manner was easy-going and jolly. He greeted us with a wide smile and a pleasant word."

Anthony fondly remembered his best customers, the Bannings, who lived on Beverly Road, around the corner; the back of their house faced the side of our barn. The Bannings had no children of their own. Consequently, they looked upon Anthony as the son they never had. Anthony learned later that Mrs. Banning would go without things she really needed to buy something from him. "No wonder she was my best customer," Anthony said. "She was a great lady, always helping someone."

Anthony's friendship with the Bannings lasted throughout their lives. He never forgot their kindness. After Mr. Banning died, his wife moved into a small apartment in Auburn. Mrs. Banning had worked long before social security was available; the meager amounts she earned in her earlier years were not adequate for her old age. Anthony continued to visit her regularly to make sure she had enough to meet her daily needs.

"It takes money to live, no matter how frugal a person tries to be," Anthony would say.

In school, Spag was well liked by other students—with one exception, a pretty junior named Olive Lutz. She told Anthony that she did not like his "garrulous manner" nor the "silly knickers he wore." (For some reason, he was one of the very few who continued to wear knickers all during high school, although they were going out of style.) Olive also complained that he fooled around too much. Her comments did not bother Anthony. He thought she was "too serious." Besides, Anthony was not thinking of settling down with one girl; he had lots of friends. They enjoyed his great sense of humor, his fun-loving and flamboyant personality, and his stream of ideas.

Bob Lutz, a classmate who happened to be Olive's brother and future assistant treasurer of SPAG'S, commented that "Anthony excelled in extracurricular activities, but his interest in Shakespeare, trigonometry, and chemistry was not that strong. However, his early background in business did make him sharp. No one ever put anything over on him, and he always knew that two and two were four."

Anthony's ability to sell things and his creative ideas for business became increasingly evident in school. Ann Bianchi, class president, recalled that "Anthony enjoyed selling tickets whenever there were tickets to sell. The fact that he did not belong to a club did not deter him; he still sold the most tickets." As expected, he also sold the most advertisements for his class yearbook.

Merle Sturtevant, Superintendent of Schools at the time, observed, "With Anthony's perseverance and exuberance, he could sell bathing suits to the Eskimos." Small wonder Anthony's classmates chose him as "the most likely to succeed in business," and described him as "the noisiest," "the most talkative," "the most argumentative," "the most romantic," and "the most helpful to the class." His classmates also appreciated Anthony's suggestion to name their class yearbook "The Last Round-up."

Anthony graduated from high school in June 1934, in the middle of the Great Depression. He told Mother that he would like to go to Harvard University. "Harvard has class," he said, "and I might as well go for the best." The family finances were not that great, however. Father had returned from the hospital, but he was not able to participate in business matters; instead, he simply puttered around the farm.

The family income depended primarily on the rental properties, but most of them were still vacant. Mother told Anthony that Harvard was out of the question. She suggested a local night school. He tried it for a month, but it held no interest for him at all. "It's not challenging," he told Ma. "It's just a repeat of what I studied in high school. So it's a waste of my time and your money."

The Jalopy

During Anthony's high school years, many changes in transportation had taken place. He and I watched as the last Boston-Worcester trolley, running on tracks parallel to Route 9 in Shrewsbury, passed into history. Buses replaced the trolleys, and more people were buying cars. We also stopped to watch as workmen poured cement on Route 9, later to be called the Boston Turnpike, making it the first four-lane highway from Worcester to Boston, just as Father had predicted.

At that time, Ford Motor Company and General Motors were selling lower-priced cars. Most people, however, could not afford them—at least not new ones. Mother, realizing that she needed a car for carrying on her business and for taking Olga to the doctor, reluctantly agreed to buy a used car. It was a very used car—a secondhand, green Buick with a rumble seat, which we called "The Jalopy."

Anthony had learned to drive the car, and, fortunately, he was a much better driver than Father had been. His only problem occurred when someone tried to give him directions. Trying to follow "left-right" directions was frustrating for him; the words "take a left at the next corner" meant nothing to Anthony. We had a few close calls before we learned to tap on his left or right shoulder for a left or right turn.

The jalopy was always in need of servicing of one kind or another. That is the way it was with cars in those days; frequent stops for repairs were the norm. We rarely went for a Sunday afternoon ride without seeing two or three disabled cars on the side of the road. The passengers usually stood by while a radiator vented a cloud of steam or a driver fixed a flat tire. Anthony carried a jack, an extra inner tube, and patches in the trunk of the jalopy; he had his share of these common occurrences.

Fireworks

Times were still tough in 1934. Anthony, now graduated from high school, did not have a job, but the big, big celebration—the Fourth of July—was around the corner. "People needed fireworks more than they needed food," he recalled. "I saw an opportunity to fill that need and an opportunity to make some money besides." In those days, it was legal in Massachusetts to buy and sell fireworks and sparklers. Young and old looked forward to the Fourth of July. They purchased fireworks either from the neighborhood grocer or from the dozens of lean-tos set up along the roadside.

With a loan from Mother in his pocket, Anthony drove into Worcester to buy firecrackers, sparklers, rockets, and cherry bombs from a man who made them in his backyard shed. He then returned to Shrewsbury, going to the now-completed garage at 193 Boston Turnpike that Mother was renting to the M&M Trucking Company. He built a lean-to alongside the garage, facing Route 9, and set up a display of his fireworks.

As Anthony noted, "Business was brisk during the three days before the Fourth." He easily sold out his entire inventory and promptly turned the proceeds over to Mother—a total of $200, which was a large amount of money in those days. He sold fireworks along-side the garage for the next six years.

Looking for the Right Job

Anthony was pleased with his profitable fireworks venture, but he needed a steady job. A few of his friends had joined the Civilian Conservation Corps, a program created by the U.S. Congress that employed young men and youths to build national and state parks and paths, as well as to work in forest conservation. Anthony wanted to join his buddies who were in the CCC, but Mother responded with a firm "no," adding, "There is plenty of work for you right here at home: the apple orchard, the garden, and the chickens."

Taking care of the chickens was no big deal for Anthony, but when it came to the unpleasant task of plucking them, that was a different story. He used to shudder at the thought of chickens hanging by their feet from the cellar beams waiting to have their feathers plucked. In later years, he groaned, "Chickens! I hated plucking chickens more than anything else." But he would do anything for Ma.

"Okay, Ma, I won't go into the CCC," replied Anthony, "but I need to do more than just the chores and the chickens. I need to find something else to do, too." Since there were no jobs available, Anthony decided that he had to make one for himself. He then asked himself two questions: "What kind of a job do I want?" and "What do I like to do most?"

His answers to those questions were, "I like to talk and I like to sell, so I should open a store and try it for a while." Years later he would chuckle while saying, "I never thought I'd be doing it for 60 years."

Mother and Father were elated with Anthony's decision to open a store. Naturally, they thought immediately of the old Emporium building that was standing empty, just waiting for an enterprising young man of eighteen. The lunch business had been a thriving one before Father sold it. Furthermore, prohibition was just ending. With that in mind, Mother and Father offered Anthony the use of the Emporium building. His response surprised them.

"I want no part of selling liquor," he said. Then he explained: "Being expected to carry it isn't for me. I know a restaurant with beer and wine would be promising financially, but I can't see making money at the expense of some of the families who would be deprived. I would feel that I had been instrumental."

Perplexed, Mother and Father asked Anthony where he wanted to have his store. "In the garage office," he answered, referring to their property on Route 9. "The front office in the M&M Transportation Company is not being used. I can set up my store there, and it's within walking distance of home."

The M&M Trucking Company, suffering the economic woes caused by the Depression, had vacated the small office in the front left side of the building. To provide access, a short flight of stairs led to a single door that opened into the 12' x 20' office with a high ceiling. Two large picture windows, one on each side of the door, faced the sidewalk and highway. A black potbelly stove, standing in front of the window on the right-hand side, was the sole source of heat. From the top of the stove, a black pipe rose toward the ceiling, and vented to the outside through a hole in the cement block wall. In a corner to the right of the stove was a four-foot square platform standing about five feet high, supported by two-by-fours. That was it.

Father agreed with Anthony. "The garage office facing the Boston Turnpike is a good place for a store."

"But, Anthony," Mother asked, "what are you going to sell?"

"I'm going to sell the stuff people need when their cars break down," he replied, "like fan belts, batteries, tire patches, spark plugs, and points. And I'm going to call it the Shrewsbury Tire and Battery Service."

The Store on the Wrong Side

The M&M garage happened to be one of the very few businesses on the west-bound side of the Boston Turnpike between Boston and Worcester. Most of the businesses were on the east-bound side of the road, going toward Boston. When neighbors and friends heard of Anthony's plan to open a store in the garage, they were quick to offer both advice and warnings. One neighbor said, "The garage is on the wrong side of the street for a store." Another stated, "It's preposterous to think of having a business on the side of the street where the traffic is moving toward Worcester." Yet another critic asked, "Why would people traveling west bother to stop where there is only one store, when they can go into Worcester and find a variety of stores and everything they need?" Still others said, "You'll never make it. People driving out from Worcester will not take the trouble to turn and cross over to one little store on the other side of the street. People are used to pulling up and parking at the curb in front of a store."

Anthony's response was, "It's what I have. It will work. If you need a dime and only have a nickel, you start with the nickel." Several years later, he noted, "They said I'd never make it where I was, on the wrong side of the highway. The place looked like a dump. You had to walk up stairs to get in. But I had to locate where I could get free rent."

In September 1934, Anthony launched his business in the garage at 193 Boston Turnpike, Shrewsbury. To furnish his store and "get going," he collected some empty wooden crates previously used as containers for large bottles of soda, long before cardboard and plastic were available. He then placed a large box upside-down to serve as a table for whatever business was in the offing. Around the "table," Anthony set up several other crates and empty, upended nail kegs to serve as seats. To display his merchandise along two of the walls, he placed two wide boards supported by crates. He also used an old apothecary cabinet, the drawers of which would in the future hold all kinds of nuts, screws, bolts, and household items.

With a 35 dollar loan from Mother, Anthony purchased his first inventory: two batteries, three sets of spark plugs, two sets of points, three fan belts, and three tube patching kits. With winter approaching, he also included tire chains and alcohol for antifreeze. "No other

YE OLDE
SCHOOLHOUSE
1985

THE WA[...]

4

TENT
1982

SPORT SHOP
1990

GAR[...]
19[...]

E

N   S

W

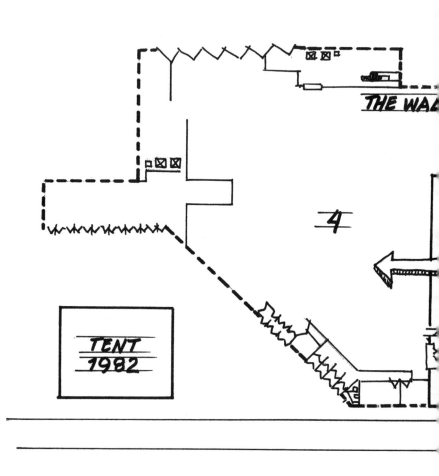
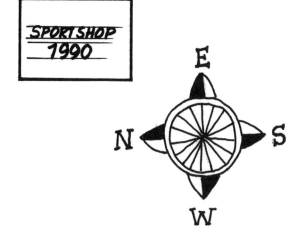

SPAG'S

193 BOSTON TURNPIKE, SHREWSBURY, MA 01545

ADDITIONS
1 – 1953
2 – 1958
3 – 1965
4 – 1993

GARAGE

B

1

A

2

BAKER AVENUE

ROUTE 9   BOSTON TURNPIKE

ORIGINAL SPACE
12' X 20'

EXPANSIONS
A – 1947
B – 1948

stores were carrying alcohol," he later recalled.

His friends—Eric Holm, Frank Viscardi, Joe Mazzari, and Bill Belanger—helped him carry his meager stock up the steps and into the empty office. There they displayed his merchandise to its best advantage. Then they all went outside to watch and cheer as the sign declaring "Shrewsbury Tire and Battery Service" went up over the door.

Those of Anthony's buddies who had not gone into the CCC congregated at the store. They had no jobs to go to, and the warmth of the potbelly stove provided an atmosphere of camaraderie. They helped by running to the boiler room in the cellar to fetch coal and wood to keep the fire going. While they were huddled around the stove waiting for customers, there was ample time for Anthony to "chew the fat with the guys" or to join them in a card game, such as pinochle or pitch. Two ladies remember entering the store one gloomy mid-morning in those early days when customers were few and far between. Anthony, who was sitting on an empty keg, stood up and greeted them with, "Boy, am I glad to see you! You're my first customers today." As Anthony often said, "If all I sold in a day was two cans of oil for 79 cents, that was a BIG day!"

How well I remember those winter days! To bring Anthony the supper that Mother prepared for him, I often had to trudge through 18 to 20 inches of snow. His lunch box contained three slices of Polini's Italian bread, generously spread with our own churned butter made from Patsy's milk; a thermos of chicken broth with Ma's homemade noodles; and, as a rule, an apple pie just out of the oven for Anthony and his buddies.

In those early days of the store, neighbors and people passing by would pause to take a look. For everyone, Anthony had a big "Hello!" and he would encourage them to stop in. "You don't have to have a reason, and you don't have to buy. Just come in and say hello. You're all my friends, and I like talking with you." He knew their pockets were as limited as his merchandise. "What the heck, none of us had any money in those days," he recalled later.

Anthony told me he wanted to get people used to the idea of coming in and looking around. "I figured one of these times when they stop by, they might need something, and might buy it from my place instead of going all the way into Worcester as they ordinarily would." Little by little, his idea caught on. Stopping in gradually became a habit with the neighbors. Some neighbors even brought frittelle, gnocchi, and other treats, which Anthony shared with his buddies. He was slowly building a customer base.

Anthony appreciated the interest and encouragement he received from his friends and neighbors, and he never forgot that they were the ones who had helped him get his start. Fifteen years later, Hugo Orizzi, one of the owners of Orlando's Market across the street from the store, would give credit to Anthony for all the area's growth. According to Hugo, "Spag brought the people to the Turnpike. After awhile, SPAG'S took off like a skyrocket, pulling trade from miles around." [1]

Oil-Can Pyramid

Eric Holm remembers how Joe Russell, the proprietor of the gas station across the street, was always happy to get rid of his empty oil cans

Orlando's Market and Joe Russell's gas station across from SPAG'S.

[1] Jack Tubert, "The Man Called Spag." Feature Parade Section, *Worcester Sunday Telegram,* 8 March 1964.

when Anthony asked for them. Eric recalled, "Spag stacked the empty cans in a pyramid and placed a full can of oil at the top. After making each sale, he discreetly waited until the departing customer drove out of sight. Then he would run across the road to Joe's and purchase another can of oil to replace the one he had just sold. When the pyramid grew beyond his reach, Spag placed a full can of oil on the floor in front of the pyramid for quick access." He was, of course, simply applying the "pile 'em high" principle he had already learned as a ten-year-old salesman.

In warmer weather, Anthony would sit outside on the front steps of the store, watch the world go by, and greet everyone as they passed. Neighborhood kids on bicycles stopped by to chat with him. He would ask them, "How's your bicycle working? Does it need fixing?" Anthony was always happy to have something to do and a chance to chat with someone. He would straighten out the front wheels of their bicycles, grease the sprockets, or attach "freebie" number plates and reflectors.

If, perchance, a customer bought something and Anthony needed more change, he would say, "Wait a minute, would you?" Then he

Anthony waiting for a customer.

would run across the street to Russell's gas station or to Orlando's Market. Customers understood and waited patiently. The pace of business was much more leisurely in those days.

Later on, Anthony found another source for getting change. Once a week, in front of the store, the newspaper boys gathered to turn in their collections and receive their pay from Harvey Raynor, circulation manager for the *Evening Gazette*. Harvey would then exchange the nickels, dimes, and pennies for the dollar bills that Anthony would take from his pocket. As time went on, Anthony replaced his "pocket cash register" with a White Owl cigar box.

Everything was scarce during the late days of the Great Depression. In spite of this, Anthony managed to add to his meager inventory, and the business was surviving; one might say it was "inching along." If "the boss" happened to be busy patching a tire, putting on tire chains, or changing oil for a customer, his buddies were always ready to jump up and serve a customer. These tasks, however, were few and far between.

Anthony changing a tire for a customer, 1936.

A tire dealer, Walter Johnson, was passing by the store one day when he noticed a few automotive accessories (two batteries, a set of chains, and inner tubes) that Anthony had placed outside in front of the store. He stopped and chatted with Anthony. As a result of that conversation, Walter offered Anthony three tires on consignment, which Anthony also displayed outside. He placed them conspicuously in front of three discarded tires to bolster the display. They sold! The initial consignment of tires marked the beginning of a successful business relationship and a long-lasting friendship with Walter. Anthony told Mother that "people are noticing the store as they pass by, and some are returning to shop."

Anthony knew and called everyone by name. This was easy at first when he waited on everyone who came into the store. Later, he would boggle the minds of thousands of his customers and vendors when he called each by name. They were even more surprised when Anthony inquired about some subject they had discussed earlier, such as an uncle's health, progress on a house bought the year before, or an anniversary trip.

The Ten-Gallon Hat

In those first years of the store, the "biggest days of the year" were still just before the Fourth of July. The sale of fireworks gave Anthony's business a financial boost. Feeling flush after a highly successful three days of selling fireworks one warm July, Anthony and a few of his buddies strolled into Worcester "to have a look around." As was their custom, they stopped in to visit Van, the Hatter, located on Front Street.

Van knew them well enough to know that they did not come in to have a hat cleaned or blocked, but he was always glad to see the fellows. Their visits and harmless horsing around gave him a breather from his steam press and from cleaning his customers' hats.

In the 1930s, men wore soft hats, usually made of felt. The brims ranged from narrow to very wide, depending upon the area of the United States where they were worn. From the width of a brim and the style, one could tell where a person lived. In keeping with the sedate character of New England, the brims of men's hats were narrow and unobtrusive, like the hats that lined the shelves behind Van, the Hatter.

On the counter next to Van, however, was a wide-brimmed Stetson with a "For Sale" sign on it. In response to Anthony's question about the hat and the sign, Van replied, "The owner died, and no one came for it. Do you want to buy it?"

Anthony picked up the hat. He saw that it was "nice and clean, like brand new, a Teddy Roosevelt style." When he tried it on and asked, "How much?" his friends laughed and guffawed.

"The price of the cleaning," Van replied.

His friends asked, "You're not going to buy it, are you?"

The reply was quick: "Of course!"

"Are you going to *wear* it?"

Above the noise of their laughing, Anthony replied, "I certainly am!"

Anthony paid Van, adjusted the angle of the hat, and led the snickering group out of the store.

When he walked into the house wearing his new ten-gallon hat, Mother looked surprised at first, then amused. She quickly commented, "Anthony, always something different!" I thought he looked silly.

He later explained, "I wanted to be different, and people did seem to notice the novelty. After a while, people began to recognize the hat and me under it. It become a natural trademark."

Anthony wore his western hat everywhere he went, and it did indeed become his trademark—first among his friends, then in the town, the county, throughout conservative New England, and abroad. When he did not have his hat on, people did not recognize him! Displayed on advertisements, programs, and letterheads, the ten-gallon hat became a familiar symbol representing "Spag, the man," and "SPAG'S, the store."

If You Don't See It...

Above the various boxes of merchandise in the store, Anthony hung signs that read "If you don't see what you want, just ask; I will find it or get it for you." He probably didn't realize at the time that people would ask for something other than auto parts. But when they did, he never hesitated to make good on his promise, nor did he stop to consider whether a store called the Shrewsbury Tire and Battery Service should carry non-automotive products. From the beginning, he recognized the importance of obtaining what his customers wanted—as well as the importance of giving good service.

Sometimes, "getting it for you" meant that Anthony had to drive into Worcester, where he could purchase the item at Cuccaro's or Waite's Hardware stores as a reseller. One day, a customer came into the store and said, "I need some wicks for my oil burner. Do you have any?"[2] Anthony did not have any oil wicks, so he replied, "I'll get 'em for you. Come back in a while." He scooped some cash from his pocket, took out enough for his purposes, and handed the rest of it to one of his buddies. He then jumped into the car and drove to Worcester. He had to do a little coaxing to get the jalopy up Belmont Hill to Cuccaro's, but he made it, bought the oil wicks, and returned to his store. When the customer returned later, the wicks were waiting for him. Everyone was happy: the customer for the accommodating service and Anthony for the good will he had generated and the few-cents profit he had made.

Customers took seriously the signs saying *"If you don't see it, ask..."* and continued to request new items. Neighbors came in look-

[2] To avoid the dangerous fumes given off by coal, people were installing oil burners for their kitchen stoves.

ing for gardening tools, such as rakes, pitchforks, hoes, and chicken wire. Then came a request for floor wax and canning equipment, such as large pots, Mason jars, and rubber rings. When filling a request for a new item, Anthony would purchase two if his scant moneys permitted. He would then place the extra one on top of one of his display crates. He noticed that "for the most part, when customers came in looking for something, it tended to be a household item. It made sense that I should carry these basic articles in the store."

Anthony's inventory probably appeared to be growing haphazardly, but underneath it all was his strong desire to meet his customers' needs. As he responded to their requests, his automotive supply store began to offer a wider assortment of unrelated merchandise, thus marking the beginnings of his variety store. Later he would say, "My store became a kind of a sort of a hullabaloo."

He continued to add new items to his inventory, pricing them as low as he could. "Quality goods at affordable prices to make everyone's life a little easier and better" became the heart and soul of his business for the next sixty years.

Nothing daunted Anthony. When some farmers asked, "How about carrying fertilizer?" he lost no time in driving the ten miles to the Worcester Rendering Works in Auburn, distributors of dried sheep manure. At first he bought small ten-pound bags, but farmers wanted larger bags of fertilizer. This presented a problem; he did not have enough cash on hand to buy the larger ones, and it was not practical to continue to drive all the way to Auburn. But for Anthony, each problem was an opportunity. "Here is a chance to establish the credit I really need," he said.

So off again to the Worcester Rendering Works he went. Joe Banks, a new salesman, greeted him with "What can I do for you?"

"I would like to purchase two fifty-pound bags of fertilizer to take with me," said Anthony. "However, I have only enough money to pay for one. I'll return tomorrow to pay for the second bag."

"Joe talked it over with his boss," Anthony later recalled, "and the boss OK'd my request with the understanding that if I didn't come back the next day, Joe would pay out of pocket for the second bag. The next day I returned, paid for the second bag, and then ordered four more." This time Anthony offered to pay for two bags and asked for the same arrangement as he had the day before. With each purchase, his credit grew, until in time he established a credit rating of $100.

Eventually, Corenco (the new name for the Worcester Rendering Works) was delivering truckloads of sheep manure to the store. This was a good seller. In those lean days, most people had a garden; just about all Italians did, and there were many Italians living near the store in the Lake-Fairlawn sections of the town. Most people did not have a car and were glad to accept Anthony's offer to deliver the fertilizer to their homes on Sunday afternoons.

A delivery of sheep manure.

Filling his customers' needs sometimes called for flexibility. An example of this was described in a letter from Jane Nicalil:

> My Dad always had a special place in his heart for Mr. Borgatti (Spag) because when he was a dairy farmer years ago and poor, he went to the store to purchase two rolls of wire fencing for sixteen dollars a roll. He only had sixteen dollars total with him. So Spag asked my Dad what he did for work. When he learned that my Dad sold eggs, Spag let him pay for the wire with eggs.

Anthony placed the cartons of eggs that Jane's father had given him on a box between the fertilizer and the shovels. They sold quickly.

At another time, a customer came to buy a roll of chicken wire. As he unrolled the wire, Anthony noticed the puzzled look on his face. He was trying to guess at the length of wire he needed for his project. Anthony told him to "take the roll home with you, and cut off what you need. When you bring the rest back, you can pay me then."

Coping With Growth

In time, customers were dropping into the store more frequently and requesting new products, such as work boots, overalls, wire, pliers, and electrical fuses. Construction workers needed all kinds of supplies, including plumbing joints, soldering irons, and couplings. Workmen from town or neighbors doing household chores and repairs were finding it more convenient to get what they needed at Anthony's store. Anthony's inventory was growing.

Carpenters came looking for hammers, saws, nails, screws, door knobs, and door hinges. At first, Anthony purchased these items at Waite's in Worcester. He was always quick to credit Vinnie Burns at Waite's Hardware for the invaluable guidance he received as a fledgling entrepreneur.

Local residents who raised chickens as a means of adding protein to their diets and a little change to their pockets requested chicken brooders, feeders, and waterers. To fulfill their requests, Anthony drove to Ross Brothers in Worcester. With the slim profit he was making on each sale, he would add these items to his inventory.

When Mr. Foxhall, a neighbor, made a request for a few pounds of birdseed, Anthony turned again to B. Palmer Hallock at Ross Brothers, who also began to supply Anthony with light farm equipment and grass seed. Anthony came to appreciate the good services that Palmer provided—as well as the birdseed. (SPAG'S now sells as much as three freight cars full of birdseed in two weeks.)

As his inventory increased, so did the need for additional shelves and bins to hold the merchandise. Anthony was not handy with a hammer, but fortunately he had a good friend who was; Folke (pronounced Fokee) Johnson, a carpenter, stopped in often on weekends and some evenings to give Anthony a hand with building shelves and bins. Anthony and Folke were well acquainted, their friendship dating back to the Emporium days. Folke, lanky and fair-haired, worked at Worcester State Hospital, and had frequently stopped at the Emporium for a college ice. Anthony was usually behind the ice cream fountain and waited on his friend. Years later, Folke told me that he got a big kick out of watching Anthony at work. "He was a chunky kid and not too tall. He was all business as he worked. When he served me the tall glass of ice cream, piled high with whipped cream and nuts, and chocolate syrup spilling down the sides, he was all smiles, hoping I would be pleased. I was."

Later, Folke and his wife, Elsie, moved into our neighborhood in Shrewsbury. Whenever they had a few minutes to spare, they would drop into the store to give a hand. As time went on, Anthony was able to pay Folke, who then became the store's full-time carpenter; he worked there for the next 40 years.

Folke built shelves that extended to the 20-foot ceiling. He also built a ladder so Anthony could reach the merchandise stored on the upper shelves. For the display of hardware, tools, and current items, Folke built three small island counters in the middle of the store. During the Christmas season, one counter held a display of his hand-made wooden trains, sailboats, cars, and knickknack shelves.

To add to the Christmas festivities one year, Anthony decided to have Santa Claus visit his store.[3] Folke reinforced the platform in the corner and built stairs leading up to it. Elsie provided a cardboard fireplace with electrified burning logs, which Anthony placed behind the rocking chair, borrowed from Folke's and Elsie's living room.

Anthony then hired Jimmie Lossano to act as Santa Claus each Sunday afternoon before Christmas. (Stores were open on Sundays and holidays then.) Hiring Jimmie at four dollars per day was expensive, but his presence created some excitement for the holidays. Anthony's showmanship was becoming apparent, as was Jimmie's acting prowess. He made a wonderful Santa sitting there on the platform in his red suit stuffed with pillows, greeting all who entered the store, and listening patiently to each child who climbed up the steps and onto his lap.

Anthony broke into a broad grin when he told us about a conversation that "Santa" had with a little seven-year-old boy:

[3] He continued to have a Santa visit for the next several years.

A youngster came into the store. When "Santa" greeted him, the boy climbed onto his lap. Jimmie then went through his regular Santa routine: "What is your name?" and "Have you been a good boy?" Then: "What would you like Santa to bring you?"

At this, the boy gave an exasperated sigh, "Why, you son of a bitch! You still don't remember! I told you twice before at the other stores! This is the third time I'm telling you!"

Anthony with Santa (Jimmie Lossano).

Sometimes the pleasures Anthony provided for his customers were simpler to arrange than a Santa Claus. As soon as his finances permitted, he bought a box of Sugar Daddies (large caramel lollipops). In an old wicker basket, he fluffed-up a cloth and piled the Sugar Daddies high to make them look like a mound of candy. In front of the basket, he placed a sign: "FREE—Take one." Barbara Hayes, a lifelong Shrewsbury resident and a youngster in those early days of the store, recalls helping herself to a Sugar Daddy each time her father took her on his weekly visits to the store.

Credit for SPAG'S

In the winter of 1939, the demand for hardware grew. Anthony needed to expand his hardware inventory, but he did not have the necessary cash on hand; he needed more credit. Having exhausted all possibilities with local hardware wholesalers, he took a bus to Boston. There he hoped to find a wholesaler who would give him a line of credit.

Dressed in his usual garb of chino pants, ten-gallon hat, and an old jacket, he got off at Park Square. Not knowing any hardware wholesalers or their locations, Anthony asked the first person he met on the street for advice. That person directed him to Decatur Hopkins, the largest hardware jobber in New England.

Anthony "walked in on big business with his heart in his hand," wrote Jack Tubert:

> Smiling and confident, he asked for credit. Frank Hopkins, the president, his son Bill Hopkins, and James Joyce, the treasurer, were impressed with Spag's enthusiasm and his ideas. They granted his request for a line of credit, and told him that Arne Furst, a Decatur Hopkins salesman, would be calling upon him.
>
> Arne Furst happened to be one of the best hardware salesmen in the east. Merchants clamored for his service. When Mr. Furst made his initial call at SPAG'S in 1939, it [Anthony's account] was the smallest of the 144 accounts that he serviced.
>
> "I had very little money, but I had the initial credit of fifty dollars, reminisced Spag. "Mr. Furst taught me to buy what my customers needed, and to buy an assortment of tools rather than a quantity of one item. Instead of six shovels, I learned to buy a shovel, pick, hoe, rake, pitchfork, and sledge hammer. In those early days, this knowledge helped me to survive. I used the fifty-dollar credit with Decatur; and, with time, they increased my line of credit. I could then order more."

Mr. Furst would come to the store, price the merchandise, place it on the shelves, and write follow-up orders. In time, he gave up the rest of his territory to devote full-time to SPAG'S and took on an assistant to write the orders. SPAG'S one account became bigger than all of Arne Furst's other 143 accounts combined. From the smallest retailer, SPAG'S became Decatur Hopkins' largest wholesale purchaser. "No jobbing house ever had so much volume," said Mr. Furst.

Bill Hopkins Sr. said later, "All that would not have happened if we had not listened to the little guy who came in wearing the baggy pants. But," added the senior Hopkins, "he accomplished it all himself..."

In addition to being Anthony's mentor, Mr. Furst also became a close friend of Anthony's. In 1950, when Anthony issued badges to his employees, he assigned Honorary Badge #1 to Mr. Arne Furst. (Anthony chose badge #100 for himself, thinking that he would never have that many employees. Today SPAG'S has over 500 employees.)[4]

Ed Hammond, the retired treasurer of Decatur Hopkins, told me about a call he had received many years later from a candy manufacturer in Pennsylvania, who inquired about SPAG'S credit. "I asked the fellow, 'How much merchandise does Spag want to purchase?' He replied, 'It's for one trailerload; it equals thousands of dollars. We've never had an order of that size before.'

"I told him that if I had an order of that size from SPAG'S, I would have only one question for Spag, and that would be, 'When do you want the order delivered?'"

Also by the late 1930s, Anthony realized that he needed to have a checking account. In keeping with his firm belief that business should be transacted locally whenever possible for the good of the area's economy, he went to the two largest commercial banks in Worcester. Neither bank was interested in serving a small retail store in Shrewsbury. They catered to large companies and individuals with large accounts.

[4] Jack Tubert, "The Man Called Spag." Feature Parade Section, *Worcester Sunday Telegram*, 8 March 1964, Section F, page 12.

A Bank for SPAG'S

The only other commercial bank in Worcester was the Guaranty Bank, which was, prior to its founding, the largest credit union in the United States.[5] It was also the first and only bank in Worcester to offer checking accounts to individuals and small businesses. When Anthony went to the Guaranty Bank in 1939, Mr. George Jeppson, the chairman, was not only interested in this aspiring and enthusiastic entrepreneur, he could also envision the future potential of the store, by now renamed SPAG'S Supply. He and, later, Mr. Roland Ericson, the president, were happy to provide banking services to SPAG'S Supply and eventually to grant Anthony the loans needed for placing larger orders.

Anthony's first account was barely in the four-digit range, but in time it grew to a significant figure. Anthony appreciated the support and the services he received at the Guaranty Bank through those early times. Over the years, several banks attempted to woo Anthony's account away with attractive propositions, but his loyalty to the Guaranty Bank was steadfast.[6]

Colorful Language

Anthony enjoyed chatting with the carpenters, plumbers, and electricians who came into the store. He admired their skills and loved to talk at length with them about their trades, their families, and their way of living. And in doing so, he began to adopt some of their earthy expressions. So it wasn't long before their colorful language became part of his permanent vocabulary.

This would not have been a problem if he had confined his expletives to the times when he was talking with these men, but he would occasionally let slip with a few "bad" words at home. We were dismayed. Mother took him to task concerning his language—without any success. It was as if he had not heard her.

One day when Father Warburton, the parish priest at St. Anne's Catholic Church, dropped in for one of his frequent visits, Mother told him that she was concerned about Anthony's language. "Anthony has started to use bad words," she said.

[5] According to Sylvio Demers, former Guaranty Bank vice president.
[6] See also Walking The Store, page 228.

Father Warburton assured her that the expressions Anthony was using were not bad, in his case. "Now, if someone else were using those same words, they would be," he added. "With Anthony, these words are just his colorful way of being a regular guy, because, as we both know, there is absolutely no malice in him. There is only goodness in his heart."

Mother understood and reluctantly accepted Father Warburton's justification, but you'd hear her "Tsk, tsk!" as Anthony sprinkled his conversation with profanity. It had surely become an integral part of his persona. There were times when I would wince upon hearing him speak. I think it might have jarred others too, because I recall hearing Mother as she related Father Warburton's explanation to one of her friends. There was probably nothing that anyone could do. Anthony was casual and matter-of-fact about it. Reporter Chris Pope noted that even when he was giving a talk, Anthony "peppered his comments with R-rated but curiously-inoffensive expletives for which he has become famous over the years."[7]

Reverend Sinclair Hart, founding father of the Trinity Episcopal Church in Shrewsbury, described Anthony this way: "Warmth is a key word for Spag. Gusto, too…Spag was always himself, no airs, 'take me as I am or not at all.' This attractive presence extended to his honesty and use of colorful language that he wore like his hat, indoors and out, in polite company, whatever."

Many times, as though to remind himself, Anthony expressed his concern to me about not wanting to change. He did not want to become "highfalutin." His colorful language certainly did dispel any such illusion. Perhaps profanity was Anthony's anchor, his means of staying the same person. In a conversation with Father Warburton, Anthony said, "The day I set myself above other men and become highfalutin, that's when I'll go out of business."

SPAG'S

When Anthony opened his store back in 1934, he had listed his full name, Anthony A. Borgatti, Jr., as proprietor, and he had named his business the Shrewsbury Tire and Battery Service. His customers, however, ignored the official name. They also ignored a subsequent sign advertising Spag's Hardware Company, preferring something more simple. "I'm going to stop in at 'Spag's Store,'" they would say. Eventually, customers simply shortened the store's name to "Spag's."

So, in 1939, when he ordered printed stationery, Anthony yielded to popular usage and changed the name of his store to "SPAG'S Hardware Supply." When he incorporated in 1966, its name became SPAG'S Supply, Inc., but customers still refer to the store as just SPAG'S.

Over the years, the name "SPAG'S" was to become a household word. Many tradespeople, customers, and acquaintances were not aware that "Spag" was a nickname, nor did they know that Anthony's

Merchandise stacked out front, circa 1942.

real surname was Borgatti. Family members called Anthony by his given name, and those of his friends who knew him before he acquired his nickname of Spag called him "Tony." But more often than not, Anthony received mail addressed to "Mr. Spag of SPAG'S in Shrewsbury." Both he and his store had become a New England institution.

Baseball player wearing shirt with sponsor's (SPAG'S) name, circa 1938.

The Working Team

The day I married Olive was my lucky day.
—Anthony

Before opening his store each morning, Anthony used to walk down to Granger's drug store, located on Route 9 diagonally across the street from White City, to buy the Wall Street Journal. Ever since high school, he had followed the stock market. But Anthony didn't go to Granger's just to buy the paper; he was also interested in the scenery there. To be more precise, he had become interested in the attractive, dark-haired clerk with the pretty smile, the same little Miss Olive who could not abide him when they were in high school. Olive Lutz was now working part-time at Granger's while she attended Worcester State College.

Anthony took advantage of the moments of conversation with Olive that he conveniently sparked with his five-cent purchases. On one such occasion, Olive must have mentioned that she sang in St. Anne's church choir, because all of a sudden, Anthony developed an interest in singing. I can remember how surprised and puzzled we were at home when he told us that he had joined the church choir. He whistled a lot, but we had never heard him sing, or even hum a song, for that matter.

During these morning conversations with Olive at Granger's, the topic of Anthony's English and the need to improve his grammar must have arisen. My guess is that Olive told Anthony that he should get someone to tutor him in English, and Anthony, always one to take advantage of an opportunity, asked her to do it. Evidently she accepted, but how much time was spent on tutoring is anybody's guess. I am under the impression that the tutoring, if it did take place, never had much effect on Anthony's choice of verb tense or pronouns; when asked about his grammar lessons, he would reply, "Who the hell cares where the adverb belongs?"

Mother smiled but said nothing when she noticed that choir practices had become less important to Anthony after he and Olive started dating. Dan Cupid had taken matters into his own hands.

Olive graduated from Worcester State College in 1939 with a degree in education, when teaching positions were at a premium. Because there were no openings available, she gratefully accepted work at W.T. Grant's 5&10 cent store downtown at the corner of Mechanic and Main Streets. She felt lucky to have a job and a happy social life with her friends—and with Anthony.

For Olive, a date with Anthony sometimes meant a drive in the Chevrolet[1] out into the country to the Worcester Rendering Works in

Auburn to pick up fertilizer. Most of the time they double-dated with Noe Benoit and Helen, his wife-to-be, or with Glenn Anderson and Ann Bianchi, who would also eventually marry. The three couples usually played cards because there was never much money for entertainment for any of them in those days. But once in a while, they did go to a movie in town.

Anthony loved to tell the story about the time he asked Olive what she would like for her birthday. "All she wanted was champagne," he said with a grin. "I had to deliver some cow manure in order to have enough money to buy the champagne."

Olive's family frowned on

Olive Lutz, graduation, 1938.

[1] The Jalopy had to be retired from service and replaced.

her budding romance with Anthony, probably because after six years in business, he was still struggling to make ends meet. He was practically penniless, and his future looked bleak. When Olive told Anthony about her family's objections, he responded with, "You don't need to worry about that. I'm going to be a millionaire some day." He must have been very convincing. Love prevailed; Olive defied her family's wishes. They set the date and the place: Thanksgiving Day, November 24, 1940, at St. Anne's Catholic Church.

Phil Regal, who was a SPAG'S supplier for the next four decades, recalled taking an order from Anthony on November 22, 1940. "The usual procedure was for Spag to pay me on the following call for the previous order. On this regular stop, however, Spag said to me, 'I'm sorry, Phil, I can't give you a check today; I'm getting married this week.'"

The wedding took place as planned. Anthony often said that "the day Olive and I got married was my lucky day." His best man was Joe Russell, and the matron of honor was Olive's friend, Helen Barry Benoit. Olive's brothers, John and Bob Lutz, Ceserina's daughter, Eleanor, and I were attendants.

After the marriage ceremony, the wedding party and guests drove to the Aurora Hotel for a reception provided by Uncle Charlie Borgatti, the hotel's chef. Uncle Charlie went all-out for the occasion with the special fixings to make it festive. Dining at a hotel was a special treat for the average family in those days.

Following the reception, Anthony and Olive boarded a bus at the Greyhound terminal for a honeymoon in New York City. Traveling by bus was cheaper than traveling by train. Their intention was to stay until their money ran out—which, apparently, it did on the fourth day, because they returned Sunday evening. They went to live on the first floor of the three-decker at 501 Shrewsbury Street, Worcester—the same house where Anthony had drawn his first breath. This was the beginning of fifty rewarding years for them.

After their wedding, Olive continued to work at Grant's—"to put food on the table," said Anthony. After their first child, Carol, was born in March 1942, he and his family moved into the house on Beverly Road where Mr. and Mrs. Banning had lived, and just around the corner from where we lived on the farm. Anthony was once again within walking distance of the store.

War and Family

The early dawn of World War II saw many young men enlist in the armed services. Even though he had a wife, a child, and a business, Anthony tried to enlist, first in the Navy and then the Army. Both rejected him because of his poor eyesight. Had the Army recruiters known that Anthony also had difficulty in responding to right and left directions (a form of dyslexia), they might have rejected him on those grounds alone. He would have been a drill sergeant's worst nightmare, for sure.

Anthony's poor vision was probably the result of too much reading in bed under a blanket with a flashlight. He was aware of the limitations caused by his weak eyesight and his need to wear glasses. When asked why he did not play baseball as a kid, he responded, "I couldn't play because I couldn't see the ball coming."

"I'll tell you how much he depended on his glasses," said Noe Benoit. "I had just met Spag when I saw him go into a shower room with his glasses on. Not knowing that he had poor vision, I said, 'Spag, you have your glasses on.' He replied, 'Hell, I've got to find my way in there.'"

Anthony felt bad about the Army and Navy's rejection of him, and over the years, he frequently mentioned it. "I really wanted to enlist and do my share in the war effort," he would say. He felt a strong allegiance to America. When he had the option of buying American or imported goods, he insisted on ordering goods "Made in America," even when the items were more expensive, and proportionately less profitable than the foreign-made merchandise.

Anthony's disappointment over not being able to serve his country was alleviated by the success of his growing business—and his growing family. Two more daughters arrived: Jean in March 1945 and Sandy on Christmas Eve 1948. Anthony eventually altered an earlier statement of his when he noted that "there was one thing I hated more than plucking chickens, and that was changing diapers." Fortunately, he did not have to do that very often.

With three daughters, Olive had her hands full, but as time permitted, she continued to run many errands for Anthony in their Chevrolet workhorse. She also arranged the display of housewares in the store, paid bills, and performed miscellaneous chores for the office, working at the table in their living room. She knew little about the actual business of running the store until April 1948, when Anthony suffered a kidney-stone attack and underwent surgery. While he was recuperating, he counted on Olive to take over.

"It was the worst experience of my life," Olive said. She had never dealt with such complex business matters before. She made up her mind then and there that she would never be in that predicament again. From that point on, she became more knowledgeable about the workings of the store.

As SPAG'S sales increased, Olive's paperwork increased accordingly. In time, Pearl Adams joined the household to help take care of the children and Fannie Melander soon came to do the cooking.[2] The extra help freed Olive for the ever-increasing store details. The business grew, and so did the traffic coming to the house—as well as the confusion. Their living room had become Anthony's office.

"We need a real office," Olive stated firmly. Anthony agreed and suggested that they build an office at the store, but Olive strongly opposed the idea. Without mincing any words, she told him, "If you want me to help, the office will have to be built here at home. The girls are going to school now. I fully intend to be here for them when they come home." She also insisted that the girls should feel free to come into the office at any time. "And, that," said she, "is final!" There was no compromise.

As a result, Anthony had a large office built just off the kitchen—the first of many additions made to accommodate the increasing store traffic and office staff. And just as Olive wanted it, Carol, Jean, and Sandy were always in and out of the office.

Home Life

When talking with Sandy about her dad, I could see Anthony's infectious smile and twinkling eyes. It was obvious that questions about Anthony evoked many happy memories. She needed no prodding when asked about life at home with her parents. Her thoughts flowed easily as she talked to me:

I loved Daddy because he made me feel special.

[2] See Extended Family, page 152 for more about Fannie.

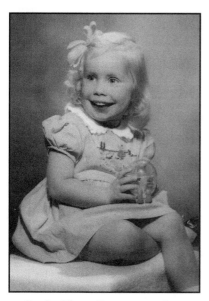

Sandra Elaine Borgatti, age four.

No matter what mistakes I made or what I did wrong, he carefully listened to what I had to say and he understood. By his example, he taught us to be kind and to share. He reminded us on a regular basis that "people are important." He appreciated nice things, but he was a collector of friends more than things. "Material things don't make you happy," he would say. "People do." He would often add, "People need each other to live."

I learned a lot by watching and listening to Father, especially when something had gone wrong at the store or when someone was angry. He was so patient, understanding, and a master of words. He would usually end a conversation by making a new friend or by turning a disadvantage into an advantage.

Father was a homebody. He enjoyed preparing Sunday night suppers, usually sandwiches. In the morning, he got Carol, Jean, and me up and off to school while Mother, who worked on the books late into the evening, caught up on her sleep. He cooked eggs, pancakes, and French toast for our breakfasts. We had to eat some of everything.

Father and Mother took their parenting in stride. Their tolerance extended to allowing us to have pajama parties in the living room. Even though their bedroom was just off the living room, they never complained about the noise that we girls made. But one morning Father did make a significant comment. As he made his way from the bedroom to the kitchen by stepping around our eight sleeping bags and pillows, looking straight ahead, he scratched his head and muttered, "I haven't had much sleep."

Father was a softie. When I wanted something, I always asked Father first. When he said, "I'll check," that meant that there was a pretty good chance I had gotten my way. I usually did get my way, except when it came to questions involving boys. In those cases, it was better to go to Mother first. She would break the ice to Father.

When a boy called and invited me to a movie at the local drive-in theater, "No! No! No!" was Father's vociferous response. Mother said, "Have him call back." Mother was much more understanding when it came to boys.

Jean agreed, and offered another perspective:

Having the office in the house just off the kitchen was neat. We saw many salesmen coming and going, but there were times when we wished it to be otherwise. Father didn't wait for private moments to take us to task. I was thirteen years old at the time. On returning from school, I went into the office as usual. The room was full of salespeople.

Father looked at me and said, "What do you have all over your face?"

Taken aback, I answered, "Lipstick. Mom said I could wear it when I was thirteen." He was straight-forward and didn't beat around the bush.

Sandy added that, for the most part, she enjoyed seeing all the salespeople:

Especially the salesman who sold dolls. The doll salesman knew how much I loved dolls, and he made sure that he came when I was at home. He knew that Father would call me in and let me choose the ones I liked the best. He would always

Carol Ann Borgatti, age eight.

order for the store the ones I chose. I guess Father figured that other girls would like the same kind of dolls that I liked. Being consulted like that made me feel a part of the store. Even more so, I liked being included in something that was important to Daddy.

Holidays were special family occasions. On the Fourth of July, we invited friends and relatives to our corn cook. The first corn of the season was steamed and served with hot dogs and hamburgers. Our parents invited all our relatives and friends. The fun part for Carol, Jean, and me was having all the people there. Everyone being together is what I liked. Everyone was so happy.

Christmas was the most important holiday. After Mass, we had breakfast. Then our grandparents, aunts, uncles, and cousins would arrive. There were always three generations there. Friends were also invited. Carol, Jean, and I could invite as many of our friends as we wanted. Our friends received gifts, too.

Gift time was spectacular. It took hours to open all our gifts. Father started by giving each of us one special present that he had selected with a lot of thought. When I opened my gift, I knew right away why he had chosen that item for me.

Father was Santa Claus! After we exchanged our special gifts, he would go down to the store to shop for his "everyone's gifts." He would pile his station wagon high with carton upon carton of items. What an assortment!

There were bath salts, clothespins, perfume, frying pans, Comet cleaning powder, Christy dry gas, rubber gloves, ear muffs, Vaseline, chap sticks, hand lotion, sponges, cough drops, fruit cake, Scotch tape, Saran Wrap, WD-40, Life Savers, stockings, light bulbs, and dust cloth packets.

When Father returned to the house, we three girls were the "gophers" running around making sure that everyone received the appropriate items. What fun! To add further excitement, Father held up his ten-gallon hat and we drew names for recipients for such presents as a vacuum cleaner, a music box, and a vase. Father loved to see the happy smiles as the winners chose their gifts.

Jean Marie Borgatti, age six.

Carol will never forget the Christmas of 1951. Here is how she described it to me:

Father returned home Christmas Eve after a busy day at the store, carrying the day's receipts in a paper bag. Being in a hurry to change and freshen up before the arrival of expected company, he placed the bag of cash in the office wastebasket.

On Christmas morning, I dutifully carried out my daily chore of emptying the wastebaskets into the incinerator. I was anxious to join the rest of the family, our grandparents, aunts, uncles, cousins, and friends at the gaily-decorated Christmas tree and the piles of gifts. After we excitedly opened our gifts, Father gathered up the wrappings, took them out to the incinerator, burned the trash, and then returned to the house. It was then that Mother asked, 'By the way, where did you put yesterday's receipts?' Father's mind drew a blank. A frantic search followed, but to no avail.

By then the turkey was ready, so we all sat down and had dinner. Then it dawned on him. He dashed outside to the incinerator. Poking through the ashes with a stick, he met the resistance of something solid. When he lifted the shiny clump of melted coins, he knew that the mystery of the missing day's receipts had been solved.

Father did not blame me, but I felt awful. I cried. Perhaps if it had been any other day, I would have noticed the weight of the basket and would have checked. But it was Christmas morning, and all the presents were waiting to be opened.

"What could I say?" Anthony explained later, "Carol had done her job."

Emptying baskets was only one of the many chores that the girls performed. Anthony and Olive believed that young people should work in their spare time after school and on weekends. Each of the girls were assigned a daily chore. "It's good for them," Anthony said. "They should learn the value of the dollar."

"When we were old enough," continued Sandy, "we had to do the filing in the office. I took over the filing job from Jean, who then went to work at the store where Carol was already working. We started at the store marking prices on goods with a magic marker. I was in 'housewares' a lot, because there were a lot of little things to be marked and they could plunk me in a corner out of the way to do it."

Jean added, "My first job at the store was making peanut butter. As we became more responsible, we were allowed to become cashiers. It was fun to be there with the other employees, our extended family."

Because the office was in the home and because both Anthony and Olive were attentive, the girls grew up in a warm, close atmosphere. Both parents had a ready ear. I know that Olive did more of the listening, because she was in the office much more than Anthony. Both of them gave unstinting support to the girls' school activities.

Mother had often advised Anthony to take time for his family, and this he did with his usual enthusiasm. Family vacations were scheduled regularly, and they all enjoyed parties and other special moments together. When the girls were teenagers, they would sometimes request permission to stay home while their parents traveled—as typical teenagers would do. They soon learned that this was not an option for them. Olive let them know that if they chose to be unhappy about going on the trip, that was okay, but they must be ready to go at departure time. (When asked about being a parent of three teenagers, Olive would say jokingly, "How do you suppose I got my ulcer?")

Sunday Mass was another must with Olive. Regardless of where their travels took them or what the difficulties might be, she would make sure that they attended church. She was conscientious; Anthony was happy with her and the family she had raised.

Teamwork

Anthony and Olive had two very different personalities. He was flamboyant and fun-loving, never taking himself too seriously. He made light of any disappointments or annoyances with an expletive or two, a wave of his hand and a shrug of the shoulder, or he would say, "Life is too short." Olive accepted that Anthony was a "people" person. She could see that he was happiest when he was surrounded by friends. On occasions when she might have been frustrated by a full house, she would quickly pass it off with "That's Spag; we aren't going to change him."

Olive, on the other hand, was serious, analytical, factual, and fair, with no time for small talk. She was fastidious in her work and held high expectations of others. Anthony admired her ability to handle the financial aspects of the business. The office system was not computerized; Olive used a common sense approach to her efficiently-kept accounts receivables and

payables and kept close track of the intricate dealings with all their suppliers. In a radio interview taped in 1989, Anthony commented on Olive's meticulous attention to detail: "Everything has to be exactly to the point with her. She is a perfectionist. She would go over the checkbook for hours to find where the missing ten cents was. I used to get her going by handing her a dime and saying, 'For Christ's sake! Here's a dime!'"

Fortunately for Anthony, Olive enjoyed being in charge of the financial details. As president of the business, she also supervised the office staff. Anthony, the treasurer, was in complete charge of operating the store, including all of the hiring, buying, and selling. They both worked long hours, focusing seriously on their individual responsibilities. As far as I could tell, they respected each other's differences, which was undoubtedly what made them such a good team.

Over the years, when he was receiving accolades, Anthony would hasten to add, "If it hadn't been for Olive, it wouldn't have happened." There is no question that Olive helped to keep it all together. Little did he know, however, that long after he married her, she would assist him in a way that he could never have imagined; she would pilot their airplane on trips to trade shows and meetings. She shared the flying responsibilities with the full-time pilots the store had hired: first Jerry Udell, then Walter Kearney, and finally Peter Woiciechowski. Anthony and Olive thought the world of their three topnotch pilots.

Olive's own interest in flying began during a vacation in Australia. After she and Anthony had returned from Australia, we gathered at their home on Beverly Road for dinner. When the meal had ended, Father, Mother and the rest of us sat around the fire, roasting chestnuts as Anthony and Olive set up their projector and showed us an interesting movie they had taken while flying over the Australian Outback in a small airplane. They had enjoyed their travels in Australia, but they were "absolutely thrilled" with their ride in the small plane. It was easy to see that they were more excited about flying in that plane than they were about the rest of their trip. So it came as no surprise when Anthony announced that both he and Olive were going to learn to fly.

Mother was the first to react. Without hesitation, she looked at Olive and said, "Olive, I'll be very glad to fly with you." Then, turning to her son, she said, "With you, Anthony, I'm not sure."

I guess Mother knew Anthony better than he knew himself! He and Olive embarked on their ground schooling, the first phase of the flying course. A short time later, on returning from an evening class, Anthony declared, "No, I can see this [flying] isn't for me. Too much bull shit, too many details."

On the other hand, Olive persevered. Within a short time, she had earned not only her single engine but also her twin engine license, and later her jet certification. Her commercial rating followed. Such a remarkable feat added to her role in the business by making her co-pilot of the company's Citation.

In 1988, Olive reported, "We attend around 25 trade shows a year all over the U.S., and we fly 100 to 200 hours a year. By having an airplane, we can spend more time on our business; we do not waste travel time. It's quite efficient when we have six high-salaried people attending a show."[3]

Between Olive's efficiency and Anthony's dedication to serving others, SPAG'S had a good team at the helm.

Olive and her Cessna Citation.

[3] Author unknown, "Olive Borgatti, President Spag's Supply, Inc. Flying Reader." *Flying* Magazine, November 1988, p. 106–107.

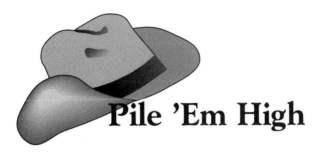

Pile 'Em High

Pile 'em high, and watch them fly!
—Spag

By the late 1940s, Anthony's pyramid of empty oil cans and the pile of worn tires were long gone. In their place, piled high and in every inch of space, was honest-to-goodness merchandise—"stuff," as Anthony called it.

All kinds of nuts, bolts, and screws filled the floor-to-ceiling shelves and bins. Checkered flannel shirts and Brown's beach (utility) jackets made in Worcester were in stock for carpenters and older men. On a counter at the back of the store next to the shelves of paint, Anthony also displayed bib overalls and other work clothes. Some "stuff" was still in the original cartons. Boxes and barrels filled all available space. Anthony piled some items on top of other merchandise or hung it from the ceiling. There was no other place to put it.

In those days, one could hardly see the front steps for all the tires, oil, hoses, rakes, and shovels that he placed outside. At closing time, all the "stuff" was carried inside for the night. In the morning, before Anthony could get into the store, he had to carry all the goods out and put them back on the sidewalk.

In the cold weather, Anthony would use a dolly to roll out a 50-gallon drum of Firestone antifreeze. Customers filled their own gallon containers using a pump and a spout attached to the drum. They pumped more than 100 gallons of antifreeze a day. (The daily volume increased later on to 10,000 gallons. By that time, however, distributors were shipping antifreeze in gallon containers.)

Because Anthony lacked a real cash register for quite a while, Bill

Belanger, Sturrie Bengston, or any friend who was handy would tally up a customer's purchase using an orange crate for a desk and their pockets or the cigar box to make change. If people were short of money, Anthony would say, "Take it home, and pay me when you can, or whenever."

Anthony standing at the door to his store, 1942.

"Pay me the next time...." was the beginning of charge accounts at SPAG'S. The tradesmen appreciated being able to pay for their supplies after their own customers had paid them for a job. Anthony trusted his neighbors to pay later when it was more convenient for them. His trust created good feelings; when customers came back to pay up, they usually bought more. In a taped recording made in 1948 during Community Week at the store, Mary Belanger talked about the extent of Anthony's trust in his customers: "If Chick [her husband] needed paint on a Sunday when the store wasn't open, Spag would give Chick the key to the store."

Benjamin Moore Paints

Back in 1942, Jim Walker, the Benjamin Moore area representative, stopped in and chatted with Anthony about taking on the Moore line of paint. Then he convinced his company that Spag would be a good risk. On that basis, the Benjamin Moore Company invited Anthony and Olive to a meeting at the Bancroft Hotel in Worcester. Jim was there with a display of Benjamin Moore paints and related items, which had been set up in a room for prospective retailers. Anthony looked at the great display of paints and said, in his direct, no-nonsense way, "I don't need all this stuff, Jim; just sell me paint."

The first order was for 80 gallons of Moore's oil-base paint. Sales for the first year totaled about 800 gallons. As paint sales grew, Benjamin Moore shipped paint to SPAG'S daily to keep up with the demand. The total sales in paint went from 800 gallons to more than 200,000 gallons a year.

In 1946, Harold Noftle became the sales representative for Benjamin Moore Company. At their first meeting, he and Anthony established an immediate rapport. Harold chuckled when he talked about his second call on Spag:

> Spag handed me a bunch of dollar bills from his pocket and said, "Mind the store, I'm going home for a while." Here I was with a roll of money. Spag didn't know me, and I really didn't know where anything in the store was, other than the paint. Luckily for me, no customers came in while I was alone.
>
> When Spag returned, I said, "Spag, I'm fairly new to you; you've only seen me a couple of times, and you trusted me with all that money and the store to boot!"
>
> "Anyone working as a salesman for your company is trustworthy and honest," was his quick reply. What a philosophy!

(Above) Harold Noftle. (Below) Shelves stocked with Benjamin Moore paint.

What trust he had in people!

Spag and I worked closely on promotions and holiday sales. He always wanted some item he could use to "get the crowd in." Any discounts we gave him on first-quality, discontinued paint items, he passed on to his customers. Spag had the right attitude. He loved to give people a fair shake for their money.

One day, Anthony turned over the responsibility for the entire paint department to Harold, saying, "Harold, it's your baby." The two men became close friends, often referring to each other as "brothers."

To make room for the paint, Folke Johnson built shelves reaching to the ceiling on the Baker Avenue side of the store. In time, the whole wall would be completely stocked with paint. Incidentally, Paul Ferrante, a longtime neighbor who lives down the street from SPAG'S, remembers buying the first gallon of Moore paint ever sold in the store.

Wheelbarrows

In the late forties, as the business grew and as Anthony began buying in quantity, he ordered a trailerload of wheelbarrows and advertised them as an early spring special. He paid $7.25 each for the 1,200 wheelbarrows and sold them for a few cents above cost.

Anthony explained, "I know I could get fifteen dollars each easily, but a lot more people will be able to buy a wheelbarrow at $7.77. By selling at a lower price, customers are able to buy more and my merchandise moves faster." Then he added the maxim he would repeat throughout his life: "I'd rather have a fast nickel than a slow dime."

The only problem was finding room to store the 1,200 wheelbarrows. Anthony stacked most of them at Beverly Road, and brought them to the store as space permitted. They were all gone by midsummer.

Hugo Orizzi, who worked in his father's market across the street from the store, shared a "Spag" story with me:

I'll never forget the day I crossed the street to shoot the breeze with Spag, who was standing out in front of his store. We were gabbing away when a truck loaded with rolls of picket fences stopped in front of us. The driver leaned his head out of the truck and asked, "Where is SPAG'S warehouse?"

Spag asked, "Why?"

"I have a truckload of picket fences here," the driver replied.

"Put them right here," replied Spag as he pointed to the sidewalk in front of the building. The driver looked askance at Spag and then, with a grimace, backed up the truck and dumped the load of fences.[1]

After the truck left, Spag and I piled the rolled fences ten to twelve feet high against the building, one row in front of the other so that they wouldn't fall over. He had to leave them out at night because it was impossible to fit them inside the store.

Anthony advertised the sale of fences at the "right" price for customers who either needed or wanted to own a picket fence. They, too, sold quickly.

"It was about that time," said Harvey Raynor, "that Anthony would buy a carload of merchandise, such as hoses, and place an ad that would appear in both the *Worcester Telegram* and the *Evening Gazette*.[2] He would sell the lot right from the sidewalk. In no time the stuff would be gone. That was when he started to become known."

Expansion Begins

In 1947, the garage's tenants, the M&M Trucking Company, notified Mother that they were scaling down their operation. They planned to vacate the building within the next year and move to new quarters in Worcester. Anthony could not wait a year for more space. As it was, customers had to work their way around a maze of cartons of merchandise piled high in the store. He needed to expand immediately.

He also needed a door for receiving goods. So he spoke with the

---

[1] Each roll of fencing when straightened out was twelve inches high and three feet long, with wire running through the middle. They were the kind used for separating a garden from a sidewalk or for placing around flower beds.
[2] See Spagtacular! for more about SPAG's advertising.

M&M manager about the possibility of using more of the garage space, preferably the area directly behind the rear wall of his store. With this expansion, his store would be using one-third of the total garage space. M&M was receptive to the idea. Anthony then talked with Mother, his private counselor and landlady, about his interim plan, as well as his desire to take over the whole garage when M&M moved out at the end of the year. Mother was supportive and agreed wholeheartedly to everything, including the rental fee of $75 per month that Anthony offered—a generous amount in the late 1940s. She was happy to see Anthony prosper.

Anthony hired the Govoni Brothers, local contractors, to remove the cement block wall at the rear of the original store and to build a temporary wall-board partition separating the store from the rest of the garage. While the work was in progress, the partially open area was breezy and cold. "To keep warm," said Vinnie Mastro,[3] "Ralph Zona and I, who worked evenings in the store, swung the sledge hammers and helped break down the wall." With this first expansion, SPAG'S had a receiving dock on Baker Avenue.

In this expanded area, Folke built more shelves and bins and restructured the existing storage space. This work included the installation of a flight of stairs located at the left-front corner of the store facing Route 9, which made the huge cavernous area on the second floor accessible for storage. Anthony could then buy merchandise in greater volume, store it upstairs, and bring it down as needed. In November of 1947, he moved some of his "stuff," including the paint department, into the new shopping area.

"When Spag began to buy in larger quantities," said Vinnie, "he and I would look at one another, shudder, and hope that it would sell. Sometimes, merchandise would arrive before we had time to think about how we would pay for it or where we would put it. With a shrug of his shoulders, Spag would say, 'It'll move quick.'"

Anthony enjoyed surprising the suppliers by placing larger-than-expected orders. Several people have told me the story about the grumpy salesman who stopped in at a Dunkin' Donuts near SPAG'S for a cup of coffee. He groaned in response to a cheery hello. "What's eating you?" the waitress asked.

He grumbled, "Some *nut* just gave me an order for a truckload of birdseed!"

---

[3] See Extended Family, page 134 for more about Vinnie.

"Where were you?" she asked.

"At SPAG'S up the road."

"Was the 'nut' wearing a big hat?"

"Yeah, why?" he asked.

"That was Spag himself, the guy who owns the place."

"You mean...that order was for real?" When she nodded, his face lit up. He hustled to a telephone to tell his boss about the great order he had just received.

More Toys Needed!

"I'll never forget the sudden burst of toy sales one Christmas season," recounted longtime friend and employee Ann Anderson.[4] She continued:

> Way back in the late 40s, I think it was 1947, we had had a "run" on all our toys. It was closing time on a Saturday night, and the shelves were bare.
>
> Looking at the empty shelves, Spag said, "We need more toys in a hurry! They'll be looking for the stuff first thing Monday morning."
>
> Vinnie agreed. Then Spag turned to Eddie Belkin, the toy salesman, and made a quick decision. "That means we'll have to go up to the house tonight, Eddie, and write up an order for a pile of toys." Thinking aloud, he added, "But we're going to need some of those toys Monday morning, enough to tide us over until your truck comes with the order on Monday afternoon." Eddie nodded, and Spag said, "So we'll go to the warehouse in Boston tomorrow to pick up toys to have on hand for Monday morning."
>
> That night, Eddie Belkin, Vinnie, my husband Glenn and I joined Olive and Spag in their home to write up the order. We sat at the dining room table, fortified with a pot of coffee and one of Fannie Melander's delicious cream cakes. We worked until

[4] See Extended Family, pages 119, 133–134 for more about Ann.

The Christmas rush, 1952.

three o'clock Sunday morning leafing through Milton Bradley, Tonka, Playskool, Barbie dolls, and Fisher/Price catalogs.

Sunday afternoon, all five of us drove to the toy warehouse in Boston to pick up an assortment of toys. It was bitterly cold. Olive, Spag, and I rode in their Kaiser Frazer. I must say we felt pretty nice in the brand new Kaiser, and a little fancy. Vinnie and Glenn drove a rental truck that had no heater. They nearly froze to death!

At the warehouse, we met Eddie Belkin, who helped us to load the car and the truck with toys. Then we helped Eddie to pile the rest of the order on the loading platform, to be picked up and delivered to SPAG'S Monday afternoon. We returned to the store with our load of toys, restocked the shelves, and collapsed—exhausted.

How right Spag was! When the store opened Monday morning, people were waiting in line to buy toys. The trailer truck arrived with the rest of the toy order none too soon. The Christmas rush was on!

The huge success of this Christmas toy sale created excitement. The SPAG crew eagerly looked forward to taking over the rest of the garage space. After M&M had moved out, Anthony needed additional carpenters to assist Folke in restructuring the store layout. Miller Henderson, another carpenter friend, and his student assistant, Jack Swedberg,[5] joined with Folke in building more counters and display racks.

At the front of the store, in the area where the truck door had been, Folke built two smaller doors for an entrance and an exit. Customers no longer had to climb stairs, but now entered at the sidewalk level and walked up the truck ramp inside the store to do their shopping. To leave, they walked down the ramp to the check-out counter and exit door. Folke and his assistants subsequently removed the front steps leading to the early store and closed in the doorway. The corner of the building where the original Shrewsbury Tire and

---

[5] Jacked worked at SPAG'S for two years, and later became a well-known photographer and naturalist.

Two exits, 1955.

SPAG'S, 1952.
One entrance, one exit (stairs removed).

SPAG'S storefront 1959.

Battery Service was first located became the housewares department.

It was about this time that Anthony had to address another important aspect of his growing business. "I can't have clerks working out of a cigar box at the checkout counter," he thought. Then he remembered the National Cash Register that had jingled each time he had rung up a magazine sale at the old Emporium. On his next daily "drop in" visit to Mother, he asked her if he could borrow the cash register stored in our attic. She, of course, was happy to have it put to good use. Anthony dusted it off, carried it to the store, and assigned it to Ann Anderson.

Ann (Bianchi) Anderson at cash register.

The M&M Company had used a steam boiler to heat the garage, but the system was inadequate for a store. To provide more heat, Anthony suspended gas heaters from the ceiling. They blew hot air, but even the gas heaters did not produce enough heat to warm the large, cavernous area during the cold months. The customers wearing their heavy winter coats and jackets did not seem to notice the low temperature, but the clerks did. The several layers of clothing they had to wear to keep warm gave them the appearance of being pleasingly plump. When they shed the extra sweaters in early spring, customers remarked about how much weight the clerks had lost!

Chicken-wire fencing stretched across the back of the store, separating the back storage area from the store itself. The hardware department expanded and moved to the furthest right-hand corner. Wheelbarrows, spreaders, lawn mowers, and supplies occupied the back of the store. Electrical supplies, carpentry tools, paint, and painting supplies spread out and took over the space in front of the fertilizer and garden tools. The shoe section expanded—and so did the number of customers.

Fertilizer started to arrive by the truckload, and Anthony also began to carry large quantities of lime and bone meal in 100-pound bags. Sometimes the bags would break open or tear during handling. Then the lime had to be weighed and put into five- and 10-pound bags.

"Bagging lime was one of the worst chores," said Vinnie. "The smell of lime and bone meal was far from the fragrance of perfume."

The early housewares section had a few toasters, pots and pans, an ironing board or two, and a few kitchen utensils. In later years, SPAG'S received countless awards from General Electric Company, suppliers of the hundreds of thousands of toaster, mixers, steam irons, and other small appliances sold at the store.

Gadabout Gaddis

With the enlargement of the store, Anthony continued to add more items. Vendors, eager to have their wares included in SPAG'S inventory, called at the office in Anthony's home or at the store. Jack Swedberg remembers overhearing a conversation between Anthony and Gadabout Gaddis, a sales representative for Shakespeare's Tackle Company. "Gad," as he was often called, was a TV personality who flew his plane up and down the coast of New England looking for lakes and streams to fish. For several years, he taped each of his excursions for later broadcast of "Gadabout Gaddis, the Flying Fisherman Show" on a Boston channel.

Jack remembered how "Spag listened to Gad as he extolled the fine features of his high-quality Shakespeare fishing rods and reels laid out on a counter for Spag's inspection. When Gad finished his spiel, he asked Spag if he would like to choose some rods and reels to display in the store. You should have seen Gad's face when Spag said in his usual casual manner, 'I'll take 'em all.'"

Later, Gad said, "SPAG'S single counter sold more rods, reels, lures than all the combined fishing tackle counters, including specialty shops throughout New England." After that initial meeting, he usually called upon Anthony in the Beverly Road office, and like other vendors, Anthony invited him to stay for lunch.

Glenn Anderson, Ann's husband, also became a full-time employee. Glenn was a great fisherman, so Anthony put him in charge of the fishing tackle counter. Fishing gear began to fill a whole wall.

Jack Swedberg recalled another unusual day at SPAG'S:

I remember the delivery of a truckload of

Flexible Flyers one hot day in July. It must have been another one of those "great offers too hard to pass up." When Spag saw that truck backing up to his receiving dock, he gathered all the help he could find. We unloaded the truck and then spent the rest of the day storing the sleds in every nook and cranny. We hauled half of them up to Beverly Road, where we filled Spag's cellar and garage. We had to pile some of the sleds against the house and cover them with a tarpaulin. In the store, Spag leaned three or four of them against a post. In spite of the heat, they sold immediately. The price was right. By continuing to display a few at a time, they moved quickly. By September, the sleds were gone.

Forward Thrusts

Anthony was carrying only workmen's boots until Bernie Hershberg came in and introduced his line of shoes. Anthony enjoyed talking with Bernie, who understood and agreed with Anthony's dedication to providing his customers with high-quality merchandise at affordable prices. My brother also appreciated Bernie's business know-how and his sensitivity to the needs of customers. His family had been in the shoe business for three generations; he knew the shoe industry inside and out.

Besides his regular line of footwear, Bernie introduced a shoe called the "Forward Thrust" made by Weyenberg. This wasn't a new kind of shoe; in fact, it was a well-known expensive shoe—that is, until Anthony stocked a few pairs and offered them at his usual low-margin price.

The designers of the "Forward Thrust" had created a shoe that moved one's weight from the heel forward to the toes. These comfortable and versatile shoes, good for both walking and standing, were ideal for businessmen, servicemen, and industrial workers who had to stand for long periods at a time. Word got around that the "Forward Thrusts" were available at SPAG'S at a great price. Customers came from diverse businesses throughout the area. "Forward Thrusts" figuratively "walked out" of the place! The expanding line of shoes soon filled the 20-foot-high shelves on a large section of the Baker Avenue wall. Anthony was delighted to have "Forward Thrust" shoes on his shelves—yet another quality item and another good buy for his customers.

To provide easy access to the shoes on the upper shelves, Folke built a 24-foot traveling ladder that he installed on a set of tracks suspended from the ceiling. The tracks ran parallel to the shelves. By positioning the ladder, which Folke set at an angle for easy climbing, clerks could reach every pair of shoes. Anthony was grateful for his master carpenter's inventiveness and fine craftsmanship.

Still More Expansion

By 1949, in addition to taking over the whole of the original building, Anthony had purchased land adjacent to the store, making it possible for him to provide off-street parking for his customers. He was well on his way.

America was in prosperity. The economy was humming; SPAG'S business was singing. "Why not get it at SPAG'S? You can't beat SPAG'S prices!" became household bywords. About this time, Anthony considered opening a store in Fairbanks, Alaska. The idea came about after talking with Jim, my husband, who had been stationed in Alaska during World War II. They talked at length about the new roads, railroads, and airports constructed for military purposes that were making the state more easily accessible.

Anthony could envision the new frontier, and he wanted to take part in its development. He could see that the new settlers would need an "everything store," such as he had in Shrewsbury. He wanted Jim to manage the store in Fairbanks, but I couldn't see myself living in the Alaskan territory, so Anthony dropped the idea.

In 1952, four years after taking over the entire garage, Anthony again found that he needed more room for stocking merchandise. So he arranged with Leo Moroney, a metal building contractor, to have a 20 foot Butler (tin-sided) addition constructed at the back of the garage. On completion, Vinnie and his workers moved the inventory into the Butler addition, which included a docking platform for two

Olive, in checkered jacket, assisting customers.

trucks. The chicken wire divider came down to make more room for the store. The new addition also included more space for merchandise, as well as a much-needed office with a door that opened on Baker Avenue.

With the extra space in the original building, the paint and plumbing department expanded. Steve Tozeski and, later, Al Proulx managed the busy plumbing area and shared their expertise with anyone who sought it. Many customers did.

Mr. Arne Furst of Decatur Hopkins and his able assistants (Ed Whalen and, later, Bob Kinchla) expanded the hardware department by stocking more items and backup inventory. With the country's economic improvement, fine quality toys—previously carried only as holiday sales items—now sold at affordable prices throughout the year. Anthony continued to add more items to the shelves throughout the store in response to the many requests made by his customers.

Buying Big

Naturally, Jim and I and the rest of the family shopped at the store on a regular basis. If I did not drop into the store every two or three days, Anthony would be on the phone asking, "What's up, Susabella?" (Sometimes I was "Joe" or "Marguerita." Anthony's family and friends became accustomed to the various names by which he addressed us.) On one of those brief visits in the early fifties, I found Anthony chuckling away to himself about some "stuff" he had bought on speculation. As we munched on some peanuts, he told me about his "illustrious order."

"The offer of a truckload of white Navy surplus pants was too good a buy to pass up," he said. "So I ordered them. Two hundred and fifty pairs of bell-bottoms just arrived, and guess what, Elsa? They're all size 29!" We both had a good laugh as we agreed that not many men had 29-inch waistlines, nor were there many who wanted to wear white bell-bottoms. Anthony got such a kick out of that shipment. "But," he said, "that's what business is all about—the problems and the solving of them."

"It's all part of the fun," he mused as he reached for another handful of peanuts to stuff into his mouth. "You try to anticipate what is on the horizon and do what is best for everyone."

Talking with Vinnie Mastro about it later, I found out that the order of bell-bottoms presented quite a problem.

"We had to scramble to find a place for them all. We piled them everywhere. Eventually, they sold for 50 cents each," said Vinnie. "Spag took a pretty good razzing on that one."

Then there was the "great" offer of wooden boxes that Anthony could not let pass. "As with the bell-bottoms," recalled Vinnie with a grin, "Spag ordered the 2,000 boxes over the telephone without having seen them. When they arrived, he discovered that each box was missing one side and a cover. What a ribbing he took! However, he never was one to be stumped. We sold them all in a couple of weeks as kindling wood."

When it came to buying, Anthony was a man of extremes. Most of his mega-purchases sold well, but an outlandish-sized order of coral jewelry he ordered while on one of his trips to Hawaii did not. He bought "tons" of it, and wound up giving most of the jewelry away.

"You know," he said, "I really thought I had made every kind of buying mistake there was, but this coral jewelry purchase is a new one. In business, there always seem to be plenty of opportunities to make new mistakes. I'm sure that I'll be making more of them."

His marketing triumphs usually outweighed his mistakes, however. One autumn in the 1960s, in anticipation of a short supply of antifreeze, Anthony ordered 25 trailerloads (12,000 gallons). When the 25 trailers arrived, he lined them up in the parking lot. That winter was exceptionally cold; antifreeze supplies ran out of stock everywhere—except at SPAG'S. Anthony purposely set a two-gallon limit per customer and, despite the shortage, continued to sell it at the regular price, $1.99 per gallon. When questioned about it, he would say, "The price is $1.99, and that's where it's going to stay!"

Dealers came to SPAG'S to buy antifreeze in large quantities, but Anthony refused to sell to them; he feared that they would jack up the price and gouge the public. Throughout the winter, he steadfastly continued to sell the antifreeze at the same price of $1.99 a gallon. The lines of customers waiting in their cars to buy antifreeze sometimes extended up Route 9, east to Harrington Avenue, up the hill past the fire station 300 feet away, and beyond the parking lot.

Dale Fair
marking prices on merchandise.

Two-Wheeler Carts

Dale Fair of Benson Brothers, who serviced SPAG'S from 1948 to 1987, began his sales career by trying to sell paper bags to a store that did not use paper bags.[7] After he had stopped by several times, Anthony surprised Dale one day by saying, "Do you have any tumblers (glasses) over at your place? I'm cleaned out and need some in a hurry."

"I told him that I would find out," recalled Dale. "I didn't know what a tumbler was. Within an hour, I returned with a box of tumblers. Spag appreciated the fast service and bought them." For Dale, that order was the first of the thousands he would be delivering to SPAG'S in the years to follow.

Dale and other salesmen had the challenge of filling the shelves while the store was still open. He described that experience for me:

> I heard rumors through the years that SPAG'S had greater dollar sales per square foot of floor space than any other store in the whole country. I believed it after having tried to get through the aisles with the two-wheelers (carts). The store was usually so crowded, I had to dance what I called the "SPAG Shuffle" to move the two-wheeler through the crowd without touching a soul. You really needed a special two-wheeler driver's permit. The more crowded the store, the more difficult it was to get goods to the counters. That's when they sold the fastest.

Whenever possible, Dale would try to get the goods on the counters during the supper hours when the store was usually less crowded. Many times he would mark up packages in the trailer or stockroom so he would not have to block the aisles as long. Then he would patiently wend his way toward the counters with lots of "nice things," as Anthony often called the merchandise.

For Dale, the following years were like a big three-ring circus. Christmas was an especially busy time, as he described it:

[7] See Making Our Lives Exciting, page 211.

Spag didn't want to run out, and Mr. Benson, my boss, didn't want much of anything left over after Christmas. I was in the middle trying to please both of them. It required a lot of planning and good luck, but somehow it all worked out well. The manufacturers knew the situation and did a great job of shipping promptly during the entire season. I think a guardian angel spent a lot of time in Worcester and Shrewsbury watching over all of us.

Customers came pouring in from everywhere and so did the deliveries. I brought in tree decorations, wrapping paper, ribbon, tags, seals, jigsaw puzzles, and toys. The SPAG'S employees were usually so swamped, they couldn't keep the counters filled….Spag never liked to see empty counters.

At the peak of the season, tree ornaments sold so fast that they would often be almost gone by the time you put the last box on the counter. The counters would be as empty when you finished as they were when you started. You would walk away wondering if you had really accomplished anything. I made repeated trips to the trailers in the parking lot, where Spag stored his backup merchandise, to haul in the "nice stuff" on a two-wheeler. I then priced the items, and put them on the step counters.

The customers would be packed around the counters so tightly; it was hard for the salespeople to reach the shelves. Caution was essential when pricing goods with a felt-tip marker. It was so crowded. Someone might bump you, and you had to make sure the marker didn't touch any customer's clothing as they reached in from all directions for the merchandise. Sometimes I felt as though I was surrounded by a giant octopus.

Anthony appreciated the extra time many of his vendors spent stocking shelves—a service that was unexpected and unusual, but one that became the norm at SPAG'S.

Filling the Wagon

Anthony often said, "You can't sell from an empty wagon." For the most part, he filled his in two ways. By the time his business really took off, he was buying half his inventory from salespeople who called on him in his office. The other half he purchased when he traveled around the country to trade shows, where suppliers from all over the world set up their booths and exhibited their products. Each show featured a different kind of merchandise, so Anthony would order hardware and plumbing here, housewares there, and so on. In this way, he was able to stock SPAG'S with bargains in sporting goods, clothing, furniture, electronics, camping equipment, gifts, and toys.

Buying this way was important to Anthony for several reasons. First and foremost, at the shows he could meet and talk with old friends in the business, make friends with new salespeople, and learn about new companies, trends, and ideas. Attending shows also made it easier for him to discuss sales promotions, to obtain special prices based on huge purchases, and to take advantage of the "incentive deals" that were available only at the trade shows.

Vinnie Mastro noted, "Spag was always on the look-out for new products, anything the store never had, or innovative ways to display items for sale. He was not afraid to introduce new items. He particularly liked merchandise that was colorful and splashy. He loved a lot of color." Anthony also liked to introduce items made in countries throughout the world, things that his customers normally would not have occasion to see, like the four-foot beer stein on display in the kitchenwares section.

As always, Anthony had his customers in mind as he shopped for the best and newest items available at prices with which they could be happy. "His judgment was always pretty much on the mark," observed Harold Noftle. "Spag had a sixth sense when it came to determining which merchandise his customers would buy." Harold accompanied Anthony when he went to paint shows. "He was continually looking for bargains on 'sundry items,' such as drop cloths, brushes, sandpaper, putty sticks—items that customers frequently requested when purchasing paint. And he also visited the booths of other paint companies to compare prices, to look for new products, and to see if he could pick up some ideas he could use."

Drills, saws, hammers, pliers: hardware galore!

Golf bags, next to plumbing.

Clothing for working men.

Anthony attended shows in cities all over the United States, including Hawaii, and as far away as Australia, but the first show he attended was a hardware show in Boston. Ernest Cuccaro, whose family ran a hardware store on Shrewsbury Street (where Anthony often made purchases) reminisced about this:

> I can remember my father, brother, and I picking up Spag to take him to the show in Boston. He wore his trademark chinos and hat. Wholesale representatives ignored Spag as he walked around looking at their displays. I suppose they assumed that he was an insignificant buyer. Then when Spag had decided on what he wanted, he surprised the reps by ordering a sizable amount.

In the store's early days, Anthony went to the trade shows by himself. Then Olive started to accompany him and in time they took along staff members, including Vinnie Mastro, John Cullen, Bill Lynch, and Frances Ruggiere. They initially traveled by train to save money, then by commercial airlines to save time. After Olive learned to pilot a plane, she flew them to trade shows throughout the country, allowing Anthony extra nap time in the air. However, when traveling to shows in Hawaii, Europe, or Australia, they took a commercial jet.

Anthony wasted no time when attending a trade show. "Spag covered all of it," said John. "He arrived early, well before the 8:00 opening, and he didn't leave until after the 5:00 closing time. He kept going until someone suggested that he call it a day."

Vinnie noted, "Spag would go until midnight, if they would let him. Sometimes he missed the last trade-show bus back to the hotel."

"He was very methodical," recalled my husband Jim, who accompanied Anthony occasionally. "He visited every booth, looked over every display, and talked with every exhibitor. If he liked what they had, he would place his order on the spot."

"At noon," added Vinnie, "we would meet for a light lunch and compare notes. Often Spag would ask the buyers to go to certain booths to purchase new or regular merchandise."

Those who accompanied Anthony on these trips agreed with Harold Noftle when he said, "Going to a trade show with Spag was a real buying and selling experience. Spag was an excellent teacher."

Gordon Prosser, Sr. talked about attending his first show:

> In January 1951, Spag and I went to the furniture show at the Trade Mart in Chicago. I was a novice. He turned me loose while he checked out other sections of the show. We were there to buy furniture for both the annual February sale and for the summer.
>
> 'Course, I was new at this, but with Spag's encouragement, I swallowed hard and ordered 150 hammocks and a large quantity of Telescope furniture—tubular aluminum chairs and tables with some wood trim. That was our first order of Telescope, but I remember that we got it at a very good price. The shipment arrived early in February. For want of display space, we hung the hammocks and other pieces of Telescope furniture from the ceiling. When all of them sold by the summer's end, let me tell you, I was greatly relieved. From then on, we ordered summer Telescope furniture every year. We sold piles of it. One time, I ordered nine railroad cars of it! The amazing thing is that there was seldom anything left at the end of the season.

"Anthony gave his buyers a free rein," added my husband, Jim. "He would say, 'If you think you can sell it, buy it!' He would send his people off on their own, and then take off and do his own buying. If he came to a booth where his buyer was placing an order, he would look over the order to see if he wanted to add more items."

"Later on," said Vinnie, "when we attended shows where exhibitors displayed many small items, Spag would make a list of the items that he wanted the buyers on his staff to see. Buyers usually started out at these shows ordering the staple merchandise, items we always carry."

In attending trade shows, Anthony was also able to indulge his love for shopping. He had not only a passion but an instinct for picking out what SPAG'S customers would most want or need. In this way, he could pile 'em higher and higher all the time.[8]

[8] For more on Anthony at trade shows, see Suppliers and Vendors, page 159.

Extended Family

Business isn't just a matter of dollars and cents; it's people.
—Spag

Anthony often said, "I wouldn't have made it without my friends in those early years." People were, in fact, the backbone of Anthony's business and his entire life, and many became part of his extended family over the years.

In the beginning, Anthony needed help moving and marking merchandise, as well as waiting on customers, especially in the afternoons and on weekends. Like Folke and Elsie, several of Anthony's friends dropped in to give a hand whenever they had some free time. Two of them were classmates from Shrewsbury High: Glenn Anderson and his wife-to-be, Ann Bianchi, who often double-dated with Anthony and Olive.

At that time, Ann was working irregular hours as a nurse's aide. Long before she was to become the first female employee at SPAG'S, Anthony would call her on the phone and ask, "What are you doing?" Then he would add, "We're kind of busy and could use your help." Or, depending upon the circumstances, he might say, "To hell with the washing! Can you come down and give us a hand? A lot of stuff just came in and it has to get marked."

When Glenn arrived home from work in mid-afternoon, he would drive Ann to the store. As time allowed, both of them worked long into the evening, marking new merchandise, filling the shelves, waiting on customers, or doing whatever was necessary.

"Working at the store was a fun thing," recalled Ann. "It was one friend helping another. That's what it amounted to. Glenn and I con-

tinued to give a hand whenever we could. When we married and settled in Shrewsbury near Beverly Road, it was so convenient."

With the first expansion of the store (in 1947), Anthony put
Ann, now Mrs. Anderson, on his payroll. He paid her when he could;
sometimes it wasn't possible for quite a while because he had other
bills to pay. But Ann would continue to be on hand for more than four
decades and would experience the tremendous changes in the business
that evolved over the years.

Anthony's first part-time employee, hired in 1943, was Ernie
Bianchi, Ann's brother. Soon after, our own brother, Bobbie, who was
thirteen, his high school pal, Vinnie Mastro, and Ralph Zona started
working part-time after school and on weekends.

Vinnie, who was our paperboy at that time, lived nearby in our
neighborhood on the corner of Caroline Avenue and Elm Street. He
was the twelfth of thirteen children in the wonderful Mastro family. He
was also a hard-working employee, and dedicated to the store; everyone liked him from the beginning. "We were one big family," said
Vinnie one day as we recalled those early days.

When Vinnie was 19 years old, Anthony
recognized his managerial skills and made him
the store's general manager, saying that "Vinnie
could manage the whole place single-handed."
Anthony was himself 33 years old at the time
and happy to hand over responsibility to such a
capable manager.

"When we think of SPAG'S," said
Anthony more than once, "we always think of
Vinnie; he was that much a part of everything."
Anthony credited him with much of the store's
success. Except for his stint in the military ser-
vice during the Korean War, Vinnie worked at

*Vinnie Mastro: dedicated, capa-
ble store manager.*

SPAG'S for a total of 49 years.

Another close friend was Moe. In the early
forties, Maurice "Moe" Rozefsky, a young businessman, made his first call on Anthony. He
was one of five brothers who were salesmen for their father Louis'
clothing business, The Rozefsky Brothers, on Green Street in
Worcester (which was founded about the same time our father opened

the Emporium). When Anthony saw the samples Moe had brought with him, he could see that carrying men's working clothes was a great idea, but he did not have money on hand to pay for the clothing. So he turned to Moe and said, "I'd like to carry your clothing, but my money is pretty tight. In fact, at the moment, I have no money."

"My father answered, 'I'll trust you,'" said Lois Rozefsky Berg, Moe's daughter, who told me this story. As she recalled it:

First Row: Jennie Fontaine, Olive Borgatti, Anthony (Spag) Borgatti, Ann Anderson, Ellen Lutz. Second Row: Ray Charette, Joe Borgatti, Vinnie Mastro, Bob Lutz, Arnie Furst. Third Row: Steve Tozeski, Parker Blakeslee, Ralph Zona, Bob Borgatti.

The two men shook hands. It was that simple. Both had grown up in the era when a man's handshake was his bond.

The first order was for work pants, woolen jackets, underwear, and socks. Some of the pants and shirts were khaki-colored. The painters' pants and jackets, however, were made of navy blue and white striped-denim. Remember, Elsa, in those days the blue dye in the denim was not colorfast and most clothing was not prewashed. The color ran! You had blue everything! Socks, underwear, and even your legs took on a bluish tinge, especially on warm, muggy days.

Men ignored the bluish tinge, and came back for more. They knew that after a few washings, the excess blue dye would be gone. The workmen's clothes, with their DAR & Five Brothers labels, soon became an important line of clothing at SPAG'S.

Anthony with Moe Rozefsky and Bernie Hershberg.

For the following 50 years, Moe continued to call on Anthony. As the business relationship between the two men grew, so did their personal friendship. Lois said, "When Father became seriously ill, he eagerly looked forward to Spag's frequent visits. Spag cheered Father by telling him stories that made him chuckle. He was a great comfort."

Another close friend was Cliff Fahlstrom, whom Anthony met in a roundabout way when the Internal Revenue Service questioned his bookkeeping abilities. Bookkeeping required an attention to detail that boggled Anthony's mind; profit and loss statements and tax forms were enigmas to him. As a consequence, an IRS agent (in a tone of voice that made it sound more like an order than a suggestion) advised Anthony to take a course in accounting *as soon as possible*.

Reluctantly, Anthony signed up for an accounting class at Worcester Junior College. When that was completed, he decided to take a course in marketing with Clifford Fahlstrom, the instructor. In addition to having an electrical engineering degree from Worcester Polytechnic Institute and a master's in business administration from Harvard University, Cliff possessed a lot of practical knowledge. Anthony often said, "I learned more about marketing from Cliff than I ever learned in books. He was an important influence in my business life."

Cliff has since died, but from his son, David, I learned that Cliff and Anthony had similar humble beginnings and shared a strong work ethic. Both of them had grown up during the Great Depression and understood the impact it had made upon people's lives. David added:

> They also shared an interest in books—books on marketing, economics, and biographies in particular—and they exchanged books often. Dad, who was an avid reader, said that Anthony was a "voracious one." Dad used to say, "I don't know how he can find the time to do so much reading, with his business, his family, and all his other activities."
>
> Occasionally, Spag invited Dad to Beverly Road for dinner, where he enjoyed the stimulating conversations on business concepts and ideas that they found in their reading. Neither engaged much in small talk. When there had been a hiatus between visits, they would pick up the conversation right where they had left off. Dad and Spag respected each other, and they were interested in each other's ideas.
>
> Dad often told me that he attributed Anthony's success not so much to his ability to sell hammers and screwdrivers, but more to his great generosity in returning to the community the benefits of his success.

I'm sure Anthony would point out that he owed much of his prosperity to friends like Ann, Vinnie, Moe, and Cliff—and also to Bill, another special friend.

Bill

In 1934, a few days after Anthony opened the store, a salesman driving by noticed the new store in the front corner of the garage at 193 Boston Turnpike. Out of curiosity, Bill M., a tall man with black wavy hair, a small mustache, and an engaging smile, stopped in to meet the new owner. He and Anthony struck up an apparently lengthy conversation. It was to be the first of many great discussions they would have over the years.

Realizing that it was past noon, Anthony said, "I have to go to lunch now. My mother's making spaghetti. Why don't you come home with me and have some?" Bill accepted the invitation.

When he returned to his home that evening, Bill enthusiastically told his wife about his chance meeting with Anthony and having lunch with his family. "Wait till you meet this guy!" he said. "He's great! He's pleasant and easy to talk with. This guy is going to go places."

Anthony and the rest of us felt the same way about Bill. He immediately became a member of our family, and from then on, he came to our house often. He would sometimes spend hours talking with Mother and Olga. Olga, who was ten years old at the time, appreciated the interest Bill took in her varied projects.

Having lost his own mother at a young age, Bill related easily and quickly to Mother and became devoted to our family. He filled a big void in our lives, too; he provided us with a father image at a time when our own father had only recently returned home on a permanent basis and was still recuperating from his illness. Thanks to Bill, we enjoyed many Sunday outings; I have happy memories of our family picnicking with him and his family at Crane's Beach.

During the Depression, many businesses had to drastically curtail production and were therefore forced to reduce their staff. It was at this time that Mother invited Bill and his family to move in with us until he found work. We all enjoyed immensely the few weeks they stayed with us.

Anthony also enjoyed having Bill for a friend. "Bill gave me a lot of solid advice," he said as he thought back to those good old days. "He was knowledgeable and experienced in the automotive-accessory industry."

"Bill was a caring person, always going out of his way to help and to do nice things for others," Anthony added. "If he saw someone walking in the other direction and the person was struggling with bundles, he would turn his car around and offer the person a ride." This made a lasting impression on Anthony, who used to mention Bill's genuine concern for his fellow man. "Bill was one of those people who inspired and encouraged others," said Anthony. "He was certainly a big influence in my life."

From the early days of the store until Bill's death following an illness 20 years later, the two men spent many hours together.

In one's lifetime, there are some people who make and leave an indelible impression on others. For Anthony and all the Borgattis, Bill M. was one such person.

The Employees

Anthony often spoke about how lucky he was to have such hard-working, loyal employees. "They give me their best. I respect and love them for it," he would say over and over. Then he'd add: "They give 100 percent! They're flexible, and they adjust their work schedules to meet the needs of the store. They're a great bunch. They don't grumble. Well, maybe they do," he would hasten to add, "but I don't hear it. Without their dedication, the store would not have made it."

To Anthony, his employees were a part of his family, and he expressed this in many ways. He often took the time to greet each employee and to ask about their families as he "walked the store."[1] By doing so, he found many ways to help them. He was genuinely concerned for his people's welfare; whenever somebody suffered a personal loss or misfortune, chances were good that Anthony would provide whatever was needed in the way of food or financial assistance.

This concern also applied to new job applicants, as was the case with Ray Bobalinski, who recalled:

> When Spag said, "Be here at 8 am tomorrow," I was happy to know that he was hiring me, but I was caught in a dilemma.
> "I can't possibly be here at 8," I replied. "I have

[1] See Walking the Store.

to see my kids onto the school bus."

"Then in that case, don't come at 8," said Spag. "Come in after your kids are on the bus. Family comes first."

That was 17 years ago. I've been working here at SPAG'S ever since.

Anthony looked out for his employees in other ways, too. One morning, around 1:30 A.M., he, Olive, Jim, and I were passing by SPAG'S on our way home after an evening out when Anthony noticed several cars in the store's parking lot. We stopped so that he could "check things out." We went in with him and saw the evening crew feverishly restocking the shelves for the next day.

"This is terrible!" Anthony gasped. "You need more help!" He decided immediately that "this is never going to happen again." At seven o'clock the next morning, he took out the file of job applicants and began making phone calls. Thirty-one people came for interviews at 10 o'clock. He hired them all and asked them to start working that evening.

Anthony was also quick to notice when an employee went out of his or her way to help a customer or did a good job on a project. He never hesitated to compliment and reward his workers with gift certificates for a night out at a local restaurant. He was also generous with his annual Christmas bonuses—yet another way he expressed his appreciation for his dedicated staff. With each bonus check, he and Olive enclosed a note. For example, their 1953 note read:

> Dear Fellow Workers,
>
> Your diligent efforts and industriousness throughout the year have made 1953 a profitable year for SPAG'S Supply. In appreciation, we wish to share the profits with you.
>
> Only your wholehearted cooperation as a team has made it possible for us to write the enclosed bonus check for you. This is what we have been able to share with you this year. Future years may not be as fruitful; God and your efforts only can produce such results.

May we at this time wish you and your families a very Merry Christmas and a healthy, happy New Year.

—Olive and Spag

Memories of Spag

When I wrote to Anthony's employees to request their suggestions for this book; their responses were overwhelming—from brief notes to full-blown articles. The following is just a sample.

Lee Zolla, Anthony's longtime secretary shared many memories:[2]

Lee Zolla: loyal and indispensable secretary.

Having worked for Spag (and Olive) for 30 years, I feel I knew the real "Spag." What you saw was what you got. He was a very down-to-earth, compassionate, loving human being—an ordinary person who, with a lot of work, dedication and desire, made good.

If Spag answered the phone when my husband, Vin, called me at work, they jokingly repeated the same conversation every time. After exchanging pleasantries, Vin would say to Spag, "May I talk to your beautiful secretary?" Spag would always reply, "Wait, I have to move her onto my other knee."

Opening the mail was important to Spag, and, of course, there was a load of it. I would open it, separate it, and put it in different piles. Then Spag would look through every bit of it. Some days, he would make up jingles using some of the names he read in the mail. He sure enjoyed everything he did.

Spag and Olive took many wonderful trips.

[2] Lee wrote a long and lovely letter; parts of it are scattered throughout the book.

Hawaii was Olive's favorite for a number of years. They went there every year, and they visited just about every place in the world... They would be away three to four weeks at a time.

When they went to Egypt, Olive wrote me a letter in which she quoted Spag as saying of the pyramids, "I never saw so many goddamn rocks." Spag always took the time to send cards to all of us. What a guy!

Paul Zolla, Lee's son, wrote an interesting letter describing his SPAG'S experiences:

> Spag and Olive and the store were a part of our everyday life. Hardly an evening meal went by without some discussion about the world of SPAG'S Supply. I have vivid memories of going to the office to pick up Mom and hanging around that crazy place. Phones were always ringing off the hook. People were rushing around, and there was this smiling guy in khakis and a cowboy hat. No matter how busy he was, he always noticed me and came over to talk.
>
> In my family, the rite of passage was the job at SPAG'S. By today's standards, the store was nepotism run amok. At one point, my mother, sister, myself, an aunt and several cousins all worked at SPAG'S. Many employees seemed to have similar family trees at the store. Spag gave a lot of kids that first entry on the résumé, and helped them get through college. I can recall how amazed my college roommates were that I always had a job waiting for me on vacations. Spag would take you back on summer and Christmas breaks whether he needed you or not.
>
> Once, on a hot Sunday afternoon, Spag called

my house and asked me to meet him down by the trailers that surround the main parking lot. It was about 90 degrees outside those tin trailers, and probably hotter inside by 20 degrees. We started going from trailer to trailer with me climbing up and telling him what was in each trailer or him asking me to look for something. One particular trailer was packed solid, from front to back. Spag asked me to tunnel back to the end to see if it was all the same stuff. After about an hour of this, I was dehydrated and exhausted. That was when we came upon a pile of wooden pallets that were in the wrong place. The right place, he said, was at the farthest point on his property from where we were standing. The only shade in between was under Spag's cowboy hat, which brought me little comfort. After struggling with those pallets and a push cart that hadn't been greased in 20 years, I finally got all the pallets into the right place. Spag thanked me for helping him, gave me a few "you handsome fella"s and then handed me a twenty-dollar bill. Now back in 1974, for less than two hours' work, twenty bucks, tax free, was a lot of money to a kid who was used to making $2.50 an hour.

June Wilson wrote about working at SPAG'S and how much she appreciated Anthony's fatherly concern for her and her children's welfare. June said she was shopping at SPAG'S back in December 1955 when Anthony walked up to her and introduced himself. After chatting a while, Anthony said, "I need some Christmas help. Would you be interested?" June shared the following about her experience:

I loved working at SPAG'S. It was hard work, but I knew that he never gave anyone a job that he himself would not do. A few days before Christmas, Anthony called me aside. His big hat still in place, he told me that he was giving me a $200 bonus that

I was to put toward my children's Christmas toys. I was overwhelmed and deeply appreciative of his generosity.

When my husband and I divorced, Anthony kept a watchful eye over me. He never let me forget that I am a good person, and he reminded me of God's love. He was concerned about me getting enough to eat. One day he made me close my register and told me to go to his house for lunch with his family.

Later when I met and married a wonderful man, Spag was so happy to know that the boys and I were being taken care of.... When, after many happy years together, Earl passed away, Anthony gave me a tremendous amount of support.

No matter how many words may be written about him, I'm not sure that any of us will ever know the greatness of this man.

On occasion, Mr. Arne Furst, the salesman for Decatur Hopkins, would bring his young son, David, with him. Dave Furst wrote about an incident that happened while he was "helping out" at SPAG'S:

Spag asked me to go upstairs to the storage room and bring down a box of light bulbs. He was waiting at the bottom of the stairs. Just as I put my foot on the top step, the box of bulbs slipped out of my hand and landed with a crash at Spag's feet. He looked at the box of smashed bulbs and then at me. I was frozen with fear. He put his hands on his hips and said, "Dave, you are one hell of a bulb carrier!" Later, when I got to my dad's car, I found twenty dollars inside and a note thanking me for my help.

At a house-warming party for my folks in their first new home, the refrigerator broke down. The next day a new one was delivered. Guess who? Spag!

Some of the letters I received had a humorous twist. Dan Corcoran, who created cartoons and drawings for the store's signs, wrote:

> When I was working at SPAG'S in the late 1950s, my oldest son, three or four years old, would hear my wife and me talking about where we got things. We would usually say we got this or that at SPAG'S. After listening to that for some time, he asked his mother, "Mommy, did you get me at SPAG'S too?" We both laughed at that comment.

In Anthony's station wagon, he usually carried several boxes of "goodies" to give "where it fits." Many people wrote to express their appreciation for the "care boxes," as Jodi Scott, an employee, called them. In her thank-you note to Anthony and Olive, she wrote: "Just knowing how much you, Olive, Carol, and John care makes my job more than a job. You all are a part of my family. Thanks again."

Lynne Carlo, one of the nurses who cared for Anthony when he was ill, wrote to thank him for a Christmas bonus he had sent, noting: "You are very generous to me. More importantly though, thank-you for your wonderful stories, positive attitude, and caring guidance. You are a great man. I only hope some of your ways will rub off on me. I idolize you."

Not surprisingly, several employees wrote about Anthony's generous Christmas bonuses. Nicky Wyman noted:

> In 1965, I became a part of SPAG'S full-time family as a cashier. Every Christmas Eve, Spag and Olive would come to the store to hand out bonus checks and personally wish us all a Merry Christmas.
>
> Every once in a while when he was extra pleased with how things were going, he would say, "You good kids!" And he would give each one of us cashiers a friendly kiss.

Prior to Anthony's death, Folke Johnson's wife, Elsie, wrote a touching memoir about the couple's fondness for Anthony:

My husband, Folke, knew Spag very well from his childhood on Belmont Street, but I met him in 1934 when he opened the quaint little store on Rte. 9 in Shrewsbury, which also housed the M&M Trucking Company.

Spag and Olive would take us on shopping trips to Boston where he would buy supplies for the store. The store was growing larger by then, and Spag was quite important to these businesses. After he finished his business, he and Olive would take us to dinner at Ye Olde Oyster House in Boston, and then on to a hockey game.

Later on, after we had moved to California, our son took us to Las Vegas for a weekend. On our first night there, we went to the Circus Casino and stood in the foyer, looking down a few steps into the vast casino. Thousands of people were gambling and talking. As we stood there, we heard a voice from the mass of people calling out. Someone was shouting, "Folke! Folke Johnson!"

We stood there, unbelieving. My son said, "Dad, look who's here! It's Spag!" Spag and Folke hugged and hugged. Then Spag went and got Olive. We were thrilled to see them.

There are so many other stories to be told about this man and the help he gave all of us. He has never changed and never will change. He is the same Spag I met in 1934 as he is today.

Elsie also noted that "Folke couldn't have been prouder [working for Spag] if he had worked for the President of the United States."

Errol Melander, like so many employees, was also proud of his job at SPAG'S:

Spag instilled a sense of pride in us, and made us feel important—that we were valuable members of his Team. When we wanted to go hunting the first week in December, he let us know that he couldn't afford to do without us. Of course, the Christmas rush had already started. He said, "If I didn't need you, I wouldn't have hired you."

On parting after an evening out to dinner one evening, shortly after I was married, Spag slipped me an envelope with two $100 bills.

Wayne McOwen, a former employee now living in Dallas, Pennsylvania, wrote the following letter to Anthony in January, 1991:

... I happened to tune in to a late-night airing of CNN's Financial News Network program that was presenting a segment on various entrepreneurs around the USA. There you were on the "platform" checking merchandise displayed in (typical) abundance, looking no different than you did on the day I first heard your cousin Joe bellow out our lunchtime code, "Spag's 42!" for the first time![3]

When the segment about SPAG'S Supply was over, I sat there for some time reliving some special memories that only the "early" SPAG'S alumni can claim. I remember being called to your house for the interview. The job was in the shoe department. You were especially concerned about my ability to handle some of those massive cases of shoes. You asked me to lift something there in your office (At age 16, I could have passed for 13.), but I managed to pass the test, and I was hired.

Perhaps you no longer have those dinner meetings for employees, but I vividly recall several that I attended. What a great gift of wit you had in the way you would deliver those constructive criticisms—like

---

[3] This code, based on Anthony's age when it was first used, was the signal to go to lunch. Joe, who was probably an actor at heart, employed such exaggeration when he called out "Spag's 42!" that everyone in the store chuckled when they heard him.

no one else could do. Even now I never throw paper towels anywhere but in the rubbish in any Men's Room, regardless of how full the container may be!

I think that you should know that there are many—I among them—who appreciate all of the "undeliberate" ways that you've helped us to grow and become responsible citizens. I was very lucky.

Judy Pickett wrote about the many kindnesses Anthony bestowed upon her and her family throughout her years at SPAG'S, including his generosity to her in-laws when they had a death in the family. She noted that "he didn't have to consider my in-laws, but he did. He went out of his way. He went the extra mile to make sure that we were happy." Judy also wrote:

Judy Pickett:
the versatile receptionist.

Shortly after I started to work in the office, Spag came to me and said, "I heard you were going to Texas to visit your parents." I said, "Yes." Then we carried on a short conversation about our families. As he was leaving, he handed me a hundred-dollar bill and said, "Take your parents to dinner with this. Tell them that they did a great job raising a special person and that I feel lucky to have you as an employee." He made my day!

At the annual retirement party in October, 1995, Spag really was not feeling well. But he made the effort to show up at the hall and say a few words to the six employees who were being honored. His presence was really appreciated. He left as quietly and quickly as he came, which was so like him, very unobtrusive and unassuming.

Mary Vilkas, a retired employee, wrote to express her appreciation for the generous pension that allows her to live comfortably:

> My fifteen years of steady work at SPAG'S are memorable ones. I know if it were not for Spag, I wouldn't be in the position I am in today. Whenever I am shopping and buying something, perhaps a little frivolous, I always think of him. I say to myself, "Spag is the one who made it possible for me to do this."

Gordon Prosser Sr., also now retired, wrote:

> Around 1952, I had decided to leave the gas station that I managed. Spag, who was a customer of mine, asked me if I would consider working for him. Here was a man who always greeted you with a smile and a good word, just like his mother and the rest of his family did. I didn't stop to think it over. I grabbed the offer. What a change in my life and in my work followed! Happiness, financial security, holidays off, paid vacations, Christmas bonuses, and a good insight into compassion, trust, and love for all people. That is what I received from Olive and Spag.
>
> Any wonder that I love and respect them?

The Cooks

To Anthony, everybody who worked for him was important, including the cooks, who provided nourishment to all who entered the Borgatti residence. I remember the enticing aromas that drifted into Anthony's office, sparking the appetites of all those in the house—family members, employees, salespersons, and anyone else who happened to be visiting at mealtimes.

The cooks served the meals in a dining room next to the office. Often when I stopped in before lunch, I would catch Anthony passing through the kitchen so that he "could be persuaded to sample every-

Top row left to right: Brad Sjoberg, Joe Borgatti. Middle row left to right: Don Valle, Elizabeth Pickett and Beverly Anthony. Left: Ron DuFault. Right: Nancy Gentile and Cindy Longval.

thing." The cooks loved to have their food sampled, and Anthony was happy to oblige by eating generous amounts of everything from the pots on the stove or from the heated trays. He ate practically a full meal before he even sat down at the table!

Consequently, as Anthony's store expanded, so did his waistline. When we brought this to his attention, he pretended that he did not know why. He cast aside any suggestions that we might make about his losing weight, saying, "You gotta catch the brass ring when it's in front of you." He would cock his head and add, "Gotta make the most of the opportunities that come your way, or life passes you by."

The kitchen staff at Beverly Road kept a busy schedule. What workers they were! Fannie Melander was the first full-time cook. As Queen of the Kitchen, she spoiled everyone who came to dinner. Fannie was already a gourmet cook when she came to work for Anthony and Olive. One of her hobbies was taking cooking lessons, and Fannie's food presentations were works of art. Her creed was "the eye eats," and this pertained to everything she prepared. The food was beautiful to look at and scrumptious to eat. Lucky for all of us!

Fannie's successor was Peggy Mastro, Vinnie's sister, beloved by all. She reigned for many years as cooking queen of the Spag household. Her happiness depended upon how well she pleased her diners, and she gauged her success by the amount of food they ate. The more we consumed, the happier she was.

Oh, how she enjoyed compliments! And, oh, how we all relished her delicious fare! Many of us ate her rich desserts supposedly "just to keep Peggy happy." Those who broke bread regularly at the Spag dining room "wore" her cooking well.

As more visitors came and activity increased on Beverly Road, so did the work in the kitchen. The days were busy, first with grocery shopping and then with meal preparation. As needed, cases of coffee and other staples arrived from the store to replenish the shelves. Every day, those from the store who were coming for lunch would call beforehand to find out if milk, crackers, bread, or anything else were needed.

During Peggy's reign, Olive hired Anna Cosky, a housekeeper, to handle the pantry detail, table setting and clearing, and other household chores. She also hired Alice Fallon to assist Peggy. When Peggy retired, Alice took over in the kitchen. She was a pleasant and handsome woman, tall and striking in appearance with pretty, neatly coifed blonde hair.

Those of us who were frequently on hand at mealtime surreptitiously glanced toward the pastry counter to see what the dessert was before taking a seat at the table. Alice was a good cook and a pastry specialist. It was easy to forget you had planned to skip dessert when Alice's platter of delicious cream puffs or any of her fruit pies were set on the table. One could never plan on having another serving later; her desserts simply didn't last that long.

In the spring and summer, when Anthony and Olive held lawn parties, Alice was in charge. The guests, any number from 25 to 125, stood patiently in line at serving time waiting for Alice's baked beans. They were the best; no one could top them!

Last but not least of the kitchen royalty, was Libby Tomaiolo. Libby had such charisma. She was the ray of sunshine who greeted each one of us. Any memories of a busy or trying day faded away when Libby extended her happy welcome.

Libby was on hand to give Alice a needed assist with the lawn parties. She also cooked when Alice was off duty. If she expected you for dinner, she would serve your favorite dish along with the meat and vegetable course. She tried to please everyone with her cooking. There would be soy chicken for the youngsters, who devoured it, a shrimp dish for Bobbie, thin-crust pizza for me, and soup for the soup lovers.

The time eventually came when Anthony's over-indulgence took its toll, and his doctor prescribed a special diet for him. Consequently, Libby provided carefully-planned meals in keeping with the doctor's instructions. As it was with Alice, Fannie, and Peggy when they were the kitchen queens, Libby's good food was hard to resist.

Thus, a splendid complement of cooks served at Beverly Road over the years, and each did her share in spoiling anyone who dined there. And like so many of Anthony's employees, the cooks mentioned often how "Spag was always good to us, and he appreciated our work."

Can't Please Them All

However much most of his employees enjoyed working for Anthony, it was to be expected that not everyone was happy at SPAG'S. Anthony received a note from one worker that read, "I quit! Working here is

Anthony, 67, checking out one of the trailers.

too continuous!" The writer evidently was frustrated because his job of stocking the shelves was never finished. Apparently, he did not have the satisfaction of completing a task because customers would grab merchandise as fast as he could put it on the shelves.

Another employee wrote: "I hereby tender my resignation. SPAG'S closes at 9:30, but letting customers stroll through the store until ten is too much for me. Thank you."

Anthony once commented, "People are different, and perhaps it's a good thing. Not everyone who came to work at SPAG'S could hack it. But I have a great bunch! They're all part of my extended family, and that's the way I want it."

And with only a few exceptions, the feeling was mutual. Those who worked closely with Anthony and knew him well appreciated his deep concern for them and for others. Lou Rossi, who was SPAG'S advertising manager for 18 years, expressed it well when he said, "You know, Elsa, he was my brother; he was my father." Lou paused and then solemnly added, "He was my dear friend."

"He was a great boss," said Vinnie Mastro, summing up. "We loved that man!"

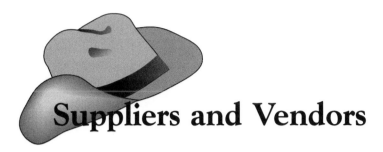

Suppliers and Vendors

What goes out must first come in.
—Spag

As important as his employees were to Anthony, so were the suppliers who provided him with merchandise to sell. He was keenly aware of the link between his customers and the tradesmen who made it possible for him to provide "spagtacular" bargains. Salespeople were an important part of his world, and he let them know it. They, in turn, appreciated his warmth and consideration, and consequently had many stories to share.

Beverly Road

Chuck Colini, a salesman, talked about his first meeting with Anthony: "I was very nervous, and he could see that. He put me at ease by saying, 'Just be honest with me, and you'll always be welcome.'"

That was Anthony. No matter how busy he was, everyone received a pleasant greeting, often with a bit of kibitzing.

Suppliers also enjoyed the congenial hospitality that Anthony extended in his home office on Beverly Road. Salespeople waiting to see him would sit in a small area near his desk. Because he liked taking phone calls, Anthony's appointments could and often did pile up. When this happened, he would call out to whomever was in the kitchen and ask for coffee to be given to his visitors. If a salesman had been to the house before, Anthony might suggest that he go to the kitchen himself. This enabled Anthony to give his attention to one person at a time.

To accommodate his business expansion and the increasing number of staff members, Anthony continued to add to the office space at Beverly Road. On occasion, he would take a visitor to another part of the house; or, if it were a spring day, they might walk outside to talk and enjoy the tulips in the garden.

Joe Banks, a salesman from the Worcester Rendering Works, sometimes called on Anthony at his home office and often had to wait. Joe recalled:

> When Spag was finally free, we would take his four dogs and go for a walk up in the woods beyond the little incline in the backyard. There we would sit on a big boulder. Both of us loved nature and the outdoors. How I treasured those walks with him! There, in the quietness of the woods, we would exchange yarns and bits of philosophy while catching a breather from the stream of visitors, some of whom came by appointment and others who were just in the area for a brief time and wanted to say hello.

Ed Hammond, retired treasurer of Decatur Hopkins, wrote about the warm reception that Anthony and Olive gave their visitors: "They treated the employees like family and their suppliers like human beings, friends and almost partners. Spag understood that the suppliers must survive if they were to continue as sources of merchandise for SPAG'S to sell." Many salespeople expressed the same sentiment and appreciation.

At lunch time, Anthony invited salespeople who were waiting in the office to join him, his family, and his staff members in the dining room. Being the people person that he was, he liked doing this. "In addition to the added sociability," he once told me, "it gives the salesmen a chance to relax and talk about their products. I get to know the vendors better and I learn more product information that otherwise might have gone by the board." Having lunch with his employees and salespeople also gave Anthony a chance to talk about the needs of his customers and the various requests they had made.

As a rule, there was a crowd in the dining room, but there was no such thing as being too crowded. If anybody else happened in after everyone had taken a seat, they made space. "Just move over," Anthony would say from the head of the seven-foot long table, "There's always room for one more." He was right! There was, although you could not imagine where; we were already wedged in. But as everyone shifted their chairs and plates, the late-comer was able to squeeze in and join the group at the table.

Having the company office in his home provided other conveniences for Anthony. Arthur Venezia, a salesman, wrote:

> One of my greatest pleasures was calling on Spag at his home in the early morning. He usually was still in his bathrobe, hair tousled and barefoot, and would greet me with a "How the hell are you and the family, Arthur?" The scene was a far cry from the usual business decorum, but that was Spag. He considered people for who they were and always looked beneath the superficial dressing.

Trade Shows

Anthony's positive relationships with vendors extended to those he met at the numerous trade shows he attended around the country.[1] However, on more than one occasion, his large orders were not taken seriously because of his casual working clothes. One buyer told me about an incident that took place at the huge Merchandise Mart in Chicago: "I was standing behind Spag, and I could see that he was placing a sizable order with an exhibitor. The rep taking the order apparently didn't recognize Spag, even though he was wearing his ten-gallon hat. I could see the skeptical look on the man's face. When Spag moved on to another booth, I asked the rep how big an order he had placed. 'Oh, a couple hundred thousand pieces,' the man said with a grimace, then added, 'You can see that guy doesn't have a nickel to his name.' I suggested that he do a little checking. He might change his mind."

Milton Frem of Anchor Plastics told me about a similar occur-

[1] See also Pile 'Em High, page 131.

rence at a New York hardware show, as related to him by the New England rep of a lawn mower company. It seems that a salesman from the Midwest, who was attending his first New York trade show, informed his sales manager at the end of day that he had received an order for $150,000 worth of lawn mowers from "a guy." When his boss asked to see the order, the salesman said that he had torn it up and thrown it in the waste basket. Alarmed, the sales manager asked him why he had done this. The rep replied that the customer was "just stringing me along."

"How do you know that?" asked his boss.

"Oh," said the other, "he looked like a hoe-poke. He was wearing khakis and a string tie."

The manager immediately became suspicious. "What was his name?"

"Oh, I don't know," said the Midwesterner indifferently, 'Spiek, Spac, or something like that."

"Spag!" his boss cried out—as he made a mad dash for the waste basket. They spent the next hour putting the pieces together to find out what Spag had ordered.

"Eventually, people did recognize Anthony wherever he went," said SPAG'S general manager John Cullen, who also noted that Anthony tried to buy something from every exhibitor:

> The vendors were happy to see him. There was always a flurry of excitement when he arrived on the scene; they knew then that big orders were coming their way.
>
> He liked to encourage new businesses. He gave many new salesmen their first order, "just to get them started," he would say. Many of them rose to important positions in their firms, and several of the new businesses became highly successful. Salesmen never forgot Spag; he was their best friend, and they looked for ways they could help him in return.

This was a recurring theme in Anthony's life. Whether he was dealing with friends, customers, buyers, or vendors, he always worked to create an environment of trust and mutual respect.

Working Together

Suppliers knew in advance that Anthony would not ask them to lower their prices; this was understood. Anthony probably remembered the stand that the grape merchant on the Reo truck took when his customers wanted to badger him on the prices he was asking for his grapes: "This is not Italy. The price on the box is the price you pay."[2] And according to Dale Fair, that was the way it was throughout the 38 years he supplied SPAG'S with Benson Brothers products—with two exceptions:

> Just before Thanksgiving one year, he asked the price of a nice looking toy I was showing him. When I told him it would cost 60 cents, he sheepishly asked if I could sell it to him for half a buck. He said that he wanted to sell it for not more than that and just break even. He explained, "When some poor guy comes into the store looking for a nice toy and has only half a buck, he could really buy something nice for his kid and feel good." I knew the toy cost 48 cents. I sold it to him for 49 cents. He made a penny, and we made a penny.
>
> Another time he called me on the phone and asked if I could trim the price of a three-ounce bathroom dispenser cup by a penny a package. A nearby supermarket was selling them for a penny less than he was paying. He said, "I hate to nick[3] you, but could you help me out?" There never was much of a profit on that item anyway, so I looked up our cost, changed the price, and both of us made a penny or two. Think of it—someone like Spag asking for a lower price only twice in over 38 years.

From what I've learned, Dale's story is not unique; Anthony's regard for his vendors was such that he invariably formed close working relationships with them. He was also quick to sense when a salesman had special concerns, as Roderick McDonah explained:

[2] See Ma, page 64.
[3] Nickel-and-dime.

I worked for Swift AgriChem Division, and we worked on a quota system. When we made or surpassed our quota, we were eligible for a bonus. Each and every year, Spag saw to it that if I were somewhere near being close to that goal, he would run a "special" or a "sale" to make sure I'd meet or surpass my quota... doing this with no pretense of helping me...

I was not the only one who relied on Spag's business intuition...and I am sure I was not the only salesman who relied on Spag to make a quota...or receive the same wonderful help and support...but again, this is the way Spag operated. Spag was truly one in a million.

Thoughtfulness

Anthony was also thoughtful when it came to his vendors' personal lives. For instance, he knew that Sumner Baker, a salesman who sold electrical tape and some plumbing supplies, worked out of his home so that he could care for his ailing mother. Occasionally, though, he would have to call on Anthony to show him something. Sumner wrote:

I would walk into his office, which was usually crowded with other salesmen. He'd spot me and take me out of turn. One time when I was leaving, Spag introduced me to the other salesmen, saying "Gentlemen, I want you to meet Mr. Baker because he's a No Bull Shit guy!"

Anthony could easily identify with those who respected and cared for their parents. I am probably correct in assuming that he took Sumner out of turn because he knew that Sumner's invalid mother was waiting for him at home.

Several salespeople have mentioned that Anthony was their mentor, one to whom they would go when they needed sound advice.

Alfred Roccanti wrote about asking Anthony for advice concerning a change of jobs:

> He took me into his living room and advised me as a true friend would.... Calling on SPAG'S was like calling on family. The office was small in those days. When you entered you were greeted by Lou Rossi [the advertising manager], Olive, the other two or three young ladies, and of course, Spag, if he was not roaming around the store. He would invite me to share lunch with the crew on an occasion or two. Perhaps that's why I felt like family....

"Spag's compassion for people included his suppliers," said Bob Lutz. "Spag would say, 'Sometimes you have to buy even when the need is not there. You remember their faithfulness.'" Bob recalled Anthony's concern for a salesman who sold picks and shovels. He had suffered a heart attack and had been out of work for quite a while. "When he resumed work again, he called on Spag," said Bob. "Although mindful that he had just bought a year's supply of picks and shovels from another source, Spag gave the man a sizable order 'to help him get started again.'"

Among some papers in Anthony's files, I found a note in which he wrote: "Regarding orders to old salesmen who helped us— even though the need for merchandise was not there, the need to help the dignity and livelihood of those past salesmen was. It is part of returning the help they gave in their younger and more successful years."

Anthony's own experiences in selling provided him with the tradesmen's point of

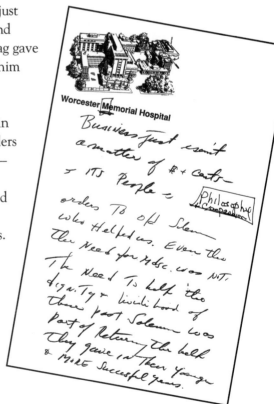

Worcester Memorial Hospital

view, which he expressed often. Edward Eckland, a Rotarian friend, said, "After Spag had placed an order with a particular salesman, I remember him saying, 'Hell! They have to make a living, too! If I can help in some little way, I will.'"

The salespeople who called on him were very much aware of the personal interest Anthony took in their well-being and that of their families. When he learned that a salesman, or anyone for that matter, was in the hospital, ill at home, or had lost a loved one, he was sure to respond in some way. Bernie Hershberg, who had introduced the Forward Thrust shoes to SPAG'S, wrote:

> From a personal point of view, I was happily welcomed when I became a patient at Newton-Wellesley Hospital. The nurses loved to have me as a patient, because they knew that Spag would be sending a truckload of all kinds of refreshments for the nursing staff and other patients as well.
>
> When I lost my parents, Spag and Olive found time to visit me. Knowing that I would miss my parents, especially on my birthday, Spag and Olive entertained me on that day. Who else would do this? I was a vendor, not a customer.

Just as he did with his employees, Anthony expressed his appreciation to his suppliers in many ways. At Christmas, he gave each salesperson a case of fruit or a goodie box. In a thank-you note to Anthony for a box of fruit he had received, Robert Hunnewell, a representative for New England Enterprises, noted:

> I can't think of another one of our accounts that has ever said "thank-you" for our services and has remembered us at Christmas with such a nice gift. Those of us who have the privilege of servicing the SPAG'S account can only feel more attached and more devoted to giving the best possible service and getting the best possible prices for SPAG'S.

Integrity and Fairness

Anthony had a strict sense of fairness when it came to both customers and suppliers. To avoid paying a vendor's commission, manufacturers occasionally tried to get Anthony to buy directly from them. He did not appreciate these offers one bit! Dale Fair told me:

> On several occasions, Spag called to tell me that somebody was offering him a big bargain, a product that he could buy direct if he wanted to. Instead of buying it for himself, he called me to suggest that I buy it with the understanding that I would then in turn sell it to him so we could both realize a profit. How many customers would pass up a good bargain and go out of his way to share the profits with a supplier?

Integrity, fairness, and loyalty to his suppliers were more important to him than saving a few dollars. At times, he actually enjoyed the challenge of responding to offers that he knew were meant to short-circuit and eliminate the salespersons' commissions. Anthony used to smile when he recalled one such incident involving Joanne Collins, a new sales representative for one of the leading oil companies.

Joanne was feeling discouraged; she was short of meeting her quota of 1,000 cases of oil even though she had called on all of her assigned number of gas stations in the New England area. Then the idea flashed through her mind, "Try SPAG'S."

She entered the store and asked a clerk if she could speak with Spag. The clerk pointed to Anthony, who was on a ladder rearranging the inventory. "That's Spag there," he said. Joanne went to the foot of the ladder, introduced herself, and exchanged some pleasantries with Anthony. Then she asked him if he would like to order some oil.

From the top of the ladder, he asked, "How much will it cost for 50 cases?" When she gave the price, he asked her, "How much for 100?" She smiled, checked her distributor's book, and gave Anthony the price for 100 cases.

"How much would it cost for 1,000 cases?" he asked. "And can you give me delivery by Thursday? I'd like to advertise it as a special."

—Courtesy of Worcester Telegram and Gazette

*Standing: James M. O'Coin and Joseph Malone with
Anthony receiving the BBB Award. May 2, 1995.*

At that question, Joanne frowned and said, "I don't know. I'll have to check with the office."

"There's a phone over there on the wall," he said, and he turned back to his work. Joanne made the call and returned with the price for 1,000 but the worried look was still there.

"They thought I was joking," she said, "They got a big kick out of it. They told me to 'Bring the check with the order, and we'll deliver the oil by Thursday.'"

Anthony gave her an order for 1,000 cases—a truckload. Joanne beamed and then suddenly her face darkened again as she wondered whether or not her boss would take the order seriously. Then Anthony added, "And I'll give you a check for the full amount to take with you." The sun broke through the clouds. Joanne smiled, thanked him, and went to the office on Beverly Road, where the check was waiting for her.

When Joanne returned to her office waving the purchase order and the check, her supervisors were stunned. Then they gasped. They were unprepared to deliver an order of that size on such short notice, but they had made a commitment. To meet it, they had to scramble. They called all the dealers in the New England area for help in filling Anthony's order. Only by emptying other dealers' shelves were they able to deliver 1,000 cases of oil to SPAG'S on the promised date.

Anthony advertised the oil in his one-inch advertisement on the front page of the local newspapers;[4] it sold quickly. The following week, Anthony gave Joanne a repeat order. With that, she became the rising star of her company. A few weeks later, Joanne called to say that her boss and two other officials were interested in meeting with Anthony. After making sure that Joanne would be coming with them, he agreed to a date.

When the group arrived at his home office, Anthony chatted with them for a few minutes, enough time to give him some idea of what they had in mind. Then he turned to Joanne and said, "I would like to order 4,000 more cases of oil."

The three men could hardly contain themselves as they thanked Anthony profusely for the huge order. Anthony heard them out; then he looked directly at them and said, "Joanne does a good job. As long as she works for you, she is the only one who sells to me. If it can't be that way, we won't be carrying your oil."

---

[4] See Spagtacular!, page 171.

The men gulped, and then agreed, "Of course, of course," almost choking as they spoke. Joanne must have been chuckling to herself. She had become the company's most valuable sales representative overnight due to Anthony's insistence on fairness in all his dealings.

Salespeople and business rivals alike applauded Anthony for his honesty and integrity—many even attributed his success to it. So it was no surprise when, in recognition of his "Integrity in Business and Commitment to the Community," the Better Business Bureau of Central New England, Inc. presented him with the BBB Torch Award.

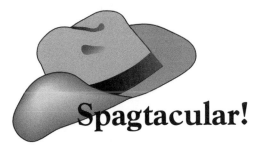

Spagtacular!

The man who whispers down a well
About the goods he has to sell
Will never reap the gleaming dollars
Like a man who climbs a tree and hollers.
—Author Unknown

During the first few years, Anthony depended on "word-of-mouth" for his advertising; but in 1938, a young rookie classified advertising sales-man, Lee Adams, convinced Anthony that by advertising his wares in the newspaper he would reach more customers.

Lee, who first met Anthony when he started his store in the garage office, recalled that:

> I sold Spag his first ad. It was a ten-word ad that was placed in the classified sections of the *Worcester Telegram* and the *Evening Gazette*.[1] The ten words featuring 'tire patches on sale' ran in both papers for three days and cost $1.05, which Spag paid for out of his pocket. He had no cash register. The ad was effective; there was a run on tire patches.
>
> As the adage goes, "From little acorns, great oak trees grow." And so did SPAG'S, which has been a million-dollar advertiser for many years. Spag grossed 100 million in sales per year.

When I asked Anthony about that first ad, he thought for a moment. According to his best recollection, the ad read:

---

[1] As previously noted, these were the two leading area newspapers; they merged in 1988 to become the *Worcester Telegram and Gazette*. In 1989, the title was shortened to the *Telegram and Gazette*.

```
┌─────────────────────────────┐
│        Tire Patches         │
│      SHREWSBURY TIRE        │
│            AND              │
│      BATTERY SERVICE        │
│   193 Turnpike, Shrewsbury  │
└─────────────────────────────┘
```

Shortly thereafter Lee went into the military service, and John Vecchiola took over the SPAG'S account. John persuaded Anthony to place a larger ad in the classified section. The following two-inch ad appeared in October 1945, under Articles for Sale:

```
┌──────────────────────────────────────┐
│             ANTI-FREEZE              │
│            $1.00 per Gal.            │
│           Regularly $1.40            │
│          RADIATOR ALCOHOL            │
│             85¢ per Gal.             │
│            Bring Container           │
│ Furnace Pipe, Stove Pipe, Window Glass│
│           SPAG'S HARDWARE            │
│           193 TURNPIKE RD.           │
│      Tel. 5-8599 - Shrewsbury, Mass. │
└──────────────────────────────────────┘
```

John has vivid memories of SPAG'S as it was in the years before it really took off. He wrote about one trip he made to the store in 1945 to talk to Anthony about increasing the size of his classified advertisements:

> I went up the steps and opened the door to walk into the place. In its center was a pot-belly stove glowing with heat; it was winter time. Against every wall, there were rows-upon-rows of small bins from floor to ceiling containing all kinds of hardware. A man was up on a ladder in a corner of the store restocking one of the bins.
>
> "I'll be right with you," he said, as he started to

clamber down the ladder. We introduced ourselves, and got down to the business at hand, the placing of an advertisement. Just then, a customer came in; Spag excused himself to wait on him. After the customer found what he wanted, he dug into his pocket only to find that he did not have enough money. Then I heard Spag's hearty laugh and Spag saying, "So pay me next time you're in for something else." That was my first impression of Spag, a generous and charitable person.

John served SPAG'S for several years. When the advertising manager transferred him to retail advertising, this was not at all to Anthony's liking; he wanted John to continue serving the SPAG'S account. John explained that he couldn't do it because he was in a different department, but Anthony persisted and hassled the manager until he gave in.

As business grew, so did SPAG'S advertising in the newspaper. Gradually, Anthony went to spot ads. Over time, the spot ads expanded to half-page, full-page, and, more recently, multi-page ads, which appeared midweek and on Sundays. The first $1.05 classified ad was just the beginning of a huge advertising budget. Anthony felt that keeping the name "SPAG'S" in front of the public was important.

Spagtacular Sales and Give-Aways

Early on, Anthony moved the date for celebrating the store's anniversary from September to February, for no reason other than that February, traditionally a slower month in the retail business, was in need of some excitement. To celebrate the store's anniversary, he advertised his "Spagtacular Sales" in large newspaper ads, and also handed out small gifts to the first ten thousand customers. The "give-aways," as he called them, varied each year. The items—spatulas, yard sticks, folded rain caps, mixing bowls, measuring cups, tape measures, or painting hats—all bore the SPAG'S logo, a ten-gallon hat with the store's name.

"And why not give?" Anthony would ask, his expressive hands

gesturing, the mannerism he exhibited whenever he was speaking, in person or on the phone. He would then add, "How much steak can I eat? How many cars can I drive? I learned a long while back that all that is necessary in life is to have enough." His give-aways reminded me of his childhood days at Bloomingdale School, when he shared his broken ice-cream cones and candy, "because it feels good to divvy."

In 1950, Anthony created another way of sharing. As he thought about a "Spring Give-Away," he remembered Father's large vegetable garden and the "Victory Gardens" that many of his customers had started during World War II.

"How about giving people tomato plants?" he asked himself. After talking with Father about growing tomatoes, Anthony realized he would have to make sure the plants would be healthy and hardened to the outdoors.

With that in mind, he located a commercial tomato farmer in Macon, Georgia, who agreed—Anthony placed his order for 25,000 tomato plants in bundles holding 25 each. The tomato farmer agreed to grow the plants outdoors so they would be "hardened" before they arrived in Shrewsbury. This would give the gardeners an early crop of tomatoes.

The timing of the Tomato Plant Give-Away was important. The farmer in Georgia had to schedule his crops so the plants were ready for shipping after the threat of frost was over in Massachusetts, but not too late for New England's short growing season. Around the last week of May, he bundled the tomato plants together and packed them in crates. After loading the crates into an air-conditioned trailer truck, he called Anthony to tell him that his 25,000 tomato plants were on the way. While in transit, the driver kept Anthony informed of his schedule and his expected time of arrival.

Anthony needed this information so that he could give gardeners time to prepare the soil for their plants. To do this, he placed an announcement in the local newspapers:

> **FREE**
> **TOMATO PLANTS**
> **DUE TO ARRIVE SOON**
> **AT SPAG'S!**

On the day the truck arrived, the ad sang out:

> **SPAG'S**
> **FREE TOMATO PLANTS**
> **ARE HERE!**
> **Bring your own wrapping**

When the truck carrying the plants arrived, Anthony was on hand to greet the people who came for them. He thrived on the excitement generated by the Tomato Plant Give-Away. The people filled the

parking lot with their cars before the store opened, and lined up at the doors, newspapers in hand, waiting for the crates of plants to be placed at each checkout counter. No purchase was necessary. Each person received one bundle, but could have additional ones if he or she needed more than 25 plants.

Waiting in line on Tomato Plant Give-Away Day.

Within a day and a half, all the plants were gone. From that year on, the Tomato Plant Give-Away became a spring ritual—and Anthony loved it! Without a doubt, it was one of his greatest pleasures. Occasionally, toward evening, he would sit in his station wagon, parked inconspicuously near the store exit, to watch the happy customers as they headed to their cars with their plants.

I asked Anthony once how many tomato plants he gave away each spring. "Pretty close to a million," he replied. "In the days when gardening was not only popular but necessary, we gave out a million plants. They were gone in two to three days." That meant that in just two to three days, 40,000 people had come to SPAG'S for their tomato plants. What excitement! What congestion!

In those days, the busy parking lot was in a state of confusion as gardeners sat in their cars with the motors running, waiting for a space to park. The "tomato" line of cars extended to Route 9 and backed up Belmont Hill for over a mile. Anthony had to hire four policemen to keep the traffic moving. As many as 4,500 people received tomato plants in the first hour alone.

The SPAG'S Tomato Plant Give-Away continues to this day. Each year, gardeners from the surrounding towns harvest their abundant crops of SPAG'S quality tomatoes. In Anthony's time, many of them wrote to thank him for the plants and to send photos of their gardens and tomato crops. Others would express their gratitude if they came upon him in person, as Bob Ballantine, the advertising director for the Worcester Telegram and Gazette, recalled from a personal experience. On Tomato Plant Give-Away Day in 1989, Bob had gone to SPAG'S to make a promotional advertisement:

—Telegram and Gazette

Free tomato plants!

When I finished the video, Spag asked me to go with him to the Quality Fish Market on Millbury Street [in Worcester]. He wanted to make a purchase there. We were waiting at the counter in the market as the clerk wrapped up Spag's order of fish when a man and his wife, standing nearby, recognized him. They came over to thank Spag for the bundle of tomato plants that they had just picked up at the store. They also thanked him for the low prices they always found at SPAG'S. While chatting with the couple, Spag stopped a moment and turned to the clerk behind the counter. Pointing to the lobsters, he whispered, "Wrap up two of them, will you?" When the clerk handed Spag the wrapped-up lobsters, he gave the package to the couple and said, "Thank you for being my customers."

The Front Page Ads

In 1950, Lou Rossi, who had joined the SPAG'S staff to handle its advertising, suggested that Anthony place a one-inch advertisement daily in the lower-right corner of the front page of the two local newspapers. Anthony must have thought that this was a good idea; he placed the following ad:

> **TODAY ONLY**
> **FREE FLASHLIGHT**
> **$1.25 Val. without batteries**
> **With any purchase of**
> **$2.00 or Over**
> 1 to a customer—2400 only
> **SPAG'S Shrewsbury**

SPAG'S daily advertisement was the only ad on the front page of the newspaper for a long time, and it appeared there regularly in the same place for decades. As time went on, Lou created the multi-page ads that appeared weekly, and also coined the word "Spagtacular" for SPAG'S.

Lou worked at the desk next to Anthony's in the home office for 18 years. They became dear friends. Anthony said, "Lou was a gem, professionally and personally. He had a tremendous sense of humor."

When I asked Lou about the front page ad, he told me:

> It caught on instantly because people read it and recognized the value of the product being offered. The ad might have featured stock items such as faucets, masking tape, rope, and light switches. Occasionally, it was a scarce item, a product like the antifreeze or a popular "hot" item like "Cabbage Patch®" dolls.
>
> The ads were eye-catchers. People noticed them as they glanced quickly at the first page. Then they got in the habit of looking for the ad to catch what was new or what SPAG'S had today.

Lou Rossi.

For many customers, "catching the ad" became part of their daily routine, lest they miss a special they had been waiting for or something they needed. Some even looked at the SPAG'S ad before reading the headlines. Many reported that the ad helped them plan their shopping itinerary.

Lou often went to the store in the afternoon to talk with employees in the different departments and to choose the products to feature in the ads. He also wanted to make sure the store was prepared for the demand that would follow an advertisement. "Spag was a stickler for having any merchandise that he advertised on hand and in great quantity," Lou noted. "He would say, 'There's to be no running out of goods after the first few hundred customers.' If the supply on hand was insufficient, we held the ad until we had enough."

Lou also pointed out that the front page ad was not always devoted to the sale of products. On occasion, they would feature a local charity event, such as the pancake breakfasts put on by the Rotary and Quota clubs, the "Spring Assembly" sponsored by the St. Vincent Ladies Guild, or the garden tours sponsored by the Shrewsbury Garden

Club. After one such advertisement in 1994, Shirley Salamy of the Shrewsbury Garden Club wrote to express her appreciation to Anthony: "You never cease to amaze me. Your fifty-dollar gift certificate was very generous, but to be able to give us all that wonderful space in your ad was above and beyond what anyone could expect."

Occasionally, SPAG'S advertised a "lost and found" article in the one-inch ads. One time a clerk found a pair of false teeth leaning against a cuckoo clock. Lou wrote an ad that read:

> **If anyone has lost his FALSIES,**
> **please come to register #4**
> **at SPAG'S**
> **to reclaim your bite.**
> **No questions asked.**

The day after the ad appeared, the owner stopped in to pick up his dentures.

Other merchants saw how effective the one-inch, front-page ads were, and eventually followed suit. Several years later, when the newspaper editors changed their policy and moved all the one-inch advertisements to the second page, the SPAG'S ad still appeared in the same position—the lower right-hand corner of the page.

The Circus

"Anything to help children," was Anthony's response when Otto Steinhelber of the Alethia Grotto[2] asked him to buy a few circus tickets to aide the Cerebral Palsy Clinic. Anthony knew several families who were bringing their children to the clinic for treatment. Happy to help in any way he could, he bought out the entire show, all 3600 tickets, for the Sunday night performance.

Several weeks before the Grotto Circus, Anthony ran a special ad in the *Worcester Sunday Telegram* announcing the availability of free tickets to the Sunday performance of the circus on a "first come–first served" basis for those who signed up in advance at SPAG'S.

People hurried to the store to reserve their circus tickets. Within a few days, all the tickets were promised and subsequently picked up at

[2] A branch of the International Grottos, a Masonic organization devoted to helping children. The primary focus of the Alethia Grotto has been their pediatric Cerebral Palsy Clinic.

the store prior to the event. This happy and worthwhile event brought back memories to Anthony of the times when he, as a boy, went with Father to the Fairgrounds to see the Barnum & Bailey Circus.

According to Mr. Gerald Steeves, a past Grand Monarch of the International Grottos, "the Alethia Grotto of Worcester, which found-ed and maintained the local Cerebral Palsy clinic for thirty years, appreciated Spag's support throughout the years as he continued to buy out the Sunday night performances." Subsequently, Anthony con-tinued to provide yearly support to the Alethia Grotto's ongoing chil-dren's charities.

The Cabbage Patch® Dolls

Anthony's insistence that large quantities of merchandise be on hand the day he advertised them presented a problem in the mid-80s when Cabbage Patch dolls were all the rage. He wanted to feature the doll in his daily ad—that is, if he could get enough of them; they had become a scarce commodity. When an opportunity to buy a trailerload of dolls presented itself, Anthony jumped at it. The load consisted of 500 cartons. Six individually-boxed dolls were in each master carton, a total of 3,000 dolls. The dolls were dressed alike, but they had differ-ent hair colors and facial expressions. Anthony figured that the trailer-load and the supply he had on hand would be more than enough to meet the demand for this popular item.

When the trailer arrived and was parked at the unloading dock on Baker Avenue, Anthony placed this one-inch ad:

> **JUST ARRIVED**
> Trailer load of
> **CABBAGE PATCH DOLLS®**
> **SPAG'S**

The night before the ad appeared, workers stacked several hun-dred boxes of Cabbage Patch dolls on the floor in the toy section. When Anthony arrived at the store shortly after it opened the follow-ing morning, he was shocked and dismayed by what he saw. He could not believe how aggressively people were behaving. From young women to white-haired grandfathers (some even with canes), people pushed, shoved, argued, and actually began to fight as they tried to reach for "just any doll." This in itself was most unusual, since customers were ordinarily very selective about what they bought. But it got worse. As the pile diminished, the frenzy mounted.

When Anthony saw the bedlam, he immediately dispensed with the customary procedure of replenishing the stock as needed. Within two hours, the pile of dolls was gone, and the store returned to its usual—though still hectic—pace.

He commented afterwards, "I would never have believed it if I hadn't seen it myself. I'm glad no one got hurt!" To avoid a repeat of that incredible scene, he had the remaining Cabbage Patch dolls discreetly placed in small quantities here and there throughout the store. Customers would then just happen upon them unexpectedly, and before the word spread, the dolls were gone.

All during the Cabbage Patch craze, both Anthony and John Cullen received telephone calls as late as 1:00 in the morning from people wanting to place orders for "a red-haired boy" or "a blond girl," etc. "Sometimes the callers were not fussy," said John. "They would say 'any kind of doll, just as long as it's a Cabbage Patch doll.'"

In fairness to all customers, rarely did Anthony or John fill the telephone requests, telling customers instead that the dolls would be on the floor when the store opened.

*John H. Cullen,
a vice president of SPAG'S*

Television Ads

In the late 1970s, Anthony bought advertising time on WSMW-TV, Channel 27, an independent Worcester-based station with a signal that reached large portions of New England. These early television spots featured views of people shopping in the crowded aisles, information about various promotions, or testimonials from customers. They invariably ended with a shot of Anthony standing on the median strip of Route 9, with the store itself in the background.

The Channel 27 ads ended in the early 1980s when the station changed owners. In 1988, Greg Lano, a representative for WBZ-TV Channel 4 in Boston, called on Anthony and introduced the idea of advertising SPAG'S on Channel 4 and tying it in with a print advertising campaign. The subsequent television spots, produced by Charles Thanas, featured Anthony telling the SPAG'S story. Anthony appeared on the screen sitting in his home, or working in his greenhouse with his grandson, Angus (each wearing a ten-gallon hat), or talking with his daughters. The ads often had themes related to the time of year, and judging by the sales increase, they were a great success.

Greg Lano told me that Anthony liked the TV exposure; in addition to reaching new customers, it also served to remind past and present customers of the good buys they had found at the store:

> Spag described the value of his television advertising efforts with the story of a man from Wellesley who bought a drill at the store years ago. The man needed to replace the drill, and after seeing a SPAG'S ad on television, he remembered that he had saved $10-$15 when he purchased the last drill. So he went to SPAG'S again. Naturally, he bought more than the drill. Spag saw the value of television advertising as making thousands of these "reminders" every day.
>
> Some of Spag's television spots ended with him emphatically delivering the line "…and you'll SAVE MONEY!!!" He became so well known as a result of these ads that many people began to throw that line back at him when they met him. Spag didn't mind; it was just further proof of the ads' effectiveness.

One series of advertisements featured surprise interviews with customers chosen at random while they were shopping in the store. One of these shoppers, Mrs. Laurie Snelson, enjoyed a momentary spell of stardom when Channel 4 aired her interview. She later wrote:

Just a note to thank you ever so much for the carton of fresh citrus fruit that was delivered to my home on Tuesday by your very courteous driver. Such a delightful, delicious surprise!

Since I haven't entered any contests lately, I assume that this must be in appreciation of the Christmas ads that were taped in your store. Guess they used my short interview for two different ads—which thrilled me beyond words!! It was absolutely hilarious how many calls we received from friends all over the state and hearing the various comments of surprise as I appeared on their screens out of nowhere. It was so much fun, and really added lots of extra spark to life for those few months… It was an easy testimony, as I merely expressed my feelings about your store, items, and prices. SPAG'S is an adventure, and I really do love your store! We take all our visitors there and watch their jaws drop in disbelief.

In 1990, Anthony began to expand his advertising into prime time and late night viewing periods on WCVB-TV as well as WBZ-TV and the results were equally positive. Viewers seemed to like the ads' folksy, homespun themes. As customer Audrey Gilkerson wrote, "My husband and I enjoy your new commercial with you and your dogs walking through the woods. You have that human touch which is fast disappearing."

T-Shirts and Travels

In addition to running advertisements on television and the radio, Anthony gave away bumper stickers with the ten-gallon hat logo. One of the SPAG'S stickers landed up on a bus in Moscow, much to the surprise of one Worcester traveler.

But it wasn't just bumper stickers that displayed the SPAG'S logo. Anthony sold thousands of hats, tote bags, and T-shirts proudly bearing a drawing of his ten-gallon hat. Customers wearing their T-shirts while traveling around the country often attracted attention. In

One of the T-shirt designs.

July 1991, Walter and Frances Poyhonen wrote to Anthony to tell him about the wonderful experiences they had while traveling in their SPAG'S T-shirts through Missouri, Arizona, and on to San Francisco. Many people who had been to SPAG'S or knew about the store greeted them as if they were old friends. Some people would ask, "How are things in Worcester?" While chatting with a couple at the Hearst Castle in San Simeon, California, another man approached them and asked, "Is it true that there's no bags at SPAG'S?"

When Walter and Frances were leaving church in St. George, Utah, a married couple formerly from West Boylston, MA, and two other travelers from Massachusetts gathered around them to talk about SPAG'S and Worcester. Walter enclosed a snapshot of the group and closed his letter by saying: "The T-shirts made our vacation so much more enjoyable."

Anthony responded to their letter by writing:

> Dear Mr. and Mrs. Poyhonen,
>
> I received your nice letter and enjoyed reading about your experiences with the various people you met on your trip. Just looking at your picture, I can see that you are the kind of people who make friends easily and enjoy every day in every way.
>
> I just returned from a three-week vacation in Alaska with my children, their husbands, and grandchildren—14 all told. I made everyone wear a SPAG'S T-shirt, because what you wrote in your letter interested me...
>
> I was absolutely shocked at the number of people from Worcester and surrounding areas, as well as other parts of the country, who came up to me in Alaska and said they were [SPAG'S] customers...
>
> I hope if you are up this way again, you will call me and stop in to see me at my office, as I would like to personally thank you and meet you both.
>
> Sincerely,
> Anthony A. Borgatti, Jr.

Evidently, the Poyhonens took Anthony up on his invitation, and did visit with him. In 1995, Walter wrote again about the friends they had made due to their SPAG'S T-shirts while traveling in Venezuela, Argentina, Thailand, and China. Walter expressed the sentiments of so many when he noted: "It is amazing how SPAG'S is so well known throughout the world!"

Making Our Lives Exciting

Someone's garage sale gone haywire!
—John Caulfield[1]

Anthony believed that people have the power to make their lives interesting and enjoyable, and this was reflected in the way he ran his store. One of the many ways he made life more exciting for himself and his customers was to add an element of surprise whenever possible. He would say, "Gotta make it exciting so they'll want to keep coming."

He would also add, "People are curious. They come to SPAG'S to see what is new. It's nice for customers to find the unexpected. Remember, yesterday's ball game doesn't count. You have to *keep on creating excitement*."

In line with this philosophy, Anthony was forever coming up with new ideas for change and variety. Customers never knew what they were going to find when they came to SPAG'S. Wherever a space could be found in a corner, or on a shelf, Anthony would add a new product. At one point, he told us he was carrying 168,000 different items. The number later increased to over 200,000 items. That is what made the store unique—and why some customers called SPAG'S "the fun store!"

Christmas Trees in July

The unusual purchases that Anthony made were a big part of what made his store so much fun. He seemed to have the innate ability of

[1] John Caufield, "The Man, the Store, the Legend." PEOPLE, *National Home Center News*, 5 August 1991, p. 89.

knowing what his customers needed and would buy. From Donald Ford Murphy of the Murphy Marketing Associates in Randolph, Massachusetts, came the following account of one of Anthony's unusual (and lucky) decisions:

> One of my favorite stories goes back to the early sixties. In 1962, Spag and Olive had come to my show room to see my artificial Christmas tree line. It was the Friday of the Fourth of July weekend, a real scorcher. Spag ordered the Christmas trees, to be shipped in November. It was then I asked him if he could take them earlier, say in late September. I would give him a special price if he would accept shipment early.
>
> We agreed on a price and he insisted that I add on my normal commission, which I did. He then floored me by saying he would take a trailerload that afternoon.
>
> "Spag!" I exclaimed, "It's ninety degrees outside! The Fourth of July is coming up. Who is going to buy trees now?"
>
> "SPAG'S customers," he replied simply. So we shipped a trailerload of Christmas trees that hot afternoon from our Boston warehouse. Just before midnight, I got a phone call.
>
> "Hi!" a deep familiar voice said. "Got any of those trees left?"
>
> "You're kidding! You picked up 700 trees this afternoon!" I stammered.
>
> "I know, but we're on a roll. I'll take whatever you got left."
>
> To make a long story short, SPAG'S sold two trailerloads of artificial Christmas trees that hot weekend. I don't believe any other retailer could equal that in one store.

Groceries at SPAG'S?

In 1968, would a SPAG'S customer have expected to find, next to the ironing boards, brooms, and laundry baskets, a large bin piled high with oranges and grapefruit? Probably not. But then again, SPAG'S was always full of surprises.

In the early winter of that year, Anthony got the idea of selling fruit when he and Olive received a box of oranges and grapefruit from their friends, Ed and Fi-Fi Lundgren, who were vacationing in Florida. While Anthony was admiring the appearance and tasting the exceptional flavor of the Indian River fruit, the thought occurred to him: "My customers should be able to enjoy this, too." (The oranges probably reminded Anthony of those Christmas mornings when we each found an orange in our stocking.)

Pursuing the idea further, he called the owner of the orchard that had shipped the citrus—Harvey Groves in Cocoa, Florida—to discuss the idea of purchasing the fruit wholesale. He also inquired about the possibility of visiting the groves. Subsequently, Anthony, Olive, and the Lundgrens flew down to Florida and met George Harvey and his wife Janetta, who welcomed them and took them to nearby Merritt Island to see the groves.

—Fi-Fi Lundren

George Harvey and Anthony in Cocoa, Florida.

That day, Anthony placed his first order of citrus fruit—a trailerload—to be delivered in early December. When the oranges and grapefruit arrived, Anthony displayed them piled high on top of their open boxes and sold them at cost. The fruit was such a big hit that he immediately ordered a trailerload to be delivered every week throughout the season. Every year, from that time on, he renewed his standing order for weekly shipments of citrus throughout the season, October to March—a total of 22 trailerloads. The store continues to sell oranges and grapefruit when in season at cost.

I had the opportunity to ask George

Oranges at cost!

about that first visit, and he remembered it with great fondness. "Spag asked every question there was to ask about the growing of citrus," he told me. "And he enjoyed helping himself to several oranges."

"Little did we realize," Janetta added, "what close friends your family and ours would become."

Anthony loved the citrus fruit; he looked forward to that first trailerload every October. But he was also a cookie and cracker muncher, so on one of my trips to the store, I should not have been surprised to see a mountainous display of Nabisco crackers and Pepperidge Farm cookies near the plumbing department—but I was. And there was Anthony standing nearby, watching me as I gasped in surprise.

"Anthony!" I cried. "Crackers and cookies! What gave you the idea?"

"Well," he replied with that pleased look he got whenever he surprised someone, "it was just a hunch."

"A hunch?"

"Yeah. Everyone likes to eat crackers and cookies, but they're expensive, 'specially for some of the older people on a limited budget. I figured that if I could make the price reasonable enough, they would treat themselves. So I decided to give it a try. I've been watching to see who's been buying them, and I can see my hunch paid off."

As it was with the oranges and grapefruit, thereafter cookies and crackers became a staple at SPAG'S.

Arthur Dobson.

One day, Anthony telephoned the Charlie Cheddar Company, area distributor for the Cabot Cheese Company, and spoke to owner-representative Arthur Dobson, whom he already knew from the Rotary Club. "Arthur," he said, "I've been thinking about selling perishables in the store. The cost of living is going up, and I want to help."

Arthur, a tall and gentle person, with intense dark eyes, was happy to oblige. A few days later, the two drove to Vermont and toured the Cabot Cheese Company. They watched as employees made cheese and maple syrup. Anthony was impressed. "I like this operation," he said, as he placed an order for fifteen cases (180 pieces) of three-pound blocks of cheddar cheese at $3.90 per block.

Anthony and Olive at the orange groves.

In preparation for the delivery, Arthur borrowed an ice case for storing the cheese. Anthony gave him space for it next to the plumbing department. When the cheese arrived, Arthur was there to mark the price and load the shipment into the case. He asked Anthony what the retail price would be for each block of cheese. "$3.99," Anthony replied. In response to Arthur's surprised look, Anthony added, "The reason I'm selling cheese for just nine cents more is because I want to help people save money on their food bill. Then they will be able to afford other products when they come in."

The 180 blocks of cheese filled the case, but not for long. Four days later, Anthony ordered more cheese. From that time on, the increasing demand for cheese kept Arthur hopping. Customers were surprised and happy to find cheese at such a low price. Within six months, the Cabot truck was delivering 100 cases [1800 pieces] at a time to SPAG'S. To provide storage space, Arthur borrowed a 36' refrigerated truck from a company in Lowell.

In due time, Anthony added milk, butter, ham, sausages, and freshly-ground peanut butter to the dairy line, and he placed another dairy case at the rear of the store near the cash registers. As sales increased, he added two more dairy counters. Then he got yet another idea. The week before Thanksgiving, he ordered 3,000 dozen eggs from the Cohen Company of Maine. SPAG'S daily newspaper advertisement featured the "Eggs Special" at 69 cents per dozen. Elsewhere, the price was 89 cents. The idea of buying eggs at SPAG'S caught on quickly! Within a year, the dairy department was selling over 5,000 dozens a week. When Anthony advertised them, over 10,000 dozen eggs passed the check-out counter each week.

During that first visit to Cabot's, Anthony had also ordered six jugs of pure Grade A maple syrup "to try," as he put it; he bought them at $2.75 per jug. Up until that time, the only place one could buy pure maple syrup was at farm stands and possibly in a specialty shop. (I've been told that "maple syrup" sold in the markets was a combination of corn syrup and maple syrup.)

The six jugs of real maple syrup were priced at $2.99 and placed on top of the cheese case—they lasted thirty minutes! From that time on, Arthur had to order hundreds of cases of pure maple syrup every month from Cabot. When the demand increased beyond their production capabilities, Arthur had to supplement his Cabot's order by buying additional maple syrup from another company. Incredible as it may seem, SPAG'S became the largest seller of pure maple syrup in the country.

A bakery was the next innovation. Arthur brought in racks of shelves, placed them next to the dairy counters at the rear of the store, and piled them high with bread, rolls, pita bread, and muffins. The aroma of freshly-baked breads and rolls attracted customers. Arthur had another success on his hands. And more and more customers were getting used to doing their food shopping at SPAG'S.

Anthony greatly appreciated Arthur's dedicated role in the growth of the dairy and bakery departments. His willingness to work long hours to keep the dairy case stocked—going above and beyond what was expected of him—provided SPAG'S customers with an opportunity to stock their pantry shelves economically (in addition to earning financial success for his Charlie Cheddar Company). Anthony also enjoyed his talks with Arthur, who became a close family friend.

Prizes!

In the late 1970s, Anthony introduced another exciting feature: prizes! Throughout the store, customers found boxes wrapped in white paper with a slot cut in the top. Next to some pencils and pieces of paper was a sign that read, "Put your name and telephone number in the box for the draw! Win a bag of fertilizer!" The prize could be anything from laundry detergent to a fifty-dollar gift certificate. When the names were drawn, a clerk telephoned the winners and told them about the products they had just won.

Lucy and Leo LaRose were among the many winners who wrote to thank Anthony for the prize they had won. Lucy wrote:

> We enjoy the give-aways yearly and try to participate. I won fifty dollars once and my husband won some fertilizer. In the last one, we won Pepperidge Farm cookies.
>
> My husband was quite thrilled to be able to shake hands with you as we happened to be the first ones at the checkout counter when you passed by

one day. We think we owe you a big "Thank You" for all the low prices you have given us over the years. We are old-timers, 81 and 84, and have been trading at SPAG'S since we moved to Worcester when we got married almost 59 years ago. We try to get down there weekly and can remember when it was just a small store.

It's all been fun trading with you and we wish you all the best in the future. We will be there as usual as long as the car and our legs hold out.

Jean Abbott was another happy customer who wrote to express her gratitude:

What a thrill it was to receive the note from SPAG'S that read: "Congratulations! You have won fifty dollars in our electrical department on our give-away." Since then, we have faithfully put our names in the numerous boxes all over the store and have won many more prizes. The real thrill, though, was winning the four tickets to the Ringling Brothers and Barnum and Bailey Circus. Because we could choose our seats, we sat in the front row. What a treat that was. We shall never forget it.

Jean Borgatti surrounded by boxes for prize drawings.

Warehouses on Wheels[2]

"Only Spag would come up with the idea of
storing his inventory in trailers; it was such a
great idea!" said Dutch Demers, a SPAG'S customer. The idea, born of necessity in 1956, provided Anthony with a solution to his storage
space problem—for instance, finding room for
the bags of fertilizer being delivered by Bruce
Ward, who ran a trucking business.

Bruce was also selling limestone. When
Anthony's customers requested limestone for
their gardens, he ordered it by the bag from
Bruce. Sales increased and it eventually became
easier for Bruce to leave his trailer at the store.
It did not take Anthony long to see that selling
from the back of the trailer would not only
eliminate his storage problem, it would also

*Donnie Morrill selling from a
trailer.*

allow him to place large orders, obtain volume sales discounts, and
minimize handling.

He lost no time in asking Bruce, "Where do you get trailers?"
Following Bruce's suggestion, Anthony called the Carl Burwick
Company in Boston.

"What kind of a trailer did you want?" Carl asked. Before
Anthony had time to answer, Carl started to list the various features of
his trailers. Anthony's reply was, "Does it have wheels and does it
run?" Hearing a "yes" to both questions, Anthony placed his first
order.

Bruce recalled:

> Spag bought that first "used" trailer for $1,000.
> When I drove down to Boston with my cab/tractor
> to pick it up, he had me haul the trailer directly to
> the Worcester Rendering Works in Auburn to pick
> up sixteen tons of Corenco fertilizer. When I
> returned to the store, Spag sold the fertilizer direct-
> ly from the truck. That load sold quickly, and he

[2] Thanks to Lucy Ward, who supplied most of the material for this section. Thanks are also due
to Bruce Ward and Bob Lutz for their contrbutions.

sent me for a second load. Spag paid me for each trip
I made hauling his trailers for him.

When Anthony ordered the next trailer, he had Bruce pick up a
load of roofing paper in Waltham. "I've ordered a full load; it costs too
much to buy a half load," he would say.

Anthony's next order was for six used trailers, 32' and 34' long, to
be used almost exclusively for hauling limestone from Lee, Massachusetts. The 34' trailers were not large enough to suit Anthony, so he
gambled and had a 34' trailer stretched to 40 feet. It worked!

"Spag sure did love his trailers!" Bruce commented:

> One day I was parking my tractor cab without a
> trailer on Baker Avenue, when Spag said to me, "Let
> me try it." I was kind of reluctant; Spag didn't know
> that much about trucks. But he climbed into the cab.
> What could I do?
>
> He started the motor and headed toward Muzzy
> Avenue, waving to everyone he saw. I kept my fingers
> crossed. "Where are you going?" I asked nervously.

Bruce Ward hauling unfinished furniture.

"Up to the house to show Olive," he replied with a mischievous grin on his face. Well, he made it there, much to Olive's surprise and to my great relief. He loved every minute of it.

Anthony was now sold on trailers. He could take an early delivery of furniture in October and park the trailer near the store until February for his "Spagtacular" sales. At inventory time, the trailerload of furniture was not included because technically it was still in transit, and not subject to the real estate tax. The law was changed later to include any inventory for which Anthony had signed a receipt.

Nevertheless, Anthony continued to buy trailers, sometimes ten at a time. On one occasion, he bought 45—he was a risk taker, for sure! Some were refrigerated trailers needed to keep dairy products, candy, oranges, and roses cool in the warm weather, and to protect them from freezing in the winter.

"When shipping by railroad became more economical," recalled Bruce, "Spag would ask us to pick up 'a railroad car full of charcoal, or wastebaskets, bicycles, or some such thing at the Crescent Street siding in Worcester.' Sometimes he would say, 'Bruce, pick up some play and gym equipment, fans, grills, or kitty litter from the Southbridge Street siding,' or it might be 'salt at the Franklin Street siding,' or it could be 'peat moss and dog food at the Blackstone siding.'"

In 1972, as manufacturing companies left Massachusetts, Bruce had to drive all over New England and as far away as Pennsylvania

Trailers lining SPAG'S parking lot.

—Lucy Ward

to haul in "housewares, garden equipment, plumbing, electrical supplies, automotive supplies, paper goods, toys, and clothing."

"Even with all those trailers, we needed more storage space," recalled Bob Lutz. "So Anthony bought property, about a half of a mile from the store—the bottling plant previously owned by Canada Dry Ginger Ale. The building became a warehouse; the 30 acres around the building provided space for expansion and room to park many trailers. At one time Anthony had more than 200 trailers."

To avoid being in the way of customers when the store was open, Bruce hauled the larger trailers to the store early every morning and returned in the evening around 9:00 to take the empty trailers back to the warehouse. Today, customers see only a few trailers lining the parking lot because trailers and trucks now unload at docks on Harrington Avenue, away from pedestrian traffic. But the trailer-storage tradition continues.

Anthony with new logo for trucks and trailers.

Growing Pains

As customers flocked to the store to take advantage of the low prices and high-quality products, finding a place to park was a challenge. Consequently, to provide more space for customer parking, Anthony continued to buy up land (and houses) on both the north and west side of the store whenever and wherever he could get it. However, as business continued to boom, Anthony found he needed more space for merchandise and customers. In 1958, he decided to use the parking

The view from Harrington Avenue.

View of SPAG'S from Baker Avenue.

space behind the store for his second addition. The land sloped down-hill from the Butler building, so Anthony had to build this new cement block addition three feet below the level of the original garage. To provide access, he had a wide ramp built through the middle of the tin addition. Now customers could proceed all the way from the origi-nal store through the Butler addition into the new section. The stocked shelves on each side of the ramp enticed them to explore the great values that waited for them elsewhere in the store.

This addition, extending the store northward along Baker Avenue, included Door 10, which allowed customers to drive their cars or trucks up to the door to have their large, heavy, or bulky articles loaded directly into their vehicles. Anthony then purchased more land to expand the parking lots.

On the Baker Avenue side of the new exten-sion, Anthony added a customer entrance to pro-vide convenient access to those customers who parked their cars in the new parking lot nearby. Three check-out counters and an exit stood next to this entrance.

Attendants at Door 10: John Firling, Walter Duffy, Dave Keeler.

By 1959, the store was again bulging at the seams with merchandise and customers. Anthony needed space not just for storage but also to allow large trailers to back up to the loading docks. He purchased some of the adjacent properties that had been zoned for business, as well as a house formerly owned by the Zona family. Most of the property owners were happy with the gener-ous compensation he offered them, but a few preferred to stay where they were.

"Spag wanted to make it easier for trailers to drop off fertilizer, lime, peat moss, and other garden materials," recalled Bob Lutz. "He wanted to remove the Zona house, and build the Garden Shop in its place, but the zoning laws laid down by the Shrewsbury Planning Board at that time required some of the original structure to be left intact. So Spag raised the roof of the Zona house, gutted the rest of it, and built his Garden Shop."

These additions gave Anthony space for expanding some depart-

Randy Case, Garden Shop.   *Bob Lutz.*

The Garden Shop—originally the Zona residence.

ments. Plumbers and handymen were now delighted to find a complete department with just about everything they needed at the right price—and, as always, the best quality.

Next Anthony enlarged the electrical fixtures area and made it into a separate department. He then added two staircases to the second floor loft, one from the electrical fixture department and one from the plumbing area, to provide access to inventories stored there. He also had a conveyor belt installed to carry plumbing and electrical supplies, toys, hardware, clothes, shoes, and housewares to the loft, where they would be readily available as needed.

The Wall

The growth continued over the following decades. Anthony had no grandiose expansion plans; he just enlarged as the need became apparent, and as both the funding and the space became available.

About 1965, he expanded the store again. The third addition was erected, creating an annex that expanded the area east and north of the plumbing department. It went up just before Christmas, in time to display the toys that had been stored upstairs and in trailers. The east side of this annex became known as "The Wall"—a key location where Anthony stacked all kinds of food and merchandise to the ceiling.

Procter & Gamble displays became a big part of SPAG'S "on the wall" business in the third addition. Chuck Civiello, Jr. of Bangor, ME, remembers working "on the wall" at SPAG'S during his college vacations. "While stacking tuna fish, paper napkins, or laundry detergent to the ceiling," he said, "we would remind ourselves of Spag's words: 'Pile 'em high and watch them fly!'"

"Gotta keep that traffic coming," Anthony would say to Bill Donahue, the affable sales representative from the Bar Soap & Household Products Division of P & G. In two weeks, Anthony bought six hundred cases of Ivory soap, each case holding 720 plastic bags of Ivory soap. The soap, twelve bars to a bag and stacked from floor to ceiling "on the wall," sold for 79 cents a bag. The Ivory soap sale brought the people in. Moving elbow-to-elbow, they made their way to the "wall." For two years in a row, the Ivory soap campaign at SPAG'S earned Bill Donahue the world record at P&G for sales to a

single retail account.

The new loading docks were not particularly successful because of the limited space for trailers backing up. They served a purpose, however, and were used until the next expansion took place. Meanwhile, Anthony purchased some of the surrounding properties. One by one, as funds permitted, he acquired houses around the immediate perimeter on Baker and Muzzy Avenues.[3] These houses were removed and the ground leveled for parking. This eased congestion in the parking lot and made room for the additional trailers he had purchased. Anthony was spreading his wings.

Making room for more parking space.

However, he came to regret a mistake he made in the earlier years of the store when a 1 1/4-acre parcel east of the store on Route 9 became available for $2200. Father, always one to foresee the future potential of property on the turnpike, had urged Anthony to buy the land "for future protection." But Anthony was adamant; he was obstinately sure that he would never need that space.

"You're passing up a golden opportunity," Father reminded him on

[3] See Map Page 10–11.

several occasions. Anthony was young; he just did not want to be told, so he turned a deaf ear to Father's advice.

A few years later, he realized that he did need more space for customer parking; it was too late. Mr. DeFalco, the new owner of the lot, had built a Frosty's and had opened the DeFalco's Car Sales business on the Turnpike side of the lot. Fortunately, the area behind the two businesses was not being used, and Anthony was able to lease that space for a parking lot, paying $600 per month. The lease later increased to $1,000 per month—a costly mistake, indeed. (As of this writing, CVS has leased the whole lot to make room for a large drug store and a parking lot.)

Loss Leaders

Eric Ottoson, a manufacturer's representative of long standing at SPAG'S, was one of many to recall another of Anthony's favorite marketing techniques:

> Spag had an unique way of discounting his merchandise. He would take a loss leader[4] to bring people in the store.
>
> One day, I offered Spag some packaged clothespins for 21 cents, instead of the usual price, 49 cents. He jumped at the offer and gave me the biggest order my company had ever received up to that time.
>
> Believe it or not, the day following the delivery of the order, in his daily front-page newspaper ad, he advertised "Clothespins for 19 cents!" When I asked about it, he replied, "A full-page ad would have cost me $1,000. The two or three hundred dollars I lost on clothespins filled the store with more customers than that ad would have. I knew they weren't going to leave with just pins." The additional merchandise the customers bought more than compensated for his losses on the clothespins.

[4] Loss Leader (aka lost leader): "A popular article that is sold at a very low price or at a loss for the purpose of attracting customers to a retail store." –*Dictionary of English Language*, 2nd Edition, p.1137, Random House.

Anthony's "loss leader" sales brought shoppers to SPAG'S, and the "wall" in the third addition became one of his favorite spots for displaying these bargains. Bill Donahue remembered that "One of Spag's favorite loss-leader specials was the Downey Fabric Softener. On more than one occasion, he bought two truckloads of family-size bottles—1,100 cases in each truck! All 8,800 bottles 'flew' off the wall and out of the store in less than three weeks."

Many people recall the mountain of LifeSavers. Three trailerloads arrived with 800 cases containing 40,000 packages—over a million and a half rolls of the candy. That sale of Life Savers was the largest ever made to a single retail store by Beechmont Company at that time. Within ten days, nearly half the candy had been sold.

Another attraction was the mountain of Halloween candy, featuring Hershey and Nestle's bars. Three trailers loaded with the candy arrived. Each trailer hauled about 600 cases, holding a total of 43,000 boxes of candy for the season, which amounted to a mountain of 2,580,000 chocolate bars. Of course, SPAG'S sold other candy, too.

Milton Frem of Anchor Plastics reminisced about the day he was sitting in Anthony's office:

> This was in the 80s. Mr. Spag was on the phone speaking with someone at the Beechmont Company. He was ordering candy and nuts for Halloween. I heard Mr. Spag saying, "I want to know how they come. Can I order by the cube?...I want to order enough to fill a trailer...I want one trailer with Life Savers and two trailers of nuts."
>
> Apparently, he was placing an order of unusual proportions. He repeated his request to three levels of order takers, and each person on the other end of the phone was telling him that no one ordered that way.
>
> With his patience tried, Mr. Spag asked in a perturbed voice for the Vice President of Marketing. Finally, someone accepted his order on his terms.
>
> Milton recalled later seeing the "monumental" displays of Beechnut candies and nuts piled high on the "wall" just before Halloween.

Both SPAG'S and Anchor Plastics benefited greatly as a result of Milton's dealings with Anthony, as he explained to me:

In our plastic business, we manufacture many specialty items. At one time, we were making various-colored plastic "milk" crates. While we were making the conversion from one color to another, the crates came out of the presses an ugly muddy color.

I called Mr. Spag and told him about the 10,000 muddy-colored crates that we had on hand. I told him that all we wanted to do was to get our product cost out of them. "How much did they cost you?" asked Mr. Spag. I told him a dollar apiece. "I'll take them all," was Mr. Spag's quick reply.

We loaded two trailers with plastic crates and shipped them to SPAG'S. Two days later, I was surprised to see in the newspaper that SPAG'S was advertising them for 99 cents each. We wondered how he could be making any money; he was selling those crates for a cent less than he paid for them.

When I saw him soon after, I asked him why he was selling the crates at a loss. "Best buy I ever made," he replied with a wide grin. "The customers are carrying them around the store and filling them up with other merchandise."

He was so logical. In less than a week, he sold the 10,000 and he was back on the phone ordering another shipment "in bright colors this time."

Without knowing who was on the phone, I overheard my clerk trying to explain to a customer that because of a backlog of orders, the best delivery date she could give him for an order of that size was three weeks. When the customer replied, "It will never do to wait three weeks," she turned the call over to me. When I heard who it was and what he wanted, I replied, "We'll fill a trailer for you, Mr. Spag."

"Okay, I'll take them if you get them to me this afternoon," was Mr. Spag's answer. We delivered those crates that afternoon.

No Frills

Customers have always been willing to experience certain inconveniences at SPAG'S that they would not tolerate in other stores. For instance, until 1996, SPAG'S had no bags for customers' purchases. Who had money to think of such frills? If customers saw something they wanted, they bought it and paid for it. All other stores provided shoppers with bags. That was the way it was. Not to provide bags was unheard of, and it was odd in the beginning for first-time customers at SPAG'S. But after making a few trips, they got used to the idea, especially as they began to appreciate how much money they saved there.

If someone happened to pick up more things than could be held, he or she could either grab an empty carton, as others would do, or ask a SPAG worker for one. The workers were obliging. They would simply

Anthony: "Need a box?"

fetch a carton from a nearby pile of empties, waiting to be fed into the box-crusher after closing time.

Eventually, regular shoppers remembered to tote their own carry-all or they reached for an empty carton as they entered the store. Most assumed they would be picking up more than they could carry in their arms. There was always that something else that was needed, and the price was right. It was surely novel and fun—just as Anthony wanted it.

A customer vacationing in Baggs, Wyoming, gave the saying "No bags at SPAG'S" an amusing twist. He sent Anthony a postcard on which he had scrawled:

> Spag,
> There is no SPAG'S in BAGGS!

Charge Accounts Discontinued

As business continued to grow, so did the number of regular charge accounts. By the late 1970s, the number of charge accounts had multiplied, and so did the amount of bookkeeping required to keep track of them. When Anthony learned that it was taking one clerk almost all his time pursuing overdue accounts and chasing bad checks, he realized that this additional expense was raising the prices of his merchandise. He asked himself, "Why the hell should a cash-paying customer have to pay higher prices to support those who are not paying cash?" He decided to put an end to it and to close out all accounts, except for town and business accounts. He notified all "charge" customers that all purchases would be on a "Cash Only" basis. Thus, Anthony added "Cash Only" to his store policy of "No Bags at SPAG'S."

A Tour of the Store

People have described SPAG'S in many ways, from the "fun store" to "a country general store gone berserk." More often than not, shopping at the store is a uniquely personal experience, as the following letters and articles demonstrate.

From Rose Alden of Marlboro, Anthony received the following

tongue-in-cheek description of shopping at SPAG'S:

> I shopped at SPAG'S long before I knew Spag himself, and I want to say this: he accomplished a consumer revolution by saving the customers money, and making them work for every penny of it. If you shopped at SPAG'S you would save money, but you had to suffer.
>
> What kind of a genius could figure this out? Imagine driving a long distance—because people come from all over New England—only to be one of a thousand people driving around a parking lot filled with tractor trailers, finally settling for a space about a quarter of a mile away from a door, just so you could come into a noisy barn and wander through narrow aisles crammed with fellow shoppers, light bulbs, tulip bulbs, tennis balls, ball-peen hammers, face paint, and house paint...looking for an empty cardboard box to hold the Scotch tape, tape measure, can of coffee, coffee pot, paint brush, toilet brush, tooth brush, tooth paste, and wall-paper paste that you want to buy.
>
> With all this stuff falling out of your box, you then struggle to the checkout counter, stand in line, (the box is heavy), pay cash, reload the box—no bags, of course—and, blinded by the sun, struggle across the parking lot to your car.
>
> No wonder everybody keeps coming back. It took a genius to figure out the right way to treat the customer, and Spag is all of that and more.

On only a slightly more serious note, Mary Eileen Foley, RGS, wrote an article on SPAG'S that appeared in the *Middlesex News*, 13 December 1986. The following excerpts are from her article, "An Alternate View of the Shopping Madness."

Have you been to Spag's yet to do your Christmas shopping? Friends told me I hadn't lived until I had been to Spag's. After my first trip there, I wasn't sure that I was living at all.

I was recently appointed buyer for the community, and I polled some local convents to see where they purchased their supplies. "Oh, we always go to SPAG'S," was the cheerful reply, and my heart sank. (I was thinking of letting my fingers do the walking.)

Well, times being what they are, I began to think of all those bargains, and was I to be outdone in the challenge? Now, armed with our own carton, my friend and I head for Shrewsbury on a regular basis. We usually start at the soap and shampoo section—always mindful of the fact that what's there today may not be there tomorrow. (Do I overbuy for the lean months ahead, or limit my purchases and risk disappointment later on—or worse, pay a higher price somewhere else?)

Once we found a director's chair located unexpectedly in the midst of the golf clubs. My friend sank into it, half-smothered by her unwieldy carton, while I went off to track down the glass wax and toilet bowl cleaner...

Carried along by a steadily-moving stream of people, I remember sailing past nails, paint cans, lighting fixtures, socks, crackers of all kinds, motor oil, and furniture. I reached out to grab a huge box of Masterpiece chocolates that I thought would solve a gift problem, but the moment had passed, and I found myself with a handful of tulip bulbs.

Sometimes I marvel at the leaning towers of goods piled high next to completely unrelated stacks of merchandise. The place defies rhyme or reason. One day I turned left at the Rubbermaid items and found an impressive array of cakes, muffins, and doughnuts behind the furniture. A delightful aroma led me to the last package of Armenian bread, which I wedged in between the calligraphy materials and the Snuggle. Later at the cash register a woman was almost in tears when told there was no more Armenian bread left. I think she would have killed for the fragrant loaf cake I held in my arms.

The elderly brush elbows with the 'yuppies' as we plow through the maze of narrow aisles, respectful of each other's quest for a bargain. No one is irritable at SPAG'S. It's the Christmas spirit all year 'round. I am buffeted about in SPAG'S parking lot in winter, and sweltering heat in summer, dodging mammoth trucks decorated with SPAG'S ten-gallon hats.

Last week as we headed home, the December darkness was perforated by gleaming headlights everywhere. At the outset that day, I hadn't felt too great, but as our car lumbered away in a scramble of Christmas decorations, I noticed that I was completely recovered!

Many salespeople who sell to SPAG'S have found that shopping at the store is irresistible. Ralph Garbutt, a salesperson for the Housewares Division of General Electric Company, wrote about the time he issued a challenge to his boss:

Whenever G.E. headquarters people came to visit, we always made "a trip to SPAG'S" a priority. We knew that GE products would be well-displayed and priced to beat competition. I also challenged these bosses. "I bet you can't go through this store without purchasing something," I would say.

My new regional manager assured me that he had fielded similar challenges in other areas and had never opened his wallet. Some two hours later and 42 dollars lighter, he left with a new fireplace screen, a cricket for the hearth, and a big pair of work gloves. He acknowledged his defeat, saying "Yes, you are right. There is only one SPAG'S."

On January 28, 1983, *The Wall Street Journal* ran a front-page article written by staff writer Liz Roman Gallese:

SPAG'S
The Cheese at Spag's
Is Next to the Rugs
—Over by Golf Balls

And All of Them Are Cheap
At Homey Discount Store
In Central Massachusetts

—By Liz Roman Gallese

SHREWSBURY, Mass.—Looking for a big bargain? The $5,199 grandfather clock is yours at Spag's for $2,950. But only if you've got it in cash. This store doesn't take either checks or credit cards.

How about a lot of little bargains, like a $25.97 corn popper for $12 or a 95-cent loaf of French bread for 67 cents? They're here too, but bring something to put them in. The store provides neither shopping carts nor bags. On the other hand, there are a lot of cardboard boxes lying around, the cartons the merchandise came in. You could grab one of those.

Both the bargains and the eccentricities are part of the formula at Spag's, a sprawling discount store along neon-splashed Route 9 in central Massachusetts. Spag's has the look of an old-fashioned general store that swallowed a growth pill. Its three adjoining buildings, covering about as much space as a football field, are crammed with almost every kind of merchandise, in no discernible order.

Jammed Shelves
The rat poison may be next to the computer, the hammers alongside the brass beds. Or, more likely, *under* them. At Spag's, brass beds are suspended from the ceiling, along with many other articles. Other merchandise is stacked on over-

crowded shelves, stuck on pegboards on the walls or heaped in piles on the floor.

Something like 10,000 shoppers a good day come to paw through this clutter. For a lot of them, the lack of organization seems to add to the experience, turning a shopping tour into a kind of treasure hunt. "Spag's is sport," says Rosanne Mercer, a bargain hunter from Boston. "I love it. I can't wait to go out there and stuff my car." She makes a pilgrimage every other month and loads up on about $100 worth of stuff each time.

Presiding over the $60 million-a-year business is Anthony A. Borgatti, Jr., a jowly man of 66 who is a bit of a sport himself. He spends his days cruising the aisles in a costume regulars know to be his trademark: a 10-gallon cowboy hat and a sheriff's tin badge. While he is catering to customers and employees, his wife, the former Olive Lutz, firmly oversees a backroom staff of 12 crowded in a gutted [expanded] living room in the couple's white frame house a half-mile away.

Prof. Padden of Brown University recalls returning a counterfeit $20 bill to the store after discovering it in his change. Spag replaced the phony bill without question and gave him a five-pound box of chocolates for calling it to the store's attention. "Other stores would have said, 'How can you prove you got it from us?'" he says.

Free Tomato Plants

Like the store itself, their merchandising technique is unique and a little baffling. The Borgattis sell unpainted furniture only in January and February, for instance, because that's the only period when they think people have time to refinish it. Every spring, they give away truckloads of tomato plants. At Christmas they sell oranges at cost, because Mr. Borgatti remembers oranges as a holiday luxury when he was a child.

As for the arrangement of goods, what logic lurks behind it doesn't explain much. In one section, the Oriental rugs are just around the corner from the cheddar cheese, which is across the aisles from the plumbing equipment, which is next to the golf balls. Golf balls are next to the plumbing because when the store decided to add a golf line, the buyer for the plumbing equipment was a golfer and wanted to handle the new line.

"There's little rhyme or reason that customers can fathom in such merchandising," acknowledges James Camyre, an assistant manager. "But regulars know where to find everything and expect it to be in the same place."

Sumner Feldberg, the chairman of Zayre Corp., the giant discount-department store chain, says Spag's gets away with what other stores wouldn't dare try. "If J.C. Penny piled up merchandise, it would be schlocky," he says, "but it isn't schlocky when Spag's does it—it's part of the image."

But the chief lure for customers probably is the price tag on the goods, which is apt to be the lowest around.

What you can beat is Spag's selection. It is far from complete on many lines, because, for the most part, the store buys merchandise only in bulk and only when the price is right. On a recent day, the back wall was piled all the way to the ceiling with cartons of Nestle cocoa mix in 24-ounce containers, but there was little to offer in other sizes and brands. And there were no paper diapers, because Spag couldn't get them at a price he figured would be acceptable to his customers.

With 400 full-time and part-time employees catering to customers, service is also part of the image. If there are still a lot of customers in the store when the 9 p.m. weekday closing time comes, Spag's just stays open a little longer.

If Spag's has a retailing philosophy, Mr. Borgatti says, it is "to serve the workingman, the person everyone else forgot." That gets back to price and profit margins, and related to them is volume. Hence, the lack of shopping carts at Spag's; as Mrs. Borgatti explains it, "Shopping carts equal half the inventory, which equals half the amount of business. Turnover is everything."

It all inspires a bit of admiration in at least one retailing rival. Jerry Ellis, the president of a privately held retail chain based in Hingham, Mass., called Building 19 Inc., says of his competitor; "Spag is one of the great retailers of our generation. He's the truest discounter in the country."

Walking The Store

… "Merchant Prince"—that's what Spag is…
—Ada Greenbaum,
Seder Foods Corporation

As mentioned previously, Anthony had his own unique way of running SPAG'S. Some people might have disagreed with his methods, but they certainly worked for him. And this was particularly true when it came to pricing. Anthony's secretary, Lee Zolla remembers:

> Employees would call from the store when they wanted to put something on sale. Spag would check what he paid for it, and off the top of his head, give them a selling price—no complicated pricing formulas for Spag. He seemed to know what would be a good price to sell the item.

It was this method of pricing that often got Anthony in trouble with the fair-trade laws, but it was also just one of the many ways that he earned both the devotion of his customers and the unsolicited title of "Merchant Prince."

In his later years, Anthony began to turn over the operation of the store to his daughters, Carol, Jean, and Sandy. As he did so, one of the most important things he stressed was to "walk the store on a regular basis; it's the only way you can know what needs to be done," he would say. Anthony's "walking the store" routine was well known to employees, customers and salespeople.

This policy was endorsed by Fred Garmon, president of Fred

Garmon Marketing Corporation, who, in 1991, wrote an article entitled, "Management by Walking Around—MBWA." Garmon noted that "Management by Walking Around (MBWA) is obviously live, visual, and effective. It is one of the best ways to find out what is really happening in the store. You get to know your people, and they get to know you." He then noted that he [Garmon] "had a rare opportunity to share in this experience not long ago with a unique retail legend, namely, Mr. Anthony Borgatti, Jr., nationally known as 'Mr. Spag,' and owner C.E.O. of a single location complex of several buildings, reportedly doing close to 100 million dollars annually." His article continued:

> I met Spag at his "Open House." He had extended this invitation to the salesmen, reps, store people, and anyone who happened to be in his office. After having lunch in his home, we drove to his store, SPAG'S Supply, nearby. For those who have never been there, SPAG'S is a collection of smaller buildings that surround the main building—a building that is constantly expanding and selling all kinds of general merchandise. Around the perimeters of several fairly large parking areas is a fleet of trailers that hold various categories of products and serve as a warehouse.
>
> With Spag leading the way, we started walking around, moving from building to building. He looked into every corner as he checked the back stockrooms. He greeted the department managers with a nod and a "How're we doing today?" He suggested a sign for a display, and added "That needs one there, too."
>
> Pointing to some fallen cartons, he asked a floor person to "move them out of the narrow aisles so customers won't fall and get hurt." Then he stopped to greet the checkout cashiers. He was constantly praising and thanking everyone personally for their good work and for their cooperation.
>
> Everywhere he went, customers stopped Spag and chatted. They either knew him or they recognized him from his homey TV ad appearances and his trade-

mark cowboy hat. They chatted with him about town business, and asked him about his health (improving after recent surgery)... Anthony "Spag" Borgatti is living proof that anything is possible in America with dedication, loyalty, simple courtesy to and from your employees, and by keeping your feet busy practicing MBWA, "Management by Walking Around."

Anthony did walk the store regularly. He strolled along the aisles, greeting some and chatting with others; he took in the whole scene. He must have had extraordinary peripheral vision—when wearing glasses, that is. With hardly a glance sideways, he did, as Garmon said, "know what had to be done." He gave a hand, made suggestions, asked questions, and gave directions to the employees.

For customers, meeting Anthony as he walked the store provided an occasional surprise. If someone did not recognize him, Anthony would walk up to the person, introduce himself, and thank the customer for shopping at SPAG'S. Sometimes Anthony would reach into a bin of cookies or candy to present the person with a gift. When he met people he knew, he took advantage of the opportunity to ask about an ailing parent, a child in college, a retirement, or some crisis in a family. By chatting with his friends, he was able to offer assistance when it was needed. Seeking out people in need was not just Anthony's hobby, it seemed to be his purpose in life.

John Lilly, a clerk in the boy's clothing department, told me about one day in late fall when Anthony was walking the store :

> Evidently, Spag overheard me speaking to a man who was talking in a heavy Italian accent and gesturing wildly. I could not understand him; he was obviously new to this country. For the fourth time, the man repeated his request and continued to point to a red flannel-lined woolen jacket on display and then to his five children (ages ranging from six to thirteen) who were standing obediently at his side. I could not figure out what the customer wanted, and he was becoming more frustrated by the minute. So was I. I couldn't make any sense out of what the man was say-

ing. Spag, on one of his "walking tours," came over to us and asked, "John, is there anything I can help you with?"

I nodded and said, "I think he wants to buy jackets for his children, but...he wants only one jacket!"

Spag spoke to the man, and listened as the man repeated his request. Then Spag turned to me and said, "He is saying that he wants one jacket that all five of his kids can share, because that is all he can afford." Without a pause, he continued, "John, fit a jacket to each kid, and one for the father too. Winter is coming. Tell him he can pay us sometime when he is able."

Then off he went, back to "walking the store."

Anthony was a real softie when it came to kids; he was always happy when he was doing something for children. A customer shared this story:

Spag was walking by the toy aisles one day when he overheard a young mother speaking to her child, who was clinging tightly to a teddy bear. "I'm sorry, Honey, but I don't have enough money to pay for that. You have to put it back." The mother seemed to be as upset as her daughter.

Spag apparently sized up the situation. He could see that the mother's arms were already laden with items to take to the checkout counter. He stepped forward, saying in a warm, friendly voice to the child, "Let me see that a minute." The little girl looked up at Spag and reluctantly loosened her grip on the teddy bear. He gently took the stuffed toy, and with a pencil from his shirt pocket, he marked the price tag, "NO CHARGE, Spag."

"There, you're all set," he said as he handed it back to the girl. "Now it's yours." Then he resumed his walking the store.

Anthony's employees appreciated his walking the store as much as, if not more, than anyone else. Vinnie Mastro, sharing some of his many happy memories, recalled:

> He cared about people. He was like a father to all of us here at the store, and a friend to everyone he met. We were always happy to know that he was in the store. The moment he stepped through the door, whistling his nondescript tune, the news would spread from one end of the store to the other, "Spag is in!"
>
> He never ordered us to do anything. It was always "Would you please..." and he always remembered to say "Thank you" afterwards. He never raised his voice.

Anthony did not have to raise his voice. He had other persuasive ways. I got a chuckle when he told us about the time he asked a young clerk to pick up some papers littering the aisle. When the clerk replied, "Oh, I get paid too much to do that!" Anthony, never short of an answer, responded with "We can take care of that for you; we'll cut your pay so you won't have that problem." The clerk moved quickly to clean up the aisle.

For Anthony, walking the store was fun, and it was a good way to stay on top of things.

Store Meetings

Two or three times a year Anthony invited store employees and their spouses to dinner meetings. He held his first store meeting in 1952 at Anfred's Restaurant. Anthony held later meetings at Tillie's, the Frohsinn Club, the Svea Gille, and, on occasion, at the Olde Mill in Westminster.

"It was a night out," said Nicky Wyman, one of the cashiers. "We had a good time, and it gave our spouses an insight into the operation at SPAG'S. It helped us to understand why last-minute schedule changes occurred sometimes."

Nancy Estaphan added, "We knew we were in for some laughs and a long night."

After dinner, Anthony would reach into his khaki shirt pocket for his notes. Sometimes he would flip the pages of his ever-present scratch pad, or pull out some scraps of paper, a pile of them. His scrib-bling was always remarkably legible to him, but not always decipher-able to others.

"When we saw a pile," wrote Errol Melander, "you could hear sub-dued moans, and then someone would mutter, 'Looks like we're going to be here all night.' As Spag adjusted the pile of papers in front of him, he would say something like, 'I have a few things to go over.'"

Vinnie Mastro added:

> Spag always started the meetings in the same way, one could say with a litany that defined his creed. He steadfastly reminded his workers, "Remember, we are here to serve customers with courtesy." Then he would add, "Without customers, there is no money coming in to buy merchandise; and without merchan-dise, the customers won't come to shop. Ours is the best merchandise, the best quality merchandise at the best price."

Anthony's opening remarks sometimes varied. In his files, I found a note that read "Hi, everyone! Everyone needs you. We need each other. My job and your job is serving customers by filling stock, keeping the floor clean, and putting legible prices on stock items for customers to read. We need to make shopping easier for the wonderful people who make my job and your job possible." He would follow this with his litany, "Remember, we are here...."

At every meeting, Anthony reminded his workers, "Customers are our first priority." He not only expected but insisted that workers be courteous and helpful, and treat everyone with respect. "Be polite. Treat the customers the way you want to be treated." He also stressed personal cleanliness. He would say, "Not new clothes, but clean. And be on time. You inconvenience others when you're not."

Anthony emphasized neatness, instructing employees to pick up papers and any merchandise they saw on the floor. He would add: "And keep the shelves full. Remember, you can't sell from an empty wagon."

"At least once or twice during the evening," recalled Errol, "as heads began to bob and weave, Spag would say, 'I don't have too much more!' Then he would keep right on talking."

Francis Kubik, another faithful employee, said:

> Yes, Spag's dinner meetings were lengthy, but
> we always had a good time. He was never at a loss for
> words. No matter how serious the subject, he man-
> aged to inject humor throughout the evening. Some
> of what he said was praise; some was not. He told it
> the way it was. He always asked for and listened to
> our suggestions. This input meant a lot to him. In
> turn, it made us feel a part of the SPAG'S family. We
> came away uplifted, and knew that we wanted to
> live up to his expectations by doing our darndest.

Anthony lectured his employees repeatedly about being respectful
of customers. He was stressing that point at a store meeting when a
cashier reported that "an African American, in line at my checkout
counter, turned to the person behind him and said, 'This is the only
store that cares about people.'"

Anthony was pleased. "It's always good to hear comments like
that," he said.

At his meetings, Anthony also placed heavy emphasis on the
importance of marking every single item on the shelves. He was
adamant about this. "Every item must be marked with its price," he
would say firmly.

In the early days of the store, employees marked prices with a
crayon. Then came magic markers, fluorescent stickers, and later, bar
codes. Marking merchandise was easy in the early days, when the
number of items was small, but as the orders increased, so did the
inventory. The task of pricing thousands of the same item became
monotonous and boring.

I wondered why a single sign on the shelf or a legible sign on the
carton holding the items would not be adequate. But I soon found out
that "marking each item" was not an idle notion with Anthony. One
day I came upon him spouting that someone had forgotten to "mark" a
carton of items. I asked him why he was annoyed.

"Hell, I want the customer who brings the stuff home to be
reminded of the good buys she got at SPAG'S," he said. "The sales slip
won't help her, because she's going to throw that in the basket. But if

the price is on the package or the item, it will remind her where it came from and the good deal she got. When she needs more she'll come back to SPAG'S, and while she's browsing she'll see more low-priced items that will stretch her dollars."

Then from his pocket, he took out a stubby pencil and a spiral note pad and made a note for the next meeting, "Mark the prices."

Banking Practices

Long before Anthony had a more sophisticated mode of transporting the day's receipts to his home, and from there to the bank, he would put the money in a paper bag, usually a crumpled one most likely retrieved from a waste basket. He would then hand the bag to Vinnie Mastro or to a friend who was going in the direction of Beverly Road. Occasionally Anthony would carry the bag home himself, or ask Father to do it. He would subsequently send someone into the bank with the paper bags of money.

The time finally arrived when the officers at the Guaranty Bank in Worcester became very concerned about the way in which SPAG'S delivered their daily receipts. For many years, they tried to convince Olive that sending the receipts to the bank in a paper bag with an employee was risky. It endangered the lives of the delivery persons as well as the personnel at the bank. When, finally, Olive reluctantly hired Brinks, Inc. to pick up the receipts, the people at Guaranty gave a sigh of relief.

Anthony remained dedicated to the Guaranty throughout his life.[1] "He never changed banks," recalled Mr. John Jeppson, the son of the bank's founder. "Later on, Spag became one of our bank directors, and we appreciated the contributions he made in this capacity. He was a shrewd and able bank director, very forthright in expressing what he thought about the decisions being made." (That may have been the understatement of the year, according to another bank director, who told me about an incident in which Anthony had objected strenuously to a path of action being considered: "Spag expressed his objection in such strong earthy terms that he shocked and astonished fellow board members.")

Mr. Jeppson also told me that "Spag attended our directors' meet-

[1] See The Wrong Side of the Road, page 91.

ings religiously. Just as a meeting was about to start, he would appear with fruit in season, candy, crackers, and cheese. We loved to see him coming."

Lee Adams, who was also serving on the Board of Directors, recalled, "We were usually all seated when Spag arrived with his box of oranges and grapefruit. He would take his place and then roll the fruit down the table to each of us. We loved it."

Charles Evans, a vice-president of the bank at that time, related the following anecdote:

> We knew that Spag usually attended meetings wearing his working garb: cotton chinos, cowboy hat, and badge. So we were pleasantly surprised when he arrived at his first director's meeting wearing a business suit, shirt, and necktie. Someone commented on the fact that his "dressing-up" for the meeting was appreciated. Anthony's reply was, "I've just come from a funeral."

That was Anthony; always one to say it like it was. He knew who he was. He knew what he believed. He had no need to impress anyone.

On one of his trips to the bank, he drove into the parking lot only to find that it was full, except for one spot with a sign that read "Reserved for the President." According to Anthony's daughter Jean, "Father turned into the spot and parked. Just as he was leaving his car, the parking lot attendant rushed over to him. 'You can't park there!' he exclaimed. 'That spot is reserved for the president of the bank!' As Father continued on his way into the bank, he calmly replied, 'But I'm the customer.'"

The TV Monitor

As the store expanded, it became necessary to find more efficient ways of communicating. By the 1960s, Anthony had installed an intercom, but it did not give him the feedback he needed. He wanted to be in touch with what was going on in all the parts of the store. Installing a television monitoring system not only solved the problem, but also provided him with a new form of amusement.

One busy evening, I came upon Anthony in the TV area upstairs where I had gone to make a phone call. There he was, seated in front of 15 monitors scanning the store below and chuckling away. I soon found out what was so amusing to him.

Since the monitors were relatively new in the store, not many people were aware of them. Every once in a while, Anthony took advantage of that by mischievously calling out on the intercom the name of someone who appeared on one of the screens. It took a couple of calls before the startled person realized that someone was speaking to him.

I listened as Anthony called out "Hi, Ed! Hi, Ed Johnson, you handsome fellah, you! Did you find the tape you were looking for? It's always good to see you." It was a lark to watch that person trying to locate Anthony almost in disbelief, especially when Anthony would repeat the person's name over and over.

The Tent

Inevitably, as SPAG'S sales continued to increase, so did the need for space. In the spring of 1982, Anthony erected a large green and white striped tent (75'x50') at the back of the store to display surplus inventory. At first, he filled the tent with shrubbery and plants—overflow items from the bustling Garden Shop. Customers made their selections and brought their purchases to a clerk manning the cash register at the tent's entrance. A security fence surrounded the tent, and during inclement weather the canvas sides came down.

Along with the original plan to display department surpluses and odd-lot bargains in the tent, Anthony added left-over winter merchandise, such as jackets, mittens, thermal blankets, and deicers. As he walked through the main store, he would say to the clerks, "Unload it! Put a good price on it and stick it in the tent! Gotta get rid of it to make room for new merchandise coming in!"

To "keep the tent interesting and add a little excitement," Anthony had sales representatives demonstrate their products, such as barbecue grills, paint, car wax, and lathes. One day I joined a crowd of people who were watching a man using a chain saw to carve a larger-than-life-size figure of Anthony out of a block of wood.

At times, the area took on a carnival atmosphere. Tortorelli's calliope would fill the air with circus music and his search light scanned the evening sky. On occasion, SPAG'S staff served frankfurters, rolls, and drinks at token prices (25 cents) to well over 4,000 people. Anthony loved to watch the people as they enthusiastically devoured their hot dogs.

Shrub sale at the tent.

Another popular attraction at the tent was free popcorn. For these occasions, Anthony bought a professional corn popper, the kind on wheels. About every three months, a staff member manned the corn popper in front of the tent. As the aroma of hot, buttered popcorn wafted through the area, people lined up to receive their bags. How Anthony enjoyed chatting with the them all! Later, Anthony had Frank the Popcorn Man take over. Frank, with his cart, added considerable color to the tent area.

In the tent, the merchandise scene was constantly changing. As items sold, job lots or surplus goods, such as shoes, glassware, slippers, towels, books, and rugs took

Two clerks, Jeff Johnson and Domenic Lanzilotti, at the tent.

their place. Shoppers browsed to their hearts' content. Customers rummaging through the tent items often commented upon the extraordinarily rock-bottom prices. "How does he do it?" they would ask.

The simple truth is that, as sole owner of SPAG'S, Anthony was free to make yes-or-no decisions quickly. He also paid his bills promptly. These factors were of prime importance to jobbers, manufacturers, and suppliers, who appreciated quick decisions and prompt payments; they would call him first with special offers. Consequently, he was able to buy merchandise for the tent at ridiculously low prices, which he passed on to his customers. This made the tent an intriguing bazaar of bargains for all who ventured in.

More Expansions

Even the tent wasn't enough to handle the overflow of merchandise and customers. Anthony had purchased another vacant property on Route 9, adjacent to the parking lot. There, in that small building, he opened SPAG'S Christmas Craft Shop. During the Christmas season, he filled the shop with holiday items: decorations, gifts, paper, ribbon, and boxes. After the holidays, he stocked it with all kinds of paints, novelty candles, huge displays of silk flowers, needlecraft, and related supplies.

When a small restaurant on Baker Avenue near the back of the store closed, Anthony rented the building to use for storage. In the summer of 1977, he stored in this small building a shipment of snow shovels—another one of his "good deals." Those shovels came in handy when the blizzard of '78, the worst snowstorm since the turn of

—Clif Nickerson

The expanded School House with offices on the second floor, 1999.

—Clif Nickerson

The sport shop, 1999.

the century, hit Boston and the surrounding areas. The Massachusetts Bay Authority (MBA) desperately needed more manpower and shovels to augment the work of the plows in clearing three feet of snow that had fallen. The overnight demand for shovels had quickly depleted the supply in the Boston area. Searching further afield, the MBA called SPAG'S and learned that the store had plenty of shovels in stock. The MBA quickly dispatched a truck and driver to SPAG'S to pick up 1500 shovels. He emptied the building.

Anthony bought the building when it became available for purchase in 1988, figuring that he needed the storage space. Even though he had many large trailers lining the periphery, he continued to use it for storage for the next two years.

At the top of the parking lot stood the red brick Artemus Ward School, the school that I had attended when we first moved into the neighborhood. It had housed grades one to six in four rooms. Standing with only its memories of children whispering and teachers giving instructions, the empty schoolhouse became the target of speculation. In 1985, Anthony purchased the property and stocked "Ye Olde School House" with school and office supplies, tools, footwear, jewelry, clothing, baby products, and finished furniture, which he had Bruce Ward truck in by the trailerloads.

Meanwhile, the office staff had outgrown the cramped space in Anthony's home on Beverly Road. With Olive's approval, Anthony had architects draw up plans for expanding the schoolhouse by extending the rear of the building and adding a second floor for office space. In 1987, Anthony, with some reluctance, moved his staff from his home to the schoolhouse office—as Lee Zolla, his secretary, noted:

> When we moved to the new main office at 35
> Harrington Avenue over the School House, it was
> quite a change. We had to 'brown bag' it [instead of

the home-cooked meals we had enjoyed previously]. After a while, I did get used to it there. Olive loved our new office, but I don't think Spag did. He spent very little time there.

Perhaps Anthony was busy planning the opening of SPAG'S Sport Shop in what had been the small storage building that he had purchased in 1988. Now enlarged and renovated, he stocked his sport shop with everything from basketballs to scuba diving equipment, just in time for the big opening day in 1990.

The Dogs

After a foiled break-in at their home, the police told Anthony and Olive that they needed to protect themselves and made several suggestions, including the installation of a sophisticated alarm system. They followed the advice given them. The part of the security plan that Anthony liked best, however, was the acquisition of a pair of German shepherd dogs. From that time on, the dogs were an integral part of the Borgatti household. Anthony took them to obedience school and spent many happy hours walking with them through the fields.

As the first pair of dogs aged, Anthony bought a second pair. At night, the four dogs slept in their individual doghouses in the laundry room. During the day, they were either roaming about the house or outdoors in the kennel.

Anthony loved his dogs, and he took good care of them, although he did find that taking them to the veterinarian was a challenge. Dr. Bill Maker, the veterinarian, recalled Anthony bringing in "three dogs, each one on a leash. At the end of each leash was a very independent free-thinking German shepherd. By the time he reached the reception room, he [Anthony] would be hopelessly entangled in the three long leashes. Suffice to say, the receptionist soon learned to block out several appointment slots for Anthony."

The dogs also loved being with Anthony, especially when he took them for a ride in his station wagon. Rarely did he ever drive around town without having two of them with him.

"Whenever I went down to the store after closing time, they

Anthony with Danka and Dutchess. In the background is his home/office.

—B. A. King

always rushed ahead and led the way into the building," Anthony said. "They did their patrolling, sniffing up and down every aisle ahead of me. I always felt safe when they were with me. I knew that there was nothing to be concerned about when I turned them loose at the store.

"But different little things can happen," he added as he reminded me about the night a man hid in the store undetected at closing time. As I recall it, in the stillness, the man selected a new outfit for himself. But unknowingly, he tripped an alarm that rang at the police head-quarters. The police, in turn, called Anthony. At his whistle, the dogs, Danka and Dutchess, hopped into the station wagon, and off they went, arriving at the store just as the police cruiser pulled up.

In the meantime, the intruder had taken off all his clothes so that he could try on his "new outfit." When he heard the key turn in the lock, he ran up a flight of stairs to the storage area and hid. As Anthony opened the door to the store, Danka and Dutchess darted ahead as usual into the building, followed by their owner and the policemen. The dogs sniffed the main floor and picked up a hot scent from the clothes left behind in a heap by the intruder. Turning quickly, Danka and Dutchess headed up the flight of stairs with the two police-men at their heels. The dogs' noses led them directly to a pile of burlap bags within minutes, and they stood, growling and snarling, as the policemen pulled the thief out, handcuffed him, and brought him downstairs. Danka and Dutchess followed, barking away, until Anthony took hold of their collars.

I can remember Anthony saying as he laughed, "God, it was funny! Talk about getting caught with your pants down...There he was with nothing on, stark naked. The poor bastard didn't even have a chance to try on his new socks. I patted the dogs and gave them some treats out of my pocket."

In addition to providing Anthony with companionship and pro-tection, his German Shepherds served another purpose: "screening" people for their owner. Anthony liked having them lying nearby when interviewing prospective employees or when talking with new vendors; the dogs would pick up on the adrenaline that would start flowing if, for instance, someone exaggerated when talking about a product or had illicit goods. Whenever they sensed that something was wrong, the dogs would become very attentive, their ears shot straight up and the fur on their backs bristled. When this happened, Anthony knew something wasn't right, and he would become aware and cautious. He told me about an incident involving his first shepherds, Anna and Ambi:

> Anna was especially aggressive. When she stared you down, you knew where the expression 'steel-blue eyes' came from. She could be intimidating. Anyway, this day two fellows in their twenties came to apply for jobs. While we were talking, the dogs, who had been lying at ease, suddenly became upset. Anna fixed her piercing eyes on the fellows. Ambi, lying at the furthest end of the office rose and walked forward. Both dogs came alongside my desk and began to growl. I thought, "Can it be that these guys are up to no good?"
>
> When the fellows saw that the dogs were close enough to lunge at them, they turned pale, real white. All at once, they decided that they had to leave. I took hold of Ambi and Anna by their collars and hung on to them as the boys rushed to the door. Wow! Those guys couldn't get out fast enough!

Anthony with Anna and Ambi in the office.

The Robbery

Anthony was as concerned for his employees' safety and welfare as he was for his own family. At every store meeting, he would say, "It's logical to expect that we might have an armed robbery. If we do have a robbery, I want you to remember: *Never resist!* Give them what they want. I can always get another bag of money, but I can't get another life for you; so to hell with the money, give it to them!"

Then one day, true to his fear, it happened. During the 1970s, at the end of a busy day, two men, one of them brandishing a pistol, entered the store at the Boston Turnpike entrance. The 30 to 40 people standing in line waiting to have their purchases checked out by Al Coté at the cash register froze where they stood. Al had just returned to work after undergoing major surgery.

Pointing his gun at Al, one of the thieves demanded, "Give us the money!" Al, remembering Anthony's orders, nervously reached for the bag of surplus cash on a shelf below the cash register. The thief, evidently thinking that Al was reaching to press an alarm button, fired two shots; Al slumped to the floor in agony. The thieves hastily grabbed the bag of money, ran out the door, and disappeared into the night.

The security officer called an ambulance, and then he called Anthony and Olive, who were attending an awards dinner in Rhode Island. They went immediately to the hospital, where they joined the Coté family. Several hours later, a doctor came into the waiting room and reported that the bullets had penetrated the area of Al's previous operation. Although the bullets had been removed, serious complications had set in, and it did not look good for Al. Anthony stayed at the hospital all night.

That next morning, unaware of what had happened, I went to the First Friday Mass at St. Anne's Church. After taking my seat, I heard Anthony's familiar cough. Looking around, I saw him bowed low in prayer in the first pew.

At the ringing of the Communion bells, we both made our way to the altar railing and kneeled to receive communion. Afterwards, everyone returned to their pews—except Anthony. Obviously, he was deep in prayer, for he remained there at the railing until Mass was over. I waited for him at the back of the church. Most of the people had left when he eventually rose, turned around, and started to walk towards me.

I was shocked at what I saw. Anthony was ashen and his eyes were swollen; they were barely open. He was stooped over. He looked twenty years older than he did the day before when I talked with him at the store.

"Anthony, what's the matter?" I asked, "Are you all right?"

With a voice hardly above a whisper, he told me about Al Coté, and concluded, "I was afraid of something like this. But God is good, and he is in God's hands now."

Al did pull through. Several months later, he returned to SPAG'S painting department where he continued to work until his retirement two years later.

Bad Apples

Thefts were to be expected at the store, but fortunately most were far less serious than the robbery which nearly took Al Coté's life. Sometimes the thieves were caught; other times they found inventive ways to get away with their crimes.

One early Sunday afternoon, I was helping Anthony and his clerks, who were taking inventory. My job was to check each shoebox to make sure that the shoe matched the information on the outside of the box, and to check it off the list. Upon opening one box, I found an old pair of shoes with the soles worn all the way through. When I showed them to Anthony, he laughed and said, "I hope the bastard knew enough to take a good pair. He surely needed them!"

Anthony talked about another couple of clever "bad apples" in a 1989 interview with a local radio talk show host. In answer to the question "What about shoplifting?" he replied:

> Shoplifting is a problem like it is everywhere else. But I think there are a lot of good customers who care, and they stop a lot of the shoplifting. We do have shoplifters, though—the young, the old, the middle-aged, different segments of society. We prosecute the person if he or she is a professional or a repeater. We prosecute because this has to be. But the good shoplifters are the ones who always come

to our store because we have the best selection to pick from. So we get them both ways.

There was a man, his wife, and baby who came in several times. Each time, the man held the baby while his wife paid for her purchases. The baby would let out a scream, and the man would hustle the baby out of the store. We became suspicious, so we watched and saw the man put something under his jacket. Then, while he was standing behind his wife at the checkout counter, we saw him pinch the baby's ass, and out they went. We caught them and found out that they had taken us for a few thousand. This is the way some people are, but, fortunately, most people are honest.

In fact, Anthony felt strongly that "99% of the people are honest," so he was philosophical about the petty pilfering and thievery that inevitably went on in the store. By and large, he trusted his customers, and they repaid his trust with the loyalty and devotion they felt in return.

His Customers: His Friends

We owe so much to our customers.
—Spag

Anthony would often stop to chat with the customers while he was walking the store and once in a while he would ask them why they shopped at SPAG'S. Their enthusiastic responses included a variety of reasons: "The prices can't be beat." "You never know what you are going to find or who you might meet there." "The good service." "The return policy." "The trust." And, invariably: "It's a fun place to shop."

Harvey Raynor, who became a staff reporter for the *Worcester Telegram and Gazette*, reminded me of the time he canvassed people in the towns east of Northboro, looking for people who might be interested in placing an ad in the newspaper. While talking with a woman in her Southboro home, he asked her if she ever shopped in Worcester. She replied: "All I know about Worcester is that it is some place west of SPAG'S!"

Harvey told me: "I quoted her response in my report to the T&G brass, and the next day it was all over the county. It was even repeated to me, the reporter."

Anthony took pleasure in such loyalty from his customers and their willingness to share their enthusiasm for shopping at SPAG'S—as did I. People who responded to my request for stories about Anthony described their interactions with him in ways I could never have anticipated.

Service and Caring

As a boy, Anthony reveled in the appreciation that the Boston-bound trolley passengers expressed for the sandwiches and drinks he sold them. Returning home with his pockets jingling, he felt a warm regard for the customers who had made his trip successful.

When he started his own store at 18, he felt the same way toward the people who came to shop there. He was eager to serve them in any way he could.

As Anthony chatted with the people who came into his store, he became interested in their lives and welfare, and he looked for ways to help them. He liked everybody; this was apparent in everything he said and did and in the way he related to all he met. He felt an especially strong allegiance to those early customers and friends who helped him get his business started. He made a point of keeping in touch with them and he tried to be there for them when they needed help solving a problem or celebrating a wedding, birth, or retirement.

The daughter of an early customer spoke warmly about her father's relationship with Anthony:

> My father shopped at the store when it first opened under the name of Shrewsbury Tire and Battery Service, and he chatted with Spag often. When he retired from Howard Brothers in Worcester, Spag gave him all kinds of gifts, things he could use when he and my mother moved to Point Judith. We were amazed.

Sometimes the only thing Anthony did was make a telephone call or pay a friendly visit, but that was enough for people like Helen Meyer, who wrote to him in June 1988:

> The nicest present I received on my 90th birthday was your phone call and visit. It meant a great deal to me. With all you have to do, you over-extend yourself.
>
> Thank you for all your surprises. I hope to see you in SPAG'S real soon.

A Far-Reaching Reputation

SPAG'S phenomenal success all started with Anthony's neighbors in Shrewsbury. Stopping in at the store became a habit for many of them, and then they brought their friends to shop. When Anthony started advertising in the local newspaper, people drove across town to take advantage of the bargains, new products, and his policy of accepting returned merchandise. Then the word about SPAG'S spread throughout Worcester County and started drawing people from all around New England. News about the store eventually extended so far that travelers in the area who came from across the country, Canada, and around the world included a shopping trip to SPAG'S in their itinerary—and still do.

While shopping at the store, you will see suave individuals in designer suits touching elbows with homespun types in utility garb. Some customers appear with lists in hand, buying for themselves and their friends. Others come just out of curiosity. Many customers have said that they "treat" their guests by taking them to SPAG'S, and often former residents of Worcester County returning to visit in the area include a stop in Shrewsbury to fill their cars with purchases. I have been told that, according to Massachusetts Turnpike tollbooth workers who answer tourists' requests for directions, SPAG'S popularity as a tourist attraction in New England is second only to Sturbridge Village. Whatever their reason, people from all over make their way to the SPAG'S parking lot and join the crowds inside the store "where your dollar buys more!"

Gordon White, who worked at Lodding Engineering, found out, however, that talking about the wonderful bargains at SPAG'S could lead to trouble. He told me what happened after suggesting to a traveling salesman that he and his wife might want to stop in at SPAG'S while they were in the Worcester area:

> The next morning when the salesman came in to Lodding, he shook his fist at me. When I asked him why he was mad at me, he stammered, "You're the one who told me about SPAG'S!"
>
> I couldn't imagine why that would give him cause to be angry. But he continued, "Well, my wife

and I went there last evening, and we bought so much
stuff!" That sounded okay too; I was still puzzled.

"But we bought more stuff than we can fit into
our MG!" said the salesman. "Now I don't know how
we're going to get it all back to Georgia!" Then he
smiled and thanked me for telling him about
SPAG'S.

Many are ecstatic when they "discover" SPAG'S. Anthony once
received a postcard from Linda Williamson, a new customer, who
wrote:

> Just want to tell you I think your store is so won-
> derful. I just moved here from Virginia six months
> ago and have never had more fun going shopping!
> My Mom and Dad came to visit and they enjoyed
> SPAG'S more than Martha's Vineyard. And that's
> the truth!

Mrs. Ralph Gray, a resident of Bristol, Connecticut, said that
when she and her husband came to Shrewsbury, a highlight of their
trip was going to SPAG'S, which they wouldn't think of missing. Her
husband ran a general store, and he would buy items at SPAG'S to
resell at his store.

The Vanherelins from Belgium wrote to say that when they visited a family in nearby Maynard, MA, they always included a stop at
SPAG'S. And according to Sherm Brickett, "when the Worcester
Polytechnic Institute Alumni Association sent out alumni reunion
invitations, they offered a tour for the spouses of the alumni. Their suggested itinerary included the Worcester Art Museum, the Higgins
Armory, and SPAG'S."

In the spring of 1963, four busloads of hardware merchants from
Paris descended upon the store and spent four hours shopping. The visitors had read about SPAG'S in an international hardware trade magazine. Their itinerary for a one-week stay was: "Arrival in Toronto; New
York City; SPAG'S, Shrewsbury, MA; back to Toronto; return to Paris."

Unfortunately, the person who had arranged the itinerary had not
alerted the store before their visit to SPAG'S. Anthony, who was at

home when they arrived, rushed down to the store and quickly turned over his public address system to the French merchants so that they could find one another as they buzzed around shopping, somewhat in a tizzy in the confusing arrangement of merchandise.

"Regrettably," said Anthony later, "I was limited in what I could do for them. If I knew ahead of time, I would have jazzed things up with a little French music and a few interpreters, and I would have had a lot of food for them."

However, they did have coffee and a light lunch, and Anthony gave each one a handful of mementos before they made a mad dash back to their buses. The bus drivers revved up their motors as a reminder to the excited Frenchmen that they had a tight schedule to keep.

News about SPAG'S also spread to Japan, according to Yoshikiyo Amaki, M.D. After he had completed his residency at the University of Massachusetts Hospital, he and his wife returned home to Japan with three Tiffany-style lamps they had purchased at SPAG'S. For the flight home, his wife wore one of the lamp shades as a hat "to get it safely to Japan." It wasn't long after that when a letter arrived from Osaka, Japan, in which Akira Aono inquired about ordering some Chanel lipstick, Christian Dior perfume, and Clinique Clarifying lotion.

In 1996, Dave Nichols of Princeton sent the following letter to Anthony's three daughters, who were in charge of the store by then:

> My assignments at Norton company took me annually to Europe. One of my regular stops was at the Norton factory located near the small town of Lillesand, Norway, situated on a small fjord on the south coast 150 miles from Oslo. Over the years I built friendships with many of the Norwegians at that factory.
>
> On one visit, two of these friends, Aners Illebeck and Arnie Corneliussen, met me at the Sjevik airport and on the way from there to Lillesand suggested we stop at a small inn for dinner. When the waiter brought the menus, I put on my new reading glasses. They were those funny little

professorial-looking half glasses that sit out on the end of your nose. You can look through them or over them.

Illebeck instantly noticed these and asked, "What have you got there?" I said, "You mean my glasses?" "May I try them on?" he asked, and of course he did. It turned out that the prescription [magnification] was just right for him, and he exclaimed, "These are great! Where did you get them?" I said, "Back in the States." With which he asked, "Can you get them at SPAG'S?"

I knew that Illebeck had never set foot in the U.S., and I said, "SPAG'S! What do you know about SPAG'S?" He answered, "Everyone knows about SPAG'S."

I was dumbfounded, of course, until Anders and Arnie explained to me that at their factory office in Lillesand, there hangs a clipboard sheet labeled "SPAG'S List" (just the same sort of thing that everyone of us around here has stuck on our refrigerator door), and that at Lillesand, it is the responsibility of any employee about to travel to Norton Company in Worcester, from Vice President on down, to take the list and shop at SPAG'S for the employees back home.

Actually, I have several stories about SPAG'S, but that's my favorite.

No Quick Stop

Most customers would probably agree that a quick stop at SPAG'S is a rarity. Shoppers never know who might be there when they run down to the store to pick up something they need in a hurry. It is easy for them to forget the ten minutes they might have allotted for an errand when they bump into a friend they have not seen for a long time and had been intending to call. Despite their busy lives, customers usually take the time to enjoy the SPAG'S community of friends and the camaraderie of its environment.

"Going to SPAG'S is a ritual for some people," said Jane T., who added that "my two sisters, Beverly and Claire, and I have been going to SPAG'S two times a week for the past fifteen years—except when we're away on vacation. There's always something to pick up and besides, we like seeing what's new and bumping into our friends. We are seldom disappointed either way."

Like Jane and her sisters, Dan Corcoran has also found shopping at SPAG'S to be a family affair:

> Our family has been shopping at SPAG'S for four generations. My father shopped there in the 1930s on; I shopped there in the 1950s and on; my sons shopped there in the 1970s and on; and my grandchildren are shopping there in the 1990s and on. It's a Shrewsbury tradition.

Over the years, people raved about the first class service Anthony provided. I asked Dr. Paul Montag, a popular and busy obstetrician in Worcester what brought him to SPAG'S on a regular basis and why he kept coming. I enjoyed his answer:

> My introduction to Spag and the store took place one afternoon when I was an intern—visiting my friend, Professor Feldman at Worcester Tech. That was in the late thirties, the early days of the store. Prof. Feldman said, "Let's go to SPAG'S. I need something."
>
> When we got there, Spag was alone in the store. Prof. Feldman asked for the item he wanted. Spag promptly climbed a ladder, which was leaning against a pile of bales, stepped onto another ladder, and disappeared into a loft. Before we knew it, he came down and handed the professor exactly what he had asked for. He did this among thousands of different items all around him. He had a phenomenal memory. I was intrigued.
>
> Since then, I have gone there at least once a

week, sometimes two or three times a week, unless absent from Massachusetts. Whenever I bumped into Spag, he always stopped to chat. One day when I was there, I asked him about a particular power mower. Spag turned to a nearby clerk and asked, "Will you go upstairs to the office where all the catalogs are piled on top of a bookcase, and bring down the green catalog?" On receiving it, Spag turned to a page without a moment's hesitation. "Is that what you're looking for, Doc?" It was precisely what I wanted, so I gave him my order.

Returns and Trust

Anthony believed that he should always stand behind his merchandise. He never, ever quibbled about accepting returned merchandise. Sometimes a brass fitting was not the right size, or the item did not do the job that the customer thought it would, or the customer just changed his mind about doing a project and did not need what he had bought. For whatever reason given, the clerk at the entrance desk accepted the returned merchandise and gave the customer a credit slip or cash (and still does).

Vinnie Mastro, a very patient person, would occasionally feel his blood pressure surge when, as far as he was concerned, a customer pushed the return policy too far. "That happened," said Vinnie, "the day two women brought in a coffee pot that they had purchased at SPAG'S ten years earlier. They claimed that it was defective. Spag gave them a refund. When I questioned his judgment call on that one, his response was, 'It's easier to give 'em a new one than to argue. What the heck! Keep the good will!'"

Anthony had faith and trust in people, and his customers responded favorably to this. Joseph Szenker no doubt expressed the feelings of most when he wrote to express his appreciation for a refund check: "Thank you for believing in me when I wrote you that I was overcharged. I really didn't have any proof, but you took my word for it. Thank the good Lord for people like you."

In January 1989, Eleanor Decker from Brooklyn, Connecticut also wrote to "Dear Spag" to thank him for a check:

> If you remember, I am the person whose daugh-
> ter did not receive her change from a cashier on
> December 27th. You thought over the situation and
> sent a check for $45.50. I thank you kindly for this,
> but even more for the lovely letter you sent me. I
> appreciate and agree with your philosophy of faith
> in others.

I remember Anthony telling us about the lady who called and left a message in which she complained about the price of perfume she had bought at the store. "Before I had a chance to call her back and tell her that we would give her the difference," said Anthony, "she tele-phoned again to say that she had learned that the size of the perfume she had purchased at SPAG'S was larger than the one she had priced at another store."

The lady, Mary Ann Burritt, subsequently wrote a letter of apolo-gy in which she acknowledged her mistake and added that she had actually saved five dollars on the perfume. She also mentioned in the letter that she was going to Poland to teach "gratis" for the summer. Anthony wrote back to tell her that SPAG'S appreciated her honesty and he enclosed a gift certificate, suggesting that she use it to buy some supplies for her students in Poland. She sent several postcards from Poland, and when she returned to the States, she sent the follow-ing note along with some snapshots that she had taken of her Polish students:

> My Polish students were very pleased with the
> materials you provided. Your giant pack of magic
> markers were well used, as the photos testify. My
> economics lesson on starting a business incorporat-
> ed their use. Again, please accept our heartfelt
> thanks and appreciation for your special generosity
> and kindness.

Another customer, Paul Anderson, wrote about an unfortunate incident involving his wife:

A short time back I wrote concerning a toy trac-
tor that I bought for my son. The box was covered
with tar that ruined my wife's clothes. Your insurance
man, George Sullivan, took excellent care of this
situation. With any other store, I can only imagine
the trouble I would have gone through. This whole
thing couldn't have been handled better.

The main reason I've been a longtime loyal
SPAG'S customer is the way in which any product
problems (although few) are handled so efficiently
and professionally. The excellent treatment we
received only proves to me again and again what a
truly professional organization SPAG'S Supply is,
and that I'm proud to be a customer of your organization.

Anthony, being a human being, had his bad days too. Following is a
letter he wrote to Roger J. Poole, Northboro/Westboro Superintendent
of Schools, who had complained about an inappropriate response on
Anthony's part during an encounter in the store:

I am very sorry for my impertinence the other
morning. Like all school boys, I needed straightening
out. I appreciate your kindness in taking the time to
do so. Many times, one cannot see the trees for living too close to the forest.

Knowing your keen powers of observation, we
would appreciate suggestions you may offer to help expe-
dite matters in doing a better job serving the public.

Your kindness in taking the time to do business
with us has proven mutually beneficial to both of us.
We hope we can always continue to serve you in this
capacity.

Mr. Poole was quick to respond:

This will acknowledge your note of October 21.
Thank you for your gracious comment. I was aware

that something must be bothering you because you have always appeared to me to be a highly skillful business man under all circumstances. I made the mental note that somebody must have been giving you a hard time that morning!

I enjoy shopping in your store whether it is on official business or merely to satisfy my personal needs.

Honesty

Anthony was honest with his customers, and he appreciated it when they were honest with him. One time he received a check for $3.99 with a note in which the writer said that he had accidentally left the store with a pair of socks which were in the corner of his shopping bag. "I had so much stuff; I just didn't see them. Sorry. They were $3.99."

Some customers even wrote to report that they had not been charged enough at the cash register. A check for $3.00 arrived with an anonymous note that read, "I was recently charged $1.69 at the check-out corner for a $4.69 item."

In September 1996, S. Douglas Winslow of Hopedale, Massachusetts, enclosed the cash register tape and a check for $6.58 with a letter in which he explained:

> Last evening I purchased a variety of items at your store. On my way home I got to thinking of the total cost and thought it very low, but couldn't reconcile the amount mentally. It wasn't until I arrived home an hour later that I itemized the tape and found I had been undercharged 60 cents for a roll of masking tape, 4 cents on a nail-set, and not charged for a $5.75 can of paint. I figured an additional 19 cents for sales tax, which totals $6.58.
>
> I like your store and wouldn't like to see you go out of business.

When cashiers mistakenly overcharged or undercharged customers, Anthony welcomed feedback. For Anthony, every incident or
experience was an opportunity to make a new friend. That also applied
when people stole items from the store. Anthony chuckled when he
received the following typewritten note:

> SPAG'S Security Dept.
>   I'm sorry for stealing from your store and putting
> you through the trouble of catching me. I will never
> steal from your store or any other store. I realize that
> shoplifting only raises the price of the products for
> other people.

When people sent Anthony money in payment for something
they had stolen, he donated the money to the Shrewsbury Public
Library,[1] and sometimes he accompanied the donation with a letter,
like the following:

> Dear Bonnie:
>   A customer came into the store recently and
> said to me, "Oh, so you are Mr. Spag... I am very
> happy to meet you. When I was a little boy, I stole
> something and I have come here hundreds of times
> since and never bumped into you. Will you please
> take this $5.00 for what I took?"
>   I was more than pleased to take the money, and
> I said he was quite a man to face up to this, even
> though it was a little thing. I thanked him, and now
> the library has another $5.00. Also enclosed is an
> additional $15.00 in cash donated to the library from
> "A Friend." These may be added to the Olive I. and
> Anthony A. Borgatti, Jr. Library Fund.
>   —Anthony A. Borgatti, Jr.

In Anthony's box of letters saved for the book he planned to write
someday, I found one in which a boy explained that he had "got caught
trying to steal some stereo equipment worth $2.90." He apologized and
promised that he would never steal from Anthony again. The boy had

[1] See also Serving Others, page 294.

signed his name, and added his address and telephone number. With the note, was a copy of Anthony's reply to the young person:

> Dear _____,
>
> I appreciated very much talking to you Wednesday night. I think it was very nice of you to send me a letter apologizing. I hope when you come into the store, you will come over and tell me who you are so I may shake hands and meet you.
>
> If I am not at the store when you are there, ask them to check my office. I would like to meet you because you know you did the right thing and you will always be glad that you did.
>
> You are a real man.
>
> Your friend,
>
> Spag
>
> P.S. Thought you might enjoy spending the enclosed [gift certificate] next time you are at SPAG'S.

Anthony, adept at turning a negative situation into a positive one, was gentle in dealing with shoplifters. He preferred to be there when clerks or security guards caught someone so that he could talk with the person himself; he did this often. The following letter from Zack Temrin[2] describes one such incident:

> I first met "Spag" in the early 1960s, when I was in my early twenties. I had recently returned from Korea, married and was attending college. We had just had our first child. We were struggling financially but were being helped by my parents.
>
> As I recall the incident, it happened as follows: I had taken a winter jacket, put it on, and without paying for it, walked nervously past the register and out the front door. Then immediately I felt an arm grab mine. A man [clerk] stated that I hadn't paid for the jacket and escorted me back into the store.

[2] The names of the person and place have been changed to protect the privacy of the people involved.

I recall walking about midway through the store, being taken up a stairway and into a room. There was "Spag" sitting there with his hat on and looking sternly at me. I had always wanted to meet him, but not like this.

He asked my name and about my background and interests. I told him that I was a Korean War veteran, married, working part-time while attending college, had re-established a Boy Scout troop—one that I had been in as a child—that had folded up, and that we had taken the boys to Treasure Valley that summer.

He seemed very interested in me and my endeavors and said warmly, as I now recollect, "That's good that you're helping those boys to become responsible young men. I'm interested in the Boy Scouts and in helping boys in need, and I've got someone assisting with two right now. You just keep up that good work. I might just call on you someday to help a few of them."

He wished me good luck with my education, family, and future, shook my hand, and said, "Goodbye." He must have said something about the taking of the jacket. I'm sure he did, but that's not what he wanted me to hear. Spag had a genuine interest in people, all people, and in me. He came across as a very unique caring person who was looking for good in all people.

As you now know, it certainly left an indelible impression on my mind. I worked for about 30 years as an educator of children—trying in my little way to help young people develop positive attitudes and caring values which I know would have pleased "Spag" very much.

We moved to Germany in the 1970s, and raised our children there. My wife and I returned to the United States in the early 1990s. While back in Shrewsbury, I visited old friends, among them Spag.

Spag had not changed. He was still the same humble, relaxed, caring person—whom I hadn't seen or
heard about in thirty years.

He invited my wife and me to the family house
in Shrewsbury, where we were welcomed. I showed
Spag a map of Germany. He knew much about it. He
stated that he had been there on a few occasions.

I remarked about how much I admired his hat.
He took it off his head and gave it to me, as well as
many T-shirts and gifts to give away here in
Germany, which I did. I recall meeting some of his
family and, in my own personal way, felt that I was
now and had been, since 1960, a part of that caring,
concerned family. I felt so relaxed there with him. I
really didn't want to leave.

Gift Certificates

Many customers have taken advantage of the opportunity to purchase
a SPAG'S gift certificate for their loved ones. These, too, generated
good will for the store in more ways than one. The following letter
from P. J. Davis concerned a gift certificate that her mother had lost:

> I wish to thank you for your consideration. I
> don't know which pleased me more: your generosity
> in replacing the lost gift certificate or the respect and
> courtesy with which you treated my mother. I have
> always felt that she deserves the best, and that is
> exactly how you treated her. Thank you.
>
> We went on a shopping spree this past Thursday.
> It reminded me of the time when I was six or seven
> years old. My grandfather gave me $10 to spend as I
> wanted. My mother brought me to SPAG'S to spend
> it. I still feel the same way—there are so many won-
> derful things from which to choose.
>
> It was easier making the decision this time. We
> bought a dresser and a few other little things. Our

home is at least half-furnished with things from SPAG'S.

If I ever find the original gift certificate, I will, of course, return it to you. Thank you again.

When the clerk in charge of gift certificates at SPAG'S sells one, she leaves the name of the person blank and therefore keeps no record of the recipients. Usually, the person who purchases the certificate fills in that information later. That was the case when a young customer named Patrick Ryan purchased a gift certificate for his great-grandfather.

In June 1991, Patrick—with his mother's help—enclosed a SPAG'S gift certificate in a Father's Day card for his great-grandfather. He also enclosed a photograph and a note that read "This photo is to show you how much I love the trucks you gave me for Christmas." Under a row of "X's" and "O's," Patrick signed his name, "Patrick Ryan," and addressed the envelope to "great grannpa [sic]."

"We had planned to deliver the card in person on Father's Day," Patrick's father later explained, "but for some reason the card was misplaced. After about a week, we gave it up for lost."

A month later, the card—with no address, no return address, and no stamp—arrived at the post office's Dead Letter Branch in New York City. Eventually, a kindly-disposed post office sleuth opened the envelope to find out who the sender might have been. Since the only clue was the SPAG'S gift certificate, he mailed the card, photo, and certificate to SPAG'S.

Upon receiving the certificate, Anthony, determined to find the sender, looked up the name in the telephone book and called each Ryan listed, but to no avail. He then asked a reporter at the *Telegram and Gazette* to assist. On September 15, 1991, Patrick's mother opened her newspaper and read a human interest story with the caption: "SPAG'S has gift for 'great grannpa'." The article's writer, Carol McDonald, described the Father's Day card, photo, and fifteen-dollar certificate, and added:

> Owner Anthony A. "Spag" Borgatti Jr., is determined to get the letter and gift certificate into the right hands. He said, "I would just like to find the

person. I know how I'd feel if it were me, not for the money, but to know that my family [the great-grandson] cared. The family is probably wondering why he [the great grandfather] never said anything about it," Borgatti added.

Within a few hours, a lady arrived at SPAG'S office with her son, Patrick. She also showed Anthony an identical photo of Patrick with his trucks. Patrick's mother wrote later in a note to Anthony:

> You can imagine our surprise when we read the article in the newspaper... It is extremely nice to know that someone cares enough about people to make the effort to get a story in the paper. Once again, we would like to say thank you.
> Fred, Lynn, and
> Patrick Ryan Mosely

Anthony smiled when he learned that Patrick's last name was not Ryan, but Mosely.

Ben Jenewin's Story

Anthony said many times, "Running a store has been great for me and my family. We owe so much to our customers. We're happy to be able to help out whenever we can." His customers were invariably grateful for his help. One of the most heartwarming stories I received was written by Betty Jenewin with regard to her father, Ben:

> I was shopping in SPAG'S sometime in 1994 when I noticed Spag walking the aisles, casually greeting and talking to customers. The scene that struck me particularly was the mutual, warm exchange that occurred when he approached an elderly couple and gave them a friendly handshake, smile, and greeting.
> I immediately thought of my father, Ben

Jenewin, and how much a greeting such as that would mean to him. He surely ranked as one of Spag's biggest fans. Ben was a natural storyteller who for decades had told and retold tales he had heard of Spag's unpublicized generosity, humanity, and home-spun wisdom.

At the time, Father was eighty-three, increasingly housebound and limited by age and infirmity. He had had two strokes; his talking and walking were limited. Because of his age and physical diminishments, trips to SPAG'S were for him a thing of the past. I knew I would have to ask for a special favor. My hope was to get permission to bring my father in for a minute or two, while Spag was working in his office at the schoolhouse, just to say hello and shake his hand.

Not only was my request immediately granted, but much to my surprise, we were invited into Spag's home for a personal visit. I had kept this all as a sur-

Ben Jenewin and Anthony swapping yarns.

prise for my father. On the pretext of going to a rescheduled doctor's appointment, we headed out
(supposedly) for Fallon Clinic. I fibbed a bit more
and told him I had to pick up a few quick things at
SPAG'S first. As we passed Spag's store, I had to tell
him that we were going to meet the man that he so
admired.

Spag welcomed us graciously and treated us to
over an hour of wonderful stories of SPAG'S-lore.
He followed that up with an invitation to stay for
lunch, and gave us some freshly-picked vegetables
from his garden to take home.

This memorable visit occurred in the twilight
of my father's life and was truly special. It gave him
the opportunity to spin out one final tale of Spag's
generosity and kindness—only this time, it was from
a first-hand perspective. Many remarked that the
old familiar twinkle had come back to my father's
eyes when he related the story of his surprise visit
with a man he held in such high esteem.

Nine months later, my father passed away. I
look back at the photos we took of him and Spag
that day with great fondness, remembering how
much that visit meant to him.

Please know how much this act of kindness on
Spag's part meant to my father and my family.

Ben's sister, Wanda Varnum, also wrote to describe the effect that
the visit with Anthony had on Ben:

Well, Ben started to tell me of the visit. As he
talked, his voice became stronger, his eyes were
sparkling, he was sitting up straighter, and he looked
twenty years younger. It was like a miracle! I
thought about it all night. The following day, I sat
down and wrote a letter thanking Spag for the miracle he had performed. He did something for my

brother that no one anyplace or anywhere could do. How many people would do something like that? On behalf of all our family, I thanked him.

And what did Spag do? He sent us, by way of his pilot, two cartons of oranges, one to us here in Brookfield and one to my brother Ben. Now, do you think we shop any place but SPAG'S? Never! SPAG'S is home to us.

And knowing my brother Anthony, I'm certain he enjoyed his visit with Ben as much if not more.

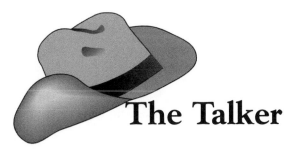

The Talker

...down to earth and practical...
—E.P. Ted Webster

"It is generally known that Spag loved to talk," recalled John Cullen. This was definitely an understatement. Anthony's propensity for talking, whether in personal conversations or informal presentations, reached almost legendary proportions. Indeed, no matter what the circumstances, he knew how to put his gift of gab to good use. He was an especially popular public speaker; he was asked to speak to all kinds of groups—professional and charitable organizations, students from grammar school through graduate school, a variety of audiences both young and old. He donated any honorariums he received to his favorite charities.

Anthony's talks were almost always "off the cuff." When asked about how he prepared for his speeches, he would grin and confess, "I just say what comes to my mind. Sometimes I learn something that way." Or: "I say what is important to me." Often while he was waiting to be introduced, he would jot down a few notes in the margins of the printed program. In his files, I found many programs with hastily scribbled notes on them. If there were no printed programs, he would reach into his shirt pocket for his spiral pad. When the topic was family values, you could be certain that he would mention Mother and his own family. When he received accolades or honors of some kind, he always passed the credit on to others.

In one talk, Anthony spoke of "women's lib."

"They have it all wrong," he said. "Women should stay up on their pedestals. They deserve it. When it comes to working, they are

smarter and they work harder than men."

Anthony's modesty and sincere regard for others were hallmarks of his talks. When E. P. Ted Webster, of the Harvard Business School Club, wrote to thank Anthony for speaking there in November 1961, he noted: "Your talk was down to earth and practical. We enjoyed your humorous anecdotes and what impressed me most was your basic philosophy (if you want to call it that), your faith and love of the people who have helped you, especially your good wife."

Anthony received many such letters after his speeches. He was warmly received wherever he went, primarily because he spoke from his heart.

Telling It Like It Is

Anthony was aware of his tendency to ramble on and on, so before starting to talk, he would take out an oversized pocket watch and place it directly in front of him on the podium to keep an eye on the time. As he talked, he jumped around from one subject to another, but the basic message was always the same: "Life isn't just dollars and cents; it's about family and people."

When invited to address young people, he was only too happy to oblige. Reporter Dave Maney wrote about the time when Anthony gave a talk regarding job-hunting to approximately 120 students at Burncoat Senior High School:

> Peering over a lectern nearly as tall as he is, Spag told the students that they shouldn't be afraid to start at the bottom. "Everybody would like to have the top job, but you can't start at the top because you'd mix everything all up. You need to start with sweeping the floor so you'll know how everything works," he said.
>
> Spag said that attention to detail can be the margin between success and failure. As an example, he told the youths that he can't stand to see the labels on cans facing the wrong way—even in stores other than his own. "When I visit other stores, I

turn the can," he said.

For young people starting out in the business world, just looking good isn't enough. Spag said. He told the students to make sure they smell good, too. "Some kids come in and they smell. They smell like they've never been near a shower or a bathtub. Make sure you don't do that."

In the question and answer period, one student asked Spag to describe the biggest merchandising mistake he ever made. After pausing to mull it over, he replied he had bought a load of padded toilet seats.

"If you went to leave in a hurry, you'd leave some of your skin with it," he said of the seats. "You kind of stuck to them."

With any luck, though, maybe some of Spag's success will stick with the members of yesterday's audience.[1]

An alumni of Worcester Polytechnic Institute, Francis S. Harvey, told me about a managerial symposium at W.P.I. at which Anthony was one of the speakers:

During the question and answer period that followed Spag's talk, a member of the audience asked, "At what level in your business do you participate?" Spag's answer was quick. "At the lowest possible level." He illustrated this by pointing to a rumpled scrap of paper lying on the floor in plain view. He walked forward, picked up the piece of litter and said, "Some of you saw it there, but you were too proud to stoop to the level of picking it up." That was how he was; no job was too menial for him. That included the job of cleaning the lavatories, which he did more often than not until it was assigned to a person hired for janitorial service. He would not ask anyone to do anything that he himself would not do.

Anthony also talked about serving others, working hard, and the

[1] Dave Maney, *Worcester Telegram*, February 3, 1988.

importance of making life exciting, among other things. He frequently expressed his common concern for "the plight of the working men, those without the means of making their needs heard." Urging people to share their good fortune and help others, he would point out, "You have to give a helping hand when it's needed. It's not much good tomorrow if it's needed today."

In one of his talks at W.P.I., Anthony encouraged the students to be risk-takers:

> If starting your own business is on your mind, do it. And if it happens that you don't succeed on the first try, so what? It's no disgrace, no dishonor to fail. You learn from the experience and from your mistakes. Everyone makes mistakes because we're all human. There'll always be mistakes; I make lots of them.
>
> If you fail, but being in business is what you want, and you believe in what you have to offer—an idea, a service, a product, or whatever your business aspiration is—grab the brass ring and go for it again.
>
> Be positive, follow your dream, act with the courage of your convictions. There is a helluva great reward in giving yourself a chance by trying, instead of wondering the rest of your life about what could or might have been if you had taken the chance.
>
> Did you ever stop to think of all the things that would be missing if the people who had those ideas hadn't forged ahead, persisted in what they set out to do, and made them happen?

Reverend Leslie Johnson wrote: "I remember my wife telling me about the time Spag came to North Shore School graduation ceremonies to speak to the graduating class. He was all dressed up in a suit. After the ceremonies, he departed for a few minutes, and then in his regular business garb he returned to have lunch with the students. He surely made an impression on all of them."

They made an impression on Anthony, too. He often remarked, "These kids have something to say. We need to listen to them."

After his talks, Anthony solicited questions from the audience—the clock permitting. He got a big kick out of the questions the grammar school kids would ask. The children in a fourth grade class were especially amusing. Their first and most popular question was, "How can I make money fast?"

"You don't," he would answer.

When they asked, "How do you make money?" he would reply, "Hard work and lots of it."

"Don't you get tired?" they would then ask, and he would say, "Oh, yes, but you feel good because you made people happy while you were doing it. You accomplished something."

Another favorite question was, "How much money do you have?" To this Anthony would simply reply, "Enough."

Sometimes questions from the adult audiences provided Anthony with opportunities for a little fun. He could not resist the openings they gave him for a quick, humorous twist. Following a talk to a group of business people, the owner of a large furniture store in town raised his hand and asked, "Why is SPAG'S, a hardware store, now selling mattresses?"

Without blinking an eyelash, Anthony answered, "Because you can have much more fun on a mattress than you can on a wheelbarrow." The whole audience cracked up at that one.

Adding the Fun

Anthony approached his talks the same way he ran his store—by introducing elements of fun and surprise. One morning, after talking to a Golden Age group in a nearby town, he stopped at my house for a cup of tea before heading into the city to address a high school class. I was preoccupied when he entered the kitchen, so he simply stood in the doorway and greeted me with his familiar, "What's brewin', Susabella?" He was waiting for the reaction he knew he would get when I finally looked up.

And he got it. I gasped, "What in the world!" In addition to his usual set of khakis and ten-gallon hat, he was wearing an outlandish tie that hung down to his ankles! The tie boasted orange, purple, and yellow colors, and was at least five inches wide.

Grinning from ear to ear, Anthony said, "You have to put some excitement into it if you want them to hear what you're saying."

Never one to refuse a request to speak, Anthony usually had several talks scheduled for any given month. He often gave two talks in a day, and sometimes as many as three—some nearby, some out of town. I don't know how he had time for them all. "You just make it," he'd say matter-of-factly when asked.

I have been told that in many cases there was standing room only at Anthony's talks —and this in spite of his colorful language. But not everyone appreciated Anthony's profanity, and he was well aware of it. In his collection of letters, I found a letter from Mrs. Mildred Griffith, who had attended a talk he gave in April 1991, at the Balmer School in Northbridge:

> I also had a mother who kept me on the straight and narrow. She told us never to use the Lord's Name in vain—that it hurts Him very much. It made me sad, and some of the others also, to hear such a great and well-respected man, such as you really are, use the Lord's Name that way (also other words). It was almost as if Lincoln had said them.
>
> Now, you probably are mad at me and say, "Who is this___? I can do as I please!" I am just someone's mother and you surely can do as you please, but dear Spag, you truly are a living legend, and an example of what can happen when a person grasps the opportunity offered by this great country. You are in the limelight; people look up to you. You have influence, especially with impressionable youth...and it places a big responsibility on your shoulders.
>
> I think that in your heart you already know these things and no one needs to tell you, and that you are grateful to God for the good things in life that have come your way. One of them is your many genuine friends, even many you don't know you have, of which I am one. Otherwise why should I bother to write to you?

At the bottom of Mrs. Griffith's letter, Anthony had scribbled a note that read: "I telephoned Mildred Griffith, apologized, and sent her a box of oranges."

A Talk Show Interview

In Anthony's box of mementos, I found a radio interview[2] taped in 1989, when he was 73 years old. The local talk show host had focused most of her questions on the store and Anthony's involvement in its success. A few excerpts from that taped interview follow:

> *Question: What do you do every day?*
> Answer: Oh, I have a pile of paper that I shuffle, and I walk around the store and the office, and I go to the warehouse and check on the merchandise, and I talk to all the different people, those who work with us and the customers and salesmen.

> *Q: So you are pretty involved in the day-to-day operation of the business?*
> A: I want to be very involved and my wife also works in it every day. She puts in a full day every day. She is exacting.

> *Q: You have become a character in yourself, almost as popular as the store. What do you attribute that to?*
> A: I like everybody; I like people. A dollar is nice to make, but the most important thing in life is people; people who work with us are people, and the salesmen are people. Our whole life is built around just people, and I love everybody—even those guys who try to give me the shaft. You learn how to handle them, and I feel sorry for them because they don't understand what life is all about. I've enjoyed every day in every way, and I take it as it comes.

> *Q: How do you decide on what you are going to sell?*

---

[2] Unfortunately, neither the name of the talk show host nor the call letters of the radio station were listed on the tape.

A: The basic principles and the basic items don't change. Customers still use nails; they still use glass; they still use hammers and saws, and all those things, and you still need paint and putty and all the bottom things; overalls, etc., all these things you need everyday. So we try to always have those in stock. We buy everything else around those things.

You don't buy things as you need them [for the store] anymore. You buy them on production. When we want mowers, we have to send out orders in the fall. If you don't have an order in when the production line is on, you don't get it. They are not interested if you are happy or not. They just don't want to have any inventory in stock. We wouldn't have a warehouse up the street if we could buy things as we needed them.

Q: *Let's talk about sales. How is it that prices for the same item differ from store to store? Something can be on sale for $50 at one store, for $39.98 at another, and at yours or another store for $24.99. Are your sales real?*

A: Well, the sales with us are real. I think most sales at stores are real.

Q: *Do you jack up the price to, say $82.95, then cross it out and mark it at $54.99?*

A: No.

Q: *Do you give special discounts to certain people?*

A: No. We like to try to have everybody get the benefit of the same deal, and we try to mark it as low as we can so that people can afford the goods. We try to price everything low, not just a few items.

Q: *Has it been difficult to keep your prices low over the past few years?*

A: Well, it is getting harder all the time between the government and its various new regulations, the insurance costs, trucking, wages, and advertising. Everything has gone up quite drastically I would say, and this has created a hard situation to cope with sometimes. But we work around it the best we can and try to avoid pushing prices up.

Q: *Let's talk a little bit about the help. They range from teenagers all the way up to 73-year-olds.*
   A: Right!

Q: *Are they caring individuals?*
   A: By far they are.

Q: *They seem happy in there. You never see a rough clerk. You never get a clerk who says "I don't know where that stuff is." Everybody knows where everything is in that place.*
   A: Well, we do have some that we hire special to insult you and tell you where it isn't so you appreciate all the nice ones we have.

Q: *You are obviously proud of the fact that your store has became a part of people's life.*
   A: I do appreciate it, and I feel pretty proud of the fact that maybe I have helped them to live a little better.

Whether he was talking on a radio show or to a class of third graders or simply to a friend, Anthony was always in his element.

"I remember the time Spag and I were at the housewares show in Chicago," said John Cullen. "We were talking as we stepped into the elevator on the 24th floor at the Sheraton. We talked on and on. Finally the door opened. When we stepped out of the elevator, we saw that we were still on the 24th floor. Then we noticed that 30 minutes had passed since we had left our rooms. We chuckled when we realized that each of us had thought that the other one had pressed the elevator button."

Anthony and Will Rogers

Yes, Anthony loved to talk—and talk he did. He especially enjoyed the casual conversations that forged friendships. Over the years, he and Roger Braley, the night maintenance man at the store, had many conversations covering topics that ranged from the store to politics, investments to amusing stories (my brother certainly appreciated a good joke). It was Roger who told me about an interesting conversation that he had had with Anthony one evening:

> Even though Spag may have walked the store earlier in the day, he usually returned every evening "to check things out." Sometimes he dropped in just as the store was closing, sometimes on his way home (perhaps after a hockey game), and sometimes it was around midnight, after his last house guest had bid farewell.
>
> When he came in, he would head for the cookies and milk. We snacked and chatted a while before taking our nightly tour of the store. Then as we whizzed up and down each aisle, Spag would write notes for himself and for the managers of the morning crew. I looked forward to seeing Spag come in. We had great chats as we "checked out the store" together.
>
> One evening, Spag came in all revved up. He had just seen a television documentary. You could see that he had been tremendously moved and was still in a state of awe. As we walked the aisles, all he talked about was this program he had seen on Will Rogers. Every so often he'd interrupt himself to quote one of Will's sayings, like: "I never met a man I didn't like." Over and over, Spag kept repeating what a great man Will Rogers was and how wonder-

ful he was. Then Spag said, "Will Rogers stressed family values, and he did so much for the working man." He went on and on, nonstop. He surely was impressed by the man.

Do you know, as I listened to Spag tell me about Will Rogers, I kept thinking about how much he, Spag himself, was like Will Rogers, the man he was admiring. And, not only that but how totally unaware Spag was of the fact that, as he talked about Will Rogers, he was describing himself.

After this conversation with Roger, I was curious and did a little research on Will Rogers. I couldn't help but come to the same conclusion that Roger did. Anthony, the son of an Italian immigrant and Will Rogers, part Cherokee Indian, were alike in many ways. Both enjoyed giving inspirational talks, and both used their own versions of the English language, as well as a lot of humor, to convey their homespun philosophies. Audiences enjoyed their flair for showmanship and fun-loving monologues. For most talks, each appeared in his usual garb: Will wore an unpretentious plain suit and cowboy hat; Anthony wore his ten-gallon hat and cotton chinos.

Both men were proud and happy to donate their services to good causes. They were avid readers, always up to date on current events. They were spontaneous, as well. When Will had a thought, it had to be executed at once. The same applied to Anthony; he would often advise others by saying, "Do it now. Don't wait until tomorrow. It might be too late. Do what fits at the moment."

"What fits" might be passing out the dollar bills that he always carried in his pockets, to help others when he saw help was needed. Imagine my delight to learn that Will did the same thing. Like my brother, he looked for opportunities to share what he had. They had a common interest in and concern for the working class people.

Thus, it may be that both Anthony and Will Rogers were popular speakers for the same reasons: because they never put themselves above their audiences, speaking *to* them, not *at* them; and because they represented decency, honor, and family values. They never met anybody they didn't like—and they were well loved in return.

Serving Others

Of all Spag's legacies, most profound was his joy in giving.
—Ann O'Connell,
President, Guild of Our Lady of Providence

Anthony and I grew up in a family where giving and sharing was one of life's greatest pleasures. Consequently, he learned at an early age that he was happiest when he was helping someone or sharing something. He also appreciated what he had received from others, especially the support of his neighbors and friends during the store's earliest years. "Without them," he said, "the store would never have been as successful as it has been."

Eager to do something for his community, Anthony devoted himself to helping others. He preferred to remain anonymous in his giving, however, saying, "Now keep it under your hat." As a result, most of the stories of Anthony's generosity were known only to the recipients and, on occasion, to those who worked closely with him. Although his memory was great when it came to business details, he consistently drew a blank when it came to discussing any of his acts of kindness or generosity. Sometimes, people would ask me to convey their appreciation to Anthony for some gift or kindness he had extended to them. When I tried to do this, or even just tried to refresh his memory about it, he would shrug his shoulders and pass it off with one of his stock replies—"I guess so," or "It must be, if they said so." If I persisted too long, he'd say, "How the hell do I know!" He just did not remember.

Fortunately, many others have remembered Anthony's kindnesses, and have shared their stories with me.

The Nursing Home

Just about every day, Anthony visited Olive's mother while she was in the nursing home. Then our dear mother, Brigie, also became a resident there. My brother Bobbie often accompanied Anthony when he visited Ma. He told me about those times:

> Anthony usually went laden down with fruit, candy, ice cream, and flowers for all the residents. On one occasion, he handed out lottery tickets to each resident, saying, 'I hope you win!' He would visit with Mother and Olive's mother first, and then he visited the other residents. As he talked with each one, he would ask, "Need anything?" They would respond with, "Oh, yes, I need..." It was usually shaving cream, hand lotion, socks, a pair of nylon stockings, postage stamps, or writing paper. Anthony jotted down each item and the patient's name on his spiral pad, and, as needed, asked for the size and color. Sometimes there were a dozen errands on the list. On his next visit, soon after, he would deliver the requested items to each person.

Whenever he could, Anthony drafted Bobbie, Jeff Hakim, or whoever was handy, to go with him and help scoop the ice cream and hand out the goodies. But Anthony happened to be by himself on the day Bill Collins pulled up to the nursing home's receiving door in his delivery truck to drop off an order—a quick errand, or so he thought. Parked ahead of his truck was a station wagon loaded with red poinsettia plants. It was the beginning of the Christmas season. Bill recalled:

> As I sat waiting and getting more impatient by the minute for that station wagon to leave, the receiving door opened and a smiling Spag came out. When he walked over to the opened tailgate of his station wagon and picked up an armful of plants, I gathered that he was in the process of emptying the wagon and offered to help.

We carried in dozens and dozens of poinsettias, placing them just inside the receiving door. "Thank you," said Spag gratefully. "Now would you give me a hand? I gotta bring 'em to the rooms."

We went from room to room. I carried the plants, and Spag handed them out. I don't know who was happier: the people receiving them or Spag giving them. What a guy! I know one thing for sure—he made my day.

Virginia Smith, RN, a nurse at the home, wrote the following letter in appreciation for all the kindness Anthony had showered on the residents and staff:

As a charge nurse at the Shrewsbury Nursing Home, then supervisor, and then director of nurses until seven months ago, I have had the opportunity over the past 16 years to see you provide so much for the staff as well as for the residents.

I remember the game tickets, the pizzas that would appear around supper time, the oranges sent each year for everyone, your "Hi, Anna Banana!" every time you greeted your mother-in-law, your so frequent cheerful visits to both your mother and Olive's mother, the hot summer nights when you'd bring in gallon buckets of ice cream, scoop it into Styrofoam cups, and pass it out to the residents.

I can see my Dad spooning ice cream into his mouth, and with a grin on his face saying, "Spag was here!" I can hear you saying to us as you'd walk by, "Hi, you good kids!" What a morale booster that was!

I guess this could be summed up by saying you are a living, doing example of what the Bible tries to teach us all regardless of our religious creeds. In your unobtrusive way with your happy grin and your cheerful greetings, you show us all what goodness and caring really are.

The Player Piano

When Barbara Hayes learned that I was putting together some stories about Anthony, she asked if I had a few moments to hear her "Spag" story, concerning her mother, Alice Martin. I was ready with pencil in hand.

Barbara mentioned that Alice, who lived in Shrewsbury, had been one of the nurses who cared for our sister Olga in her frequent stays at Hahnemann Hospital. Anthony was appreciative of the wonderful care Alice and the other nurses had given Olga. Consequently, they had become good friends. As Barbara told the story:

> Spag was also aware that my mother was an accomplished piano player. He had heard her play many times, especially during the holidays when she entertained the residents at the Shrewsbury Nursing Home, where Spag visited regularly.
>
> In later years, Spag became concerned when he learned that Mother had to part with her piano. She and my father had moved into housing quarters for the elderly, and there was not enough room for a piano. Spag called Mother on the phone and said, "Alice, I have made an appointment for you at the Worcester Piano Store. Mr. McCrohan, a salesman there, is expecting you. Go in and choose a piano for the recreation room in your housing facility."
>
> When Mother arrived at the store, Mr. McCrohan greeted her and told her that Spag was on the phone waiting to talk with her.
>
> "You can choose any piano that you want, Alice, but you might think about having a player piano, one that the other residents can play when you are not in the recreation room. If you do choose a player piano, Alice, do me a favor and select a hundred music rolls, too."
>
> Mother was delighted! She chose a player piano and the music rolls. They were a source of much pleasure to all the residents in the recreation room.

When I mentioned this story to Anthony, his response was, "What player piano?"

"The one you bought for Alice's recreation room," I replied.

He seemed puzzled. "I did?"

"Yes, don't you remember?"

"Must be if you say so," was his reply. That was the way it was with anything that Anthony did. His happiness was in the sharing and doing for others then and there, in the moment. Beyond that, he never gave it another thought.

The Rotary Club

"Spag was a dedicated Rotarian," recalled the Reverend Leslie Johnson. "He attended meetings faithfully. Every year, he held the annual cookout at this home for the Rotary Club and guests. Spag would hire a band. He and Olive loved to dance, and they would encourage others to join them in dancing on the parking lot in front of their home."

The Rotary Pancake Breakfast was one of Anthony's favorite times. Arthur Dobson, also a Rotarian, marveled, "He probably sold 500 tickets, and he furnished most of the raffle prizes." In the weeks prior to the breakfast, Anthony kept his pockets stuffed with tickets. Each morning he would replenish his supply from the pile stacked on his desk. He peddled his tickets every chance he had.

But for Anthony, flipping the pancakes was the most fun. Rev. Johnson wrote, "I was working at the counter while Spag was flipping pancakes on the grill behind me. He was thoroughly enjoying it. His joy was contagious!"

Rev. Johnson said that he had heard stories of Spag's generosity, and in 1987, he personally experienced it after having just returned home from the hospital after surgery:

> Spag called and asked, "Would it be convenient for me to stop by for a visit?" I assured him that it would indeed. He came to the door. Then he went back to his car and returned with two boxes of goodies; delicious fruit, a large selection of cheeses, maple

Anthony flipping pancakes for Rotary Breakfast.

syrup, Hershey candy kisses, and my favorite cookies. His generosity was beyond comprehension.

Surprises

Anthony's giving extended from large, magnanimous gestures to simple little pleasures. Often he would give just to enjoy people's happy,
surprised reactions. "I love to see the expressions on their faces," he
used to say. "Surprises make life exciting."

He delighted in creating excitement, and often acted on impulse.
To produce a happy surprise, Anthony might thrust a bunch of roses at
someone he happened to meet while walking by a bin of flowers in the
Garden Shop. Other times, he might hand someone a can of peanuts.
Some people found money in their palms when they stopped to shake
hands with Anthony as he walked the store.

Stories about Anthony's spontaneity and his joy in giving are
numerous. One such account came from Sophie Petrakis, proprietor of
the Owl Tobacco & Candy Shop in downtown Worcester, who
recalled:

> He used to stop in regularly to purchase boxes
> of Hebert candy. He and I usually talked shop while
> I wrapped up a half-dozen boxes for him. He was
> always interested in the other people who happened
> to be in the store. When senior citizens came in,
> Anthony would purchase several extra boxes of
> chocolates and present one to each person. The sur-
> prised looks and then the smiles on their happy faces
> were heartwarming.

Passing out boxes of chocolates unexpectedly to others was one of
the many ways that Anthony had fun. Mary Borgatti was with
Anthony one day while he indulged in this source of enjoyment. She
had driven him to Worcester for a dentist appointment. Following the
appointment, she and Anthony stopped to make several purchases at
the Owl Shop, from which Anthony emerged carrying a large bag of
Hebert chocolates.

Mary remembered the experience well:

> As we continued towards the City Hall, a woman walking in our direction recognized Anthony. She stopped to greet him and introduce herself. While Anthony was returning the greeting, he reached into his bag and handed her a box of chocolates.
>
> "Enjoy," he said. The woman, surprised at first, became ecstatic and then thanked him profusely.
>
> As we walked on, I said, "Anthony, that woman was so elated. She probably feels lucky to have bumped into you today."
>
> "No," he replied without hesitating, "she wasn't the lucky one. I was; I had the pleasure of seeing the happy look on her face when I handed her the candy."
>
> We proceeded on to the City Hall plaza, where several people were waiting at a bus stop. Once there, Anthony presented each person with a box of chocolates and said, "Enjoy!"
>
> He certainly knew how to make a trip to the dentist a pleasurable experience.

The Eight Clergymen

In addition to responding to individual and family needs, Anthony was available for any clergy—rabbis, ministers, nuns, and priests—as well as representatives of clubs and organizations engaged in charitable endeavors. Arthur Dobson was frequently asked to help:

> Over the years, Spag would call me and ask, "Arthur, will you come in early Sunday morning and give me a hand? People are coming in for children's presents." Each group came at a scheduled time and had the store to themselves—a quiet and private time to shop. As one group left, another arrived.

When each group came in, Spag would greet them, thank them for coming, and say "Select anything you want in the store." I would give each person a four-wheeler cart. Quite often, Spag would go with the group and help them by suggesting toys, clothing, games—invariably the more costly items. The more they took, the happier he was. When they had filled their carts to capacity, I helped them to pack their gifts into empty cartons and load them into their station wagons or trucks.

When an unscheduled group called at the last minute for "help," Anthony would sometimes ask a store employee to give a hand. Lori Jardarian, a store manager, was working late at the store one evening when Anthony called. As Lori recalled it:

Spag called to say that he would be coming later that evening with eight clergymen. He then asked if somebody would be there. I offered to stay and help. At 10:30 p.m., Spag and the clergymen arrived. He gave each person a cart. Then, with the clergymen pushing their carts behind him, Spag went from aisle to aisle, stopping along the way to suggest items that he thought they could use. He'd hold up a toaster oven, and say, "What do you think of this?" Pointing to another item, he would say, "How about a few of these?" Toys, clothing, appliances, plumbing equipment, they had their pick. "Whatever might fit," he would say. He went non-stop until each cart was piled high with gifts. I stood in absolute awe, watching him give to his heart's content. He couldn't have been happier doing it. There had to be hundreds of dollars of merchandise in each cart!

I asked Spag, "Shall I make out record slips?"

"Nope, nope! No slips," he replied. "Everything's taken care of. We're all set." No records were ever kept, and this was only the first of the hundreds of similar shopping sprees in which I was involved. Spag's answer was always the same when asked if record slips were to be made. "We're all set," he would say. Spag was just happy that he could share.

"We kept no record of these donations, not even for a tax write-off," Lori added. "And, boy, did they foul up our inventory records!"

Vinnie Mastro and Lori Jardarian on the job.

Reading to Children

Anthony enjoyed sharing his love of books with children; he took special delight in going to schools to read to them and talk with them, and he treasured the many letters children wrote to thank him for his visits. Following is a sampling of the letters I found in his box of mementos.

> Thank you very much for visiting us. You are funny. I like the stories you told. I go to SPAG'S all the time. It is usually crowded. I bet you like that when it happens, huh? $$$ I am the one who drew the bird on your card. I am a good bird drawer. It must have been exciting when you went on all those trips.
> —Tabatha LaMer

> I like the funny poems you told us. It was real cool to have you come and read for Community Reading Day. Thanks for the signature. I'll never lose the signature, only if my mom throws it in the waste basket.
> —Brian Merchant

> Thank you very much for the cookies and ice cream. They were really good! I also want to thank you for coming to our musical "When the Hippo Crashed the Dance." I also want to thank you for coming to our class on Community Reading Day. If you never came, none of this would have ever happened.
> —Juliet Muzere

The tomato plants Anthony brought to a class evoked some interesting letters:

Thank you for bringing my teacher those tomato plants for our class. They are not dead yet. All the
kids got to plant a couple or one. I really like tomatoes. They're my favorite vegetable.
—Lora Carreau

I didn't know that tomato plants were so interesting. I like the mulch pile in the garden. It is
loaded with worms.
—Your friend, Dane

One student was quick to pick up on one of Anthony's experiences with apartheid:

Thank you so much for coming to read funny
poems. You had a lot of neat things about all your
trips that you told us…. When you went to South
Africa, that was very mean when the person told you
to go in the white people's door. I love your store and
I go there a lot.
—Elizabeth Favulli

Somehow the students found out that Anthony had a birthday
coming up. One drew a picture of herself and added the following
greeting:

HOPE YOUR BIRTHDAY DOESN'T LEAP
BY!!! My name is Jesse. I love your store. The prices
are great! Happy birthday.
—Your friend, Jessica Motyl-szary
(My last name is Polish.)

Rainbows, smiling faces, and a drawing of a large trailer truck
bearing the SPAG'S logo decorated Melissa Rhim's card. She wrote:

Your store is awesome. It's so big! Fifteen ele-
phants can come in. I'm glad my family shops there
because it's so clean, and the products are so neat,
especially the toys! Happy Birthday!
> —Your friend, Melissa

Work for Young People

Anthony loved to talk with young people, and he was always happy to
help them achieve their goals. He also liked to encourage the work
ethic. High school kids were often found working around the house,
planting or weeding in the flower gardens, and cleaning the swimming
pool. Many area college students could be assured of part-time and
summer jobs at SPAG'S. Olive and Anthony were also responsive to
those students who needed help with tuition fees. So it wasn't surprising to learn that Anthony had assisted a young high school student,
who was interested in space science and astronomy.

Mrs. Helen May, an earth science teacher at Worcester North
High School, wrote to tell me about Diep Vu, a Vietnamese student.
Noting Diep's serious interest in becoming an astronaut, Mrs. May
made arrangements for him to attend a "Space Camp" in Huntington,
Alabama, along with several other students from Plymouth,
Massachusetts. Mrs. May wrote, "There was a fee for attending the
camp and the privilege of wearing a version of astronaut clothing. The
camp offered a simulation of space travel, from weightlessness to eating food prepared for a gravity-free environment, etc."

To obtain funds for Diep's expenses, Mrs. May contacted several
possible sources, but was unsuccessful—until Mr. Bouley, the principal,
suggested that Diep write a letter to Anthony. Mrs. May's letter continues:

Diep wrote a lovely letter to Mr. Spag, and sure
enough, Mr. Spag responded immediately with the
total amount. Consequently, Diep spent a week dur-

ing the Spring vacation at the Space Camp, where he and the other students were given many tasks, like calculating, inventorying, preparing food and cleanup, for which they were graded. At the end of the week, one girl and one boy were chosen for the "Right Stuff" award. Diep won the [the boy's] award, which he accepted humbly. Upon returning home he wrote a gracious letter of thanks to Mr. Spag.

Anthony did not expect to receive expressions of gratitude for anything he did, but he was very pleased to receive letters from young people such as Diep.

Anthony seemed to be there for the Boy Scouts, as well. John F. Knipe, III, of Shrewsbury Troop 227, wrote this note of appreciation:

Thank you very much for your generous donation to my Boy Scout Eagle Project at Shrewsbury's Camp Winnegan. With your donation, I was able to buy all of my supplies for the project. Thanks to you, Shrewsbury now has a camp restored for Boy Scouts, Girl Scouts, and families to enjoy for many years. The camp has nature trails, campsites, and a building which can be used to teach children of all ages about the beauty of nature.

After John Taylor of WXOL-Worcester announced on the air that anyone who had a Spag story or anecdote to share could write to me, the telephone started ringing early that same morning and several letters followed, including this one from a Scout leader:

Our Boy Scout troop wanted to go on a winter camping trip during the February school vacation. We needed camping supplies and equipment, but our troop finances were limited.

On learning of our need, Spag invited my whole troop, all 50 of us, to come to the store in the evening after the store was closed.

It was like Christmas in February! He furnished

us with sleeping bags, stoves, mess kits, and other equipment needed for our winter camp-out.

There When Needed

Anthony seemed to have a network of "scouts" who let him know when someone was in need. Sophie Petrakis told me about Anthony's response when she contacted him about the plight of a mother and her child who had been paralyzed in an accident:

> I called Spag one evening to enlist his aid. I had read in the newspaper about a woman who needed $2,100 to build a ramp and install bath facilities in her home so that she could care for her invalid son when he returned home from the hospital.
>
> When Spag answered the phone, I realized, from the gaiety in the background, that a party was in progress. I suggested that I should call him at a more opportune time. Spag graciously assured me that he was "happy to hear from me." After I explained my mission, his immediate response was, "There'll be a check in the mail tomorrow."
>
> Not only was there a check in the mail the next day, but also a beautiful letter thanking me and admiring my concern for others.

Irja Hofschire, who sat on the board of trustees for the Rehabilitation Center of Worcester in its infancy, shared the following with me:

> Spag probably learned about the Center and its need for financial support through Dr. Edie Hunter, a physician in Shrewsbury who referred many patients to us for therapy. I was impressed not only by his generous offer to "pay the rent" for several years, but also by the fact that he insisted that we "keep it quiet." I didn't know that there were those kinds of people still around.

While Kay M. Marquet was Executive Director of Worcester Community Foundation, Anthony made significant contributions to the non-profit programs sponsored by the Foundation. "When I think about the ideal community donor, there was no better example than Spag," said Kay. "He truly exemplified the spirit of sharing and volunteerism."

Irma Trinder would agree. She was active in the St. Anne's Women's League at the time they were holding card parties to raise funds. Anthony always insisted on providing the prizes. Irma noted, "If Spag happened to read in the church bulletin that we were going to hold a card party, he would call me and say, 'When are you coming for prizes?' When I went to get them, I often had to tell him, 'That's enough! That's enough!' He was so generous."

Helen M. Knight talked about Anthony's "human caring and thoughtfulness. He invited the ladies of the Women's Club to come to the store after hours so that we could avail ourselves of gifts for Christmas baskets to be given to the less fortunate. The important part was that he did not donate 'leftovers.' We had anything in the store." Anthony also provided personal support to Helen after her husband died. "One can be friends, but the 'second mile' is not often taken," said Helen. "Spag always considered the feelings of others."

People went out of their way to tell me about the many times Anthony had helped them over a difficult period in their lives. "Karen" was one of them.[1]

"He was there for us," Karen said almost guardedly. She was expressing her gratitude for the help that Anthony had provided after she and her family had endured a terrible tragedy that had been followed by a great deal of sensational publicity in the newspapers. Karen continued:

> To ward off the curious and to protect the privacy of our family, our doctor advised us to remain in seclusion for a month or more. He told us, "There are only two people you should allow in the house—your parish priest and Spag." We followed our doctor's advice, and kept the door locked to all others.
>
> Spag came every day. Every single day, Spag came. Of course, he never came empty-handed. He

---

[1] The name of the person has been changed to protect her privacy. I admire Karen, and deeply appreciate her willingness to tell her story.

always brought bread, jelly, cheese, and other goodies, a box full, always something. He would ask, "Now, can I get you anything? Do you need something? Do you need to go anywhere?" If we did need to go somewhere, he would drive us wherever we had to go.

Spag was sitting at the right hand of God doing for our whole family.

Anthony's heart went out to anyone in need, in pain, or suffering in any way. This included people he had never met. Connie Hubbard of Westford, MA, wrote to convey her appreciation for the support and comfort he had extended to her and her husband:

I must start by saying, I have not had the privilege or honor of meeting Anthony (endearingly known as "Spag") personally. Most of our association was by telephone. Anthony truly has enriched the lives of both my husband, Bill, (now deceased) and myself with his loving, caring, and sincere interest in our lives, our health, and handicaps.

Anthony originally called us in response to a letter I wrote requesting information about accessibility to the SPAG store by wheelchair. I wrote to tell him I was handicapped with muscular dystrophy and missed being able to shop in my "Most Favorite Store"—because of crowds and stock.

He called to let me know that I could shop (in my wheelchair) anytime, and even before the store actually opened for more convenience. His thoughtfulness and concern was overwhelming, and left its mark on both my husband and myself.

A few months later (without any acknowledgement beforehand), Anthony sent a personal driver to our home with a gift of Florida oranges and coffee. Something I will never forget, as this gift of Love and Kindness came at a time when both my dearest Bill and I needed a thoughtful good deed and a HUG of Love—as Bill had been diagnosed with prostate cancer and had been hospitalized. He was recuperating at home from the surgery.

Once again, I sent a note of thanks to Anthony for his wonderful and uplifting kind deed, and told him how grateful we were for his generous gift of love. He, in turn, answered my note with another lengthy, most caring, informative, telephone call—giving us so much of his valuable time. He was so concerned about Bill's health. He gave so much of himself to us that day, sharing his life experiences trying so hard to help us through our trying time.

He talked about his childhood (humble beginnings) and the store. Then with his heart full of Love, and Grief, he talked about his dear, devoted wife (his heart-break at losing her), about her full life, and about his children and grandchildren with SO MUCH PRIDE!!! What a proud and loving husband and Dad!

He also talked to us about his own illnesses and how he searched for the best doctors for his bladder problems, etc. All this personal information to help us cope with our problems. He gave us the name of a personal doctor friend who also has prostate cancer and does much research of the same. He later sent us a newspaper clipping regarding this doctor's research and the new drugs being tested.

Anthony's sharing of himself, all this personal information helped us realize we were not alone with our struggles. Anthony (Spag) is by far "1" in a Billion! A very special man with a heart so Big, only God knows of all the good he has done for his fellow-man, and always anonymously.

Mrs. Blute's Story

During a visit with my friend, Anne Marie Blute, our conversation turned to Anthony and the many stories I had received about him. "I have a story, too, Elsa," said Anne Marie.

"You do!" I replied.

"Yes, about Susan and Leonard."[2] She continued:

> Susan's husband held a high-profile position until he unexpectedly lost his job during a corporate merger. Discouraged, with no job offer in sight, Leonard suffered a mental collapse requiring lengthy hospitalization.
>
> When Leonard returned home, he was still nervous and insecure. Missing his job, he clung closely to Susan. He was constantly at her heels, following her from room to room. If she moved from the sink to the stove, he would move with her. With no solution in sight, Susan was about to climb the walls.
>
> Somehow, Anthony learned about Susan's situation [from one of his scouts, no doubt]. He did not know the family, but he wasted no time in calling. When Susan answered, Anthony said, "I need a hand to help with cars in the parking lot. I was thinking that your husband might like to give it a try...say, a couple hours a day...a couple days a week."
>
> A few days later, equipped with warm and appropriate clothing supplied by the store, Leonard reentered the employment ranks, directing traffic in the parking lot at SPAG's. The "couple days a week" were extended, and eventually Anthony gave Leonard an indoor job, one that lasted until his retirement.

Later, in talking with Vinnie Mastro, I learned that Leonard had also become more self-confident with each day. Vinnie added, "He was very knowledgeable about plumbing, and he became a valuable employee."

---

[2] To protect the privacy of the individuals involved, names have been changed.

The Friend

Anthony related to people of all ages, and his circle of friends continued to expand with each year. One of his closest friends was Father Bernard Gilgun of St. Anne's Church, who has done so much for those in need and who has followed his religious convictions into arenas of conflict. I asked Father Gilgun if he would like to write something about his friendship with Anthony; he sent me the following letter:

Spag deserves a beautiful book. I have known him for over forty years, and right from the beginning, I realized that he was loved, respected, and admired by most of Shrewsbury. Many years later, when I spoke at the Centrum in Worcester on the anniversary of the store, I saw at a glance the whole scope of his influence and the reason for it. The fact that his managers, salesmen, clerks, and countless friends were with him for a half-century and more is an indication of the love and loyalty he inspired in those who worked for him or came to know him. He inspired loyalty because he prized loyalty above all else. He lived it, and he proved it to me personally.

Father Bernard Gilgun at the 50th anniversary of the store.

During my first eight years in Shrewsbury, as a young, newly-ordained priest, I made many friends. I was very popular. But when a new assignment from the bishop put me in a Worcester parish with many poor black families (in the early sixties when the Civil Rights struggle was on), things began to change. My support for the cause of justice and truth brought some nasty letters and dirty looks from some former friends. And then, the few friends I had left also seemed to disappear when I, for the sake of the Gospel, said "No" to the War in Vietnam.

I was distressed, discouraged, and worried. I'll never forget how low I felt that Sunday morning when Spag came into the sacristy at St. Anne's in Shrewsbury. He slipped into my hand a few bills for the House for the Homeless I had in Hubbardston, then he was strangely quiet.

I began to tell him my troubles. Sort of a litany about those who were giving me a hard time. It got to him. It hurt him. He was angry. He loudly interrupted me.

"What the hell do you care what anybody says or thinks? You have your work from God to do. If I let them bother me, I'd be out of business long ago."

What a lift he gave me. What a friend! Loyal and true to the end. Thanks, Anthony.

Buffets and Books

Starting back in 1944, several years before the store was showing much of a profit, Anthony started to provide refreshments for the town's bereaved. Whenever a Shrewsbury resident died, Anthony arranged with a caterer to have a lunch delivered to the family's home. A great many families in the town of Shrewsbury have, at some time over the last 50 years, received this nourishing and uplifting gesture.

Anthony's files contain hundreds of grateful letters he received throughout the years from the bereaved families he had helped. Typical was the following letter from Jeannette Couillard:

> Please accept our sincere thanks for the buffet meal which you provided on the occasion of my dad's funeral. Your generosity is legend. We are among the lucky ones to have experienced the reality behind the legend. In a country where cutthroats

and ruthless people command the attention of the media, you are a breath of fresh air.

Keep up the good works. Your reward will be great in heaven.

As a memorial, Anthony also donated a book that reflected the deceased's interests to the Shrewsbury Town Library.[3] In 1956, he and Olive started a library trust fund for the acquisition of books and materials; eventually the fund amounted to more than $250,000. They also purchased a bookmobile for Shrewsbury, saying, "If it has kept just one child out of trouble by giving him the incentive to read, it has been worthwhile." In Anthony's files are numerous letters from townspeople who used the bookmobile, including those who were confined to their homes because of illness, expressing their appreciation for having access to the great collection of books at the library.

Help in Devastating Times

Anthony was always happy to help others at any time. When asked to donate to a charitable organization, you would think they had just invited him to a party. But he was particularly concerned and responsive whenever tragedy struck a family or community. In 1953, when a tornado ravaged a broad path through Worcester County, Anthony and Olive, accompanied by Glenn and Ann Anderson, rode through the devastated area to determine what needed to be done and ways in which they could help.

"The next day," said Errol Melander, "Spag gave tools, tarpaper, and nails to those who came for materials to repair the damage to their homes, and Spag himself helped the people load the stuff into their cars and trucks."

Mary Johnson told us about a friend of hers who lived in Worcester:

He had lost his home in a fire. The family lost everything. This man went to Spag and told him his story. Spag furnished the whole family with clothes. Spag took the man at his word, having never seen him before.

[3] As of this writing, the family has donated over 7,000 books to the library.

Similarly, Thomas McGrail wrote to tell me about the time he and his family were wakened by their kitten, Patches, to find that their house was on fire. "Just before the house was engulfed in flames" his family escaped with no shoes on their feet and just the clothes on their backs. His letter continues:

> Our neighbor, Mrs. Macatee who worked as a cashier at SPAG'S, told my folks to go down to the store the next Sunday morning—someone would meet us at the front door.
>
> That morning my parents, my brothers and sister, and I went down to the SPAG'S store. Well, someone did meet us at that door, and to my amazement, as an eight-year old, boy, there stood Mr. "SPAG" himself... wearing his cowboy hat. To me he stood like a giant. He told us to come in and he helped us to pick out socks, shoes, clothes, and whatever else we needed.
>
> To this day and especially around Christmastime, I often think about Mr. Anthony A. "Spag" Borgatti and his kindness and generosity that he showed toward my family and me in our time of need.
>
> Mr. "Spag" talks of values. Well, he taught me a lesson on values that day— something that you can't put a price tag on and one that I will carry always. That is the value of compassion and caring for others, especially those who may be less fortunate than yourself, and not only at Christmastime, but all year long.
>
> On behalf of my family and myself, I thank Mr. Borgatti, for his kindness and generosity.

Pleasure in Doing

Some people have wondered how Anthony could afford to be so generous, especially in the early years, before the business really took off. But whenever anybody questioned the wisdom of his generosity, he would simply reply, "What difference does it make if I lose it all? I started with nothing."

Giving was as natural to Anthony as breathing. I can see him now, flashing his dimpled smile, and I can just hear him saying: "If I want to give the store away, I'll give the store away. And if I should lose it all, they can't take away my memories or the joy I have in giving."

Money Isn't Everything

You gotta catch the brass ring when it's in front of you.
—Anthony

I thought I knew my brother well, yet as I collected stories and information for this book, I became even more aware of his multi-faceted personality and his variety of interests. He led a full life, and he injected fun, excitement, or a strong sense of purpose into whatever he did—as the following stories illustrate.

The Dancer

All the Borgattis had "dancing feet," and Anthony was no exception. He loved to dance; he was light on his feet and had a good sense of rhythm. When there was music, it was hard for him to remain seated, "letting good music go to waste," as he often said. He would jump up at the first opportunity, grab the hand of whomever might be available at the table, and head for the dance floor.

For me, dancing with Anthony was always enjoyable because I knew that he had "seized the moment" and was having a wonderful time. The waltz and fox trot were his specialties, but he danced to all kinds of music, no matter the tempo. Music was music, and he was there to dance. If one was on the floor with Anthony, dancing is what one did.

Occasionally, he would "get fancy" and put in a few extra twirls. Without warning, he would depart from his routine and do whatever popped into his mind. My, oh, my! The contortions we would go through! More than once I thought my right arm had been pulled from its socket. When this happened, I could see his puzzled look as he tried to figure out why our twirling worked sometimes but not others. He had a way of passing it off graciously. We'd get untangled and go on dancing until the music stopped at the end of our set.

Anthony and Elsa dancing.

Sometimes Anthony's love of dancing brought out the mischief in him, which he demonstrated during an important family event. He and Olive planned a post-nuptial party for a pair of newlyweds: their daughter, Jean, and her husband, Donald Morrison.

"Wait'll you see," said Anthony with an amused smile and knowing look on the morning before the party. He obviously had to share his secret with someone, so he glanced over his shoulder, then leaned and whispered in my ear. I giggled. What a surprise he had in store!

That July afternoon was sunny and warm. A breeze gently caressed the family and friends, about 250 of us, who were gathered in the yard on Beverly Road. The guests were standing around and chatting gaily while Jerry Conte and his band set up their instruments. Suddenly, a faintly audible sound of music off in the distance caught our attention. We cocked our ears to listen. It seemed to be coming from the direction of Route 9, a five-minute walk away. As the music became more audible, we heard the distinct sounds of bagpipes.

The guests were puzzled. The sound, which was getting louder by the minute, doubled in volume when the Worcester Kiltie Band—19 men strong in full Scottish regalia—turned the corner and marched briskly onto Beverly Road. They proceeded to the front of the house, and faced the door. As they came to a halt, Anthony, also dressed in Scottish attire, stepped out onto the landing. There he stood, showing off his knobby knees below his pleated plaid skirt and sporran, his tam-o-shanter cocked to the side of his head. His toothy grin seemed broader and his dimples were deeper than usual. He was obviously delighted to the hilt and reveled in the excitement his surprise had created.

All afternoon and into the twilight hours, the festivities continued with an abundance of food, spirits, and both Scottish and Italian music. Guests danced the highland fling and the tarantella. At the party's end, Anthony let out a big sigh of contentment. Whether it was work or play, he certainly enjoyed fanfare and surprises! And all for the love of it.

Anthony in Scottish attire with Mary Borgatti.

The Whistler

Anthony had been a whistler ever since I could remember. Whether he was opening the store, stocking inventory, or making change, he was usually whistling. Anthony whistled the same tune when he was a young boy arranging pyramids of oranges and apples on the counter or making college ices for waiting customers. He also whistled as he swept up the sawdust from the floor of the Emporium, and whistled on his return trolley trip with his pockets jingling.

Jenny Rosiello, a neighbor, could tell the time of day by the sound of his whistling as he passed their homes on his way to and from school. Whistling was Anthony's companion. Even if you could not see him, you could tell when he was near; Anthony was the only one who whistled that unidentifiable tune.

One day when I went looking for him, the sound of his whistle took me to the grove of trees near the pond at his home. There I found him leaning back on a bench under the shade of a flowering crab-apple tree.

Always happy to have company, he invited me to join him on the bench and admire his sea of multicolored tulips. "Your whistling gave you away," I said.

"That's good, Elsa," he replied. "I'm happy to have a few moments to chat with you."

A visit with Anthony in his garden.

—Jim Tivnan

"Why is whistling so much a part of you, Anthony? No one else I know whistles. At least, not the way you do."

He blinked for a moment, as though it had never occurred to him that his whistling was that important. "Well," he said at last. "When I was a kid, it gave me bravado to walk in the dark with just my flashlight, say if I had to go out in the back yard to get something. Then, during the day, whistling kept me company when I walked to the bus or wherever I was headed until I got there. It got to be a habit, I guess. Then with the store, I always liked to whistle so the help would know I was coming, just in case they were doing a little fooling around or had goofed off. What the heck, we're all human."

"There's no question," said Errol Merlander. "The whistle really served a good purpose. When I look back now, I grin when I think of how Spag would come into the store. He had that loud meandering whistle—no particular tune, just a whistle. Whether he knew it or not, it worked very well in breaking up the B.S. sessions and coffee breaks. 'Here he comes,' one would say, and everyone would scurry off and get back to work."

"When we heard Spag's whistle," said Vinnie Mastro, "it made us want to work harder. He was so good to us; we wanted to do our best for him."

The Mad Hatter

From the day Anthony purchased his first ten-gallon hat from Van, the Hatter, he wore it wherever he went, whether he was working or going to a dinner at which he was to receive an award or traveling for either business or pleasure. Inevitably, the hat became an icon for both the store and the man. Dale Fair commented on this:

> In the 1950s, he became a well-known figure in the community due primarily to his talks, newspaper articles and photographs, and people telling their friends about the store. In the store, I often would hear one customer telling another, "See that fellow over there in the cowboy hat? That's Spag." It was usually spoken in an undertone of awe.

"The Mad Hatter."

Hats, hats, more hats!

Anthony's travels took him around the world, and wherever he went—Japan, England, or Hawaii—there was always someone who recognized him by his hat. Jim and I were strolling with Anthony in the Galleria in Milan, Italy, one day when a gentleman walked up to him and said, "Excuse me, sir, aren't you Spag?" Anthony nodded. The man continued, "You wouldn't know me, but I know you by your hat. I've seen you at the trade shows in Chicago and in other places too."

Eventually Anthony started to collect hats—all kinds of hats. His collection ranged from the sublime to the ridiculous. The materials used to make them ran the gamut from the beautiful felt in a Barcelino to straw, silk, denim, plaid, and leather. Someone had even given him a ten-gallon hat made of mink. Some (a fez, a yarmulke, or a derby) he wore with dignity, and others he wore with a grin, choosing colors to match the season, a holiday, or special occasion. He wore a handsome Panama for a summer wedding; a purple one adorned with a cluster of flowers for Easter Sunday; a bright holly-green hat bedecked with Santa, sleigh, and reindeer; an emerald-green for St. Patrick's Day, and, when he felt roguish, a hat decorated with light-bulbs that flashed the word "Spag." How he liked to catch people off-guard with that hat as he stopped for a moment to chat with them!

As Anthony acquired each new hat, he placed it, along with his others, in the family room on a bookcase, credenza, or on a chair in his office or in the laundry room, where he tossed them on the dryer. When people started to give Anthony hats, he ran out of places to put them. To solve the problem posed by his expanding collection, Olive converted a bedroom into a hat closet. She had shelves built in tiers on two sides of the room; Anthony cheerfully stacked his hats, each one in a box marked for easy access.

He wore each of his hats with grace and aplomb, except on one occasion. He and Olive, dressed in caps and gowns, were sitting on the stage at Worcester State Teacher's College among other guests waiting to receive honorary doctorate degrees. Soon after the program started, the mortar board cap on Anthony's head posed a problem. Try as he might, he could not adjust it to his head comfortably. The tassel kept hanging in front of his eyes blocking his vision. Never one to dodge an issue and always up-front in behavior, Anthony nonchalantly took the cap off and placed it on his lap where it remained for the rest of the ceremony. His comment later was, "The son of a bitch of a thing wouldn't stay on. I was getting cockeyed from the tassel which kept jiggling, so I took it off." That hat was, no doubt, added to his collection.

Yet despite his attachment to his hats, on occasion he would part with one without a second thought. Anthony was also willing to part with a hat when requested to do so for a fund-raiser auction. At these events, his ten-gallon hat was a big attraction, especially when autographed. In one auction, Anthony realized that two final bidders were dragging out the bid, so he offered a second hat; both would be autographed. The bidders happily accepted the offer. The final tally was two successful bidders on the hat, double coffers for a charitable cause, and a grateful organization.

The Shopper

Anthony's love of shopping on behalf of SPAG'S did not end there. He was always on the proverbial busman's holiday. While traveling on vacations, he checked out merchandise, prices, the different store setups, and displays. For Anthony, shopping anytime and anywhere was fun, and he was happiest when he found something that was new and unusual. When he did find something he liked, his habit of buying in large quantities prevailed.

Anthony often bought earrings, cuff links, tie clasps, and pleasing little trinkets. He would sometimes buy an item just because he liked it or thought it was novel. Other times he bought "just to have it on hand to give someone when the occasion fits." Rarely did he return from a vacation trip when his bags did not bulge with an assortment of presents.

He did not always have someone in mind when he bought something; it could be for anyone and everyone—family, friends, and even sometimes strangers. In Hawaii, he bought presents to give to the domestic staff on his floor at the hotel. In Quebec, it was the two men on the desk and the outdoor gardeners who received gifts. And so it went, on and on. His "family" was always expanding.

When asked about it, Anthony would say, "I want to give them a little something. You gotta give! You gotta share! What good is it [money] if you don't spread it around?"

When shopping for himself, he inevitably bought hats and neckties. How quickly he could spot an unusual tie on the racks! He never wasted time deliberating, and he seldom bought only one; a half dozen was more likely. Without hesitation, and to the delight of the salesperson, he would nonchalantly say, "Wrap 'em up. I'll take 'em all."

Anthony's collection of ties, at least 750 of them draped on racks in his shoe closet, made a colorful array. Many of them were sassy as well as bright. His passion for bright ties (the brighter the better) was obvious—a little too obvious for some people. But for Anthony, beauty was unquestionably in the eye of the beholder. That was why he consistently chose to wear his silk "Marilyn Monroe" tie instead of the silk Missoni ties that I gave him.

Shopping with Anthony was always fun, especially when he was looking for hats. During a vacation in Bologna, Italy, Jim and I accompanied Anthony on one of his "window-shopping" expeditions. We followed him as he darted into a men's specialty hat shop, and watched him as he walked around the store glancing quickly at the various hat styles, including a collection of fedoras that lined the shelves and counters.

The salesman bowed, smiled and greeted us with a charming, "Bon giorno, cari amici." (Good morning, dear friends.)

It didn't take Anthony long to "zero in" on a display of beautiful fedoras. As he paused briefly to look at them, he lifted up a Barcelino that struck his fancy. The salesman's big smile melted into a disturbing frown, which deepened when Anthony placed the fedora on his head. The clerk spoke firmly: "Per favore, signor, non toccate la merce." (Please, sir, do not handle the merchandise.)

There was no mistaking the message; however, Anthony appeared to be completely unaware of it. He checked the fit in a mirror, slowly placed the hat back on the counter, and tried on a second Barcelino.

The shop keeper waved his hands, shook his head, and stammered vociferously, "Signor! Per favore, non toccate la merce!"

Again Anthony kept a straight face. After he had looked at some other fedoras, he matter-of-factly went back and reached for the two Barcelinos that he had tried on, handed them to the still-harried shopkeeper, and said, "Wrap 'em up, please."

Wow! What a "quick change artist" that shopkeeper was! His smile returned, this time from ear to ear, as he patted Anthony on his back in approval of his fine selection. He then carefully placed the

Barcelinos in two hat boxes, which he tied together with a cord.

We followed Anthony out of the store as he left carrying his purchases. As soon as we rounded the corner from the shop, he chuckled and said, "I knew he was upset, but I also knew I was going to take them."

Anthony liked any and all kinds of shopping. Occasionally he would take a ride up to C&S Wholesale Fruit Company in Worcester, to shop "for the house." There he would load up his station wagon with large quantities of fruits and vegetables: cases of honeydew, a few crates of grapes, cherries, and blueberries—whatever might be available at the time.

When he returned home, he piled the boxes and bags of produce on every available counter space in the laundry room, just inside the back door entrance. The fruit and vegetables Anthony brought home overwhelmed the cook and the housekeeper. "Where do we put it all?" they would exclaim.

Anthony figured that someone or other would be dropping in, and he was usually right. Then he would tell them to "grab some stuff on your way out." That helped solve the storage problem somewhat.

After one of his "food-shopping" excursions, Anthony stopped at my house with two cases of artichokes. They were big and choice, and the season on them is brief—but I was left with 48 artichokes! I was delighted, of course, since they were always a special treat for me, but I was taken aback by the quantity. Anthony caught my look of surprise.

"Oh," he said, dismissing it casually with a wave of his hand, "They were too nice to leave there." Jim and I subsequently spent several hours preparing the artichokes for stuffing; then, during the next several days, we had a feast with our friends. And, no—Anthony did not have a single artichoke. He always said, "They're more bother to eat than they're worth."

In the early fall, Anthony was apt to stop at my home on his way to the Elbe Peach Farm in Northboro. "Why don't you take a ride?" he would suggest.

At the peach orchard, we enjoyed chatting with the folks there, whom we knew well, and tasting the various kinds of peaches. Then Anthony would fill his station wagon with baskets of peaches to give away. What pleasure he derived from a little shopping trip to the peach orchard.

"It's the simple things in life that are fun," he said as we headed back home.

The Gardener

"It's not mine. It doesn't belong to me," Anthony exclaimed as he waved his out-stretched hand in the direction of what he called his "yard," a little park beside his house on Beverly Road. "I am merely its keeper while I am here on this earth," he added.

As "keeper," Anthony had lovingly transformed the wooded area and fishpond into a quiet sanctuary. He had cleared the underbrush and planted grass and a wide assortment of flowers; he loved flowers of all kinds. Close to the house, a magnificent Japanese red maple, which nature seemed to have sculpted for its location, bowed gracefully with several hanging plants of bleeding hearts and begonias. Dozens of other tuberous begonias enjoyed the shade of the maple tree. Tall oaks, majestic pines, azaleas, rhododendrons, and blueberry bushes adorned the grassy slopes that led down to the fishpond, about an acre in size.

—Jim Tivnan

Anthony checking out his tomato plants.

Anthony continued to expand the little park, and as he did, the work increased. He enlisted the help of Diep Phan and his son, Way, who diligently and artistically tended the gardens. According to Way, there were 22 beds of varied flowers. One rose garden held 300 bushes. Thousands of tulips and impatiens dotted the meadows and hills wherever one looked.

Way said, "We were always running up to Marston's and McGoldrick's greenhouses to pick up a load of plants." (McGoldrick's supplied SPAG'S Garden Shop with plants.) Roger Braley, who worked night maintenance at the store, added:

After the store closed in the evenings, Spag came and selected his bulbs very carefully, especially for the garden plots in front of his house. He usually took 500 bulbs at a time, carefully labeling the bags, not only by the contents but also by their height and colors. Spag would say as he made his selections, "I enjoy the way they look. People enjoy them, too."

Fred Van Bourgondien, who was the largest distributor of Dutch bulbs in America, furnished all the tulips carried in the store. He visited Anthony at home one afternoon when the "yard" was in full bloom. As he looked around, Fred told me, "This display of tulips is the largest I have ever seen in this country."

When the tulips and other early plantings waned, flowers in season took their place. Anthony loved his flowers, and he took great joy in sharing them with people who came to see them. I recall one glorious day in early June, when the Shrewsbury Garden Club was meeting at his home.

"It's for everyone's enjoyment," he said. "Anyone who cares to come here is welcome." He was responding to Barbara Greene, who had graciously acknowledged his kindness in extending the use of his "yard" to us. I and other members of the garden club's fund-raising committee were meeting at Anthony's home to plan a tour of some of the gardens in town. On the day of the tour—which included Anthony's garden—the

—Jim Tivnan

Shrewsbury garden club members. Left to right: Shirley Salamy, Barbara Green, Elsa, Marvin Lainer, Anthony.

club members served bagged lunches to the guests sitting at the colorfully-set tables scattered about his "little park."

In addition to his flower gardens, Anthony had a vegetable garden large enough to feed ten families. This was the same garden that Father had tilled and planted when he was younger. It extended from behind our parents' house to the area behind Anthony's house and further.

Sandy spent many long hours working with her father in the gardens. "I used to go and squish bugs for him, a job I hated, but he was there, and I would do it just to be with him," she said. "He grew bushels of tomatoes, zucchini, squash, and other vegetables, much to the dismay of the cook who had to make room for them."

In response to the cook's reaction, Anthony would just say, "Ah, just a little extra to give away. I like to do it for the fun of it."

The Son

Anthony was devoted to our parents, as they were to him. Different as they were from each other, he had gained something from both of them. Like Father, Anthony was short; and also like Father, he developed a portly figure. Both had blue eyes, fair skin, and strong physiques. As a child, however, Anthony had light blond hair, which over the years thinned out and turned honey-colored. Most of the time, his hair had a rumpled look.

Mother was Anthony's barber throughout his high school years. Other boys in their teens would have put up a big fuss if their mothers had cut their hair, but Anthony never complained. He sat patiently on the step-stool while Mother wrapped a towel around his shoulders. With hand-clippers and a little help from a pair of scissors, she trimmed his curly hair—sometimes successfully, sometimes not. I recall seeing Anthony wince silently when the clippers pinched at his scalp. Too many pinches, and the result would be an unevenly-tapered haircut that shrieked home-style rather than a barber's cut. No matter: as Mother put the clippers down and carefully removed the towel covered with hair trimmings, Anthony always said, "Thank you, Ma."

When Anthony's friends saw the uneven "steps" of his haircut, they razzed him by asking, "Spaghetti, which bowl did your mother use today?" His friends told me that he always laughed good-naturedly when they teased him. Apparently their kidding did not faze Anthony in the least; in fact, he may have liked the attention.

After he married, Anthony visited Mother every day, unless he was out of town. He came to share with Mother the day's happenings step-by-step. As he groped and stumbled, he related the most minute details of the business and its progress over the years as he parlayed SPAG'S into the huge operation that it became.

Anthony also showered Mother with gifts throughout the year. When she thanked him and asked, "And what is this for?" he would

—Marvin Richmond

The Borgatti Family. First Row, left to right: Olga, Mother, Father.
Second Row: Anthony, Elsa, and Bobbie Borgatti.

point to her and say, "Ma, any day is the right day to give you something."

Like Mother, Anthony was patient with Father. Pa loved to buy farm gadgets although he wasn't mechanically inclined and probably wouldn't use them. But he was forever cornering Anthony to tell him about yet another piece of small machinery he "needed." No matter what Father asked for, Anthony would buy it for him. Once in a while, though, when the request was rather farfetched and Pa was not in earshot, Anthony would ask us, "What the hell does he want with that?" Then with an amused shrug of his shoulders, he would add, "What's the difference? As long as it makes him happy."

When little anxieties crept into Pa's thinking (one of the scars from his former illness), he would say quietly to Anthony, "I have to see you for just a moment." Anthony patiently talked to Pa, usually for ten or fifteen minutes, and gave him the reassurance he needed to allay his fears. Time did not enter into it, even when Anthony had intended the visit to be a quick one. He applied his motto, "You gotta do it [listen] now when it counts." Then, compassionately, he would add, "I feel sorry that Pa gets that way, poor guy."

But as I look back, I can see where Anthony and Pa were alike in many ways. Both of them had plenty to talk about, and I might add that Father's embellishments, especially vivid when telling a story, couldn't be beat. As I think about Father at the Emporium, surrounded by people and congeniality, I can see where Anthony got both his love of people and his love of fun. He also probably picked up his business skills from Pa; I recall Mother telling me of the high regard in which Father was held by the Worcester community for his acumen and impeccable business principles.

Both Pa and Anthony had huge appetites—to put it mildly! But their zest for food was second only to that of dancing. When the music started at a party, food was forgotten; Father and Anthony were among the first to grab a partner and head for the dance floor.

How true it is that "the apple doesn't fall too far from the tree."

Fun and Relaxation

Anthony had a busy schedule, but unlike Father, he also knew how to relax and be good to himself. He took the time for such enjoyable pursuits as reading, viewing the gorgeous dahlias in his garden, swimming in his pool, flying with Olive, or cross-country skiing. He and Olive were devoted sports fans and attended many games together, especially hockey and baseball. They also often flew to Lake Placid for the bobsled competitions.

When it came to snowmobiling, Anthony was a reckless demon. On one of the few times I rode with him, he took a sharp turn, tipped over, and landed us in a snow bank. We laughed so hard, we couldn't get up.

Anthony found many ways to have fun and to be good to himself, and he never hesitated to indulge in his special pleasures when he felt it was necessary. For instance, stamp collecting was a lifelong hobby of Anthony's. When new issues came out, I would happen upon him at the post office as he stood in line waiting to make a purchase.

As mentioned previously, gardening was a quiet pursuit that helped to keep him going. His secretary, Lee Zolla, noted:

> Like the cats that slept on our desks, Spag knew
> how to relax, no matter how busy he was. On any
> given day, he would just say, "I am taking no calls
> today." That meant that he had decided to either

—Lee Zola

(top) Anthony guest conductor, German band. (middle left) Anthony assisting Richard Salem, pig roast. (above) Anthony with grandchildren. (bottom) Four generations of Borgattis.

visit some old customers and friends—bringing
them boxes of fruit or "goodies," or work in his
flower garden. I might look out the office window
and see him, his sweat band on his head, working in
the soil. I have a photo of him doing just that.

In addition to turning to the soil for revitalization, Anthony
went, as often as his schedule permitted, to the Bancroft Salon in
Worcester for massages; he felt that massages were important to his
well-being. Steven "Tank" Tankinow, the owner of the salon, took
Anthony at a moment's notice, mindful of how busy he was.

Tank said, "I came to know Spag first as a client, then as a friend,
then as a surrogate grandfather." The two of them enjoyed the great
camaraderie that developed between them, and when Anthony
became ill late in his life, Tank visited him faithfully at Beverly Road.

Delegating Responsibility

"How did he find the time to do all the things he did?" was a question
posed to me often whenever Anthony became the subject of conversation. I myself used to marvel at how much he accomplished in a day.
He did so much, yet to watch him you never got the impression that
he was in a hurry.

In addition to the store, he took time for his family, traveled
extensively to attend trade shows, enjoyed vacations, read incessantly,
made countless phone calls, gave talks, threw parties, attended sports
events, read to school children, and went out of his way to keep in
touch with his friends, including employees and tradespeople. He also
worked in the garden and found time for extra indulgences, such as a
massage or a sauna and swim. Even then, he still found the time to
call on people who were ill or needed help.

So how did he do it all? I think that the answer may be that he
was able to delegate responsibility and authority to others. He had
hired a top notch crew, in large part because he used his sixth sense
when interviewing job applicants. He could tell almost at once
whether or not a person applying for work at SPAG'S would "fit." He
also had a knack for recognizing the potential in his employees. Even

during the store's early years, he was quick to recognize a certain young man's talents and capabilities, and knew instinctively that in Vinnie Mastro he would have an efficient and dedicated store manager.

As many of his employees have pointed out, Anthony focused on their successes and honored their accomplishments. They also appreciated that he drew from the ranks when creating new positions or replacing retiring employees. Some employees have told me that "he welcomed our ideas and made us feel important to the success of the store." And, of course, they were. Anthony was fully aware of how much the store's success depended upon his employees and he took advantage of every opportunity to give them their due. As for his own role, he would only say, "I was lucky!" That was my brother—humble to the core.

The net result was that Anthony had a responsive and responsible crew who took care of the "details" at the store, making it possible for him to devote more time to larger issues—and to pursue his hobby of helping others.

Human Frailties

Those who knew Anthony have repeatedly said that he was the kind of person who crosses one's path probably once in a lifetime. While he was indeed a rare individual, there are, after all, no saints among us. We all have shortcomings—my brother included.

Lest I be biased in my story of Anthony, I decided to question those who knew him best. Harold and Edith Noftle were close friends of Anthony's, both socially and in business, so I called Edith, now widowed. I told her that I was looking for stories about my brother's flaws and faults. I explained that I wanted to capture the whole person, and added that I regretted Harold's absence because no one knew Anthony better than Harold.

Edith quickly replied, "You would never have gotten it from Harold. All he ever did was sing Anthony's praises, especially after one of his weekly visits. As you know, Harold loved him like a brother."

I also searched through past memories for times when Anthony and I might have argued or disagreed. After all, siblings rarely have perfect, peaceful relationships. However, I can truly say that, aside from a few episodes in our childhood and teen years, we got along very well. Anthony rarely, if ever, displayed anger toward me. However, he did express disappointment in me when I occasionally refused his lavish gifts, like the time he wanted to give me 36 five-piece place settings of china— 180 pieces in all! Where could I put them? Six place settings would have been more than adequate; I wound up with a service for twelve.

I guess Anthony's lack of anger was due to the fact that he just did not have an ego problem. He didn't take things personally, nor did he harbor grudges against anyone. Whenever anyone asked him if he were angry with a person who had given him a hard time, he would say, "Anger consumes you." On occasion, however, employees did hear him blast off. If a clerk at the store did not respond to his request promptly, he would let that person know about his disappointment in unmistakable terms. He kept his composure, but he aggressively pursued the matter.

Once I was walking with him through the store when he noticed that a rack of mops and brooms was only half filled, and the clerk in charge was busy socializing. Bristling with annoyance, he turned to the clerk and said, "I just came from the warehouse where I saw piles of mops in stock. I see we are all out of Sla-dust. Goddamn it! Our customers don't go to the warehouse; they buy what they see on the shelves. They can't buy it if it isn't there. Will you see to it that someone hustles up to the warehouse and gets this shelf filled?" The clerk took off in a hurry to the nearest phone.

Some situations at the store could only be corrected if Anthony displayed firmness. Paul Zolla recalled one such occasion:

> I remember one time Spag was making one of his "walk-throughs." When he came through my aisle, he stopped. I was marking some merchandise. There were a couple of empty boxes from the stock I was pricing lying on the floor. He noticed them. "Hey, you handsome fella! You want to take care of those boxes for me?" he asked. "Sure, Spag," I replied, "as soon as I finish marking these." His tone changed immediately as he said, "No, why don't you do it right now?" I did. He made his point calmly and effectively. There was never any question as to

who was in charge at SPAG'S.

For the most part, it was not in Anthony's makeup to have ill feelings toward anyone. "Everyone has a reason for the way they behave and for what they do," he would say. When things didn't go the way he wanted, he would just shrug his shoulders and say, "Sometimes, the worst thing that could happen to you turns out to be the best thing that could have happened."

Like all people, Anthony had some bad habits. Among other things, he ate far too much ice cream and other desserts, and he worked such long hours that he frequently exerted himself beyond his limitations, drawing upon energies that he often did not have at the end of a full day. When he was cautioned about this and told he should slow down, he would say, "I'm doing what I want to do. What the heck! I want to die with my boots on."

Anthony had another bad habit which drove me and others up the wall. He thought absolutely nothing of keeping the world waiting. Time meant nothing to him. An appointment meant "as soon as I can make it." He could have an office full of people waiting to see him, yet he was capable of casually reaching for his hat and jacket and saying to everyone, "I'll be back in a couple of minutes." Then off he would go, perhaps to a wake, or a "quick run" to Dr. Maker, the vet, with one of the dogs. Tradesmen who came to the office were accustomed to lengthy waits, sometimes by the hour. He went along at his own pace and did what he had to do.

Anthony could also fall asleep at a moment's notice. When fatigue overcame him, he would quietly disappear from the office for a half hour nap in the family room. Meanwhile, everyone waited. When he returned, he was ready to resume work. Salespeople and visitors surely had to have patience when they called on Anthony!

His family had to be patient, too. When Anthony and Olive joined us to go out for an evening, Jim usually did the driving, which meant that we would go to Beverly Road to pick them up. Rest assured that our arrival was merely Anthony's signal to "change my shirt" or to make a "couple quick calls"—even though there was no such thing as a "quick call" as far as Anthony was concerned. We would wait in the car with the motor running, ever hopeful of only a few minutes' delay. Finally, he would appear, unhurried and seemingly unconcerned about keeping us waiting. In response to my grumbling or my exasperated sighs, he would say, "Take it easy. Take it easy!" Then he would change the subject and start talking about what had gone on in his day.

Out for an evening—Anthony and Jim.

I loved my brother, but without hesitation, I can tell you that Anthony's profanity was his worst habit. It was never music to my ears, nor to those of many others. I chided him for it often, and asked him why a man of his stature would resort to such language. I would say, "It's demeaning to you, Anthony. It perplexes me, and it is so unnecessary. Why do you speak this way?" His answer was usually the same: "Oh, it just comes out"—which I did not accept, because I knew that he didn't swear when he talked to children. I really think that he swore sometimes just to see people squirm, often for his own amusement. He did have a contrary streak; he admitted it. He once said, "Sometimes, I like to throw people a curve by saying just the opposite of what they expect. You know, to have a little fun. The expressions on their faces are priceless!"

Anthony had another habit that might not have met with everyone's approval; he seemed to have a great fascination for women's bosoms. When an amply-endowed woman came into sight, he would roll his eyes, grin ear-to-ear, and whisper a muffled "Wow!" Those around him would exchange knowing glances and look away. But one day, when he didn't know that a friend and I were standing nearby, we could see that he didn't particularly notice a buxom woman who had just passed by him. That was when I realized that he put on that act just to be funny and get a reaction from others.

Anthony was well aware of his own mistakes and shortcomings. And, according to a note I found in his files, there were times when he was not easy on himself:

> A man came to me. He looked seedy. I felt that he was going to ask for a hand-out. But he told me that he "took the bus from Marlboro to come up to buy two Bisell carpet sweepers." He peeled off the

money from a roll that would choke a horse.

And then there was the time a man wanted to talk to me. I felt he was going to complain, but he came in to tell me that he had visited stores all over the United States, and we topped them all. I was prejudiced, but I kept still.

He had entitled this note "Secret Prejudices."

The Cadillac Story

No book on Anthony would be complete without the "Cadillac" story. The original circulated around town, and as it was passed on, with each telling, it became more dramatic. Eventually a single Cadillac had become three Cadillacs. When I told Anthony about the three variants of the story I had heard, he chuckled and admitted that he also had heard several versions. "Well, what *did* happen?" I asked.

"Well," he said, "I had been waiting for the arrival of the new models of Cadillacs [in Worcester]. When I heard that they were in, I drove to the agency on Shrewsbury Street, intending to get one that day."

I might add that Anthony was wearing his usual chinos. They were neat, but not custom-cut by any means. Atop his head, as usual, was his wide-brimmed, ten-gallon hat. He continued:

> I went into the showroom. One salesman was busy with a customer, and two others were in a deep conversation at a desk. After the other prospective customer left, the first salesman joined the other two at the desk.
>
> In the meantime, I looked at the several Caddies on the floor, as one would do, all around the outside. Then I opened the door and took a look inside. I had decided to buy the car. I waited about fifteen minutes for a salesman to come and take my order. No one came, so I left.
>
> As I said, I had decided earlier that I wanted to get a Caddie that day, not some other day. I like to get

done what I set out to do, because tomorrow might be too late. So I drove into Boston and right over to the Fuller Cadillac Agency on Commonwealth Avenue and went into the showroom.

This time the reception was a little different. A salesman promptly came toward me, and, after exchanging greetings, he asked me if he could be of assistance.

"Yes," I replied. "I came in to buy a car." We meandered over to the new models. After a quick look, I paused to ask a couple of questions about one car in particular. At this point, the salesman held out a set of keys, saying, "Try it. Take it for a spin around the block and get the feel of it for yourself." This I did. On returning with the car, I handed the keys back to the salesman and said, "I'll take it, and I want to pay cash."

When the paperwork on the transaction was completed, the salesman said, "You have a Cadillac dealer in Worcester. Why didn't you buy it there?" I told him what had happened earlier in the afternoon.

I heard later that, after I left the Boston Cadillac showroom, the salesman lost no time calling Cadillac in Worcester. He said, "Say, can you send me down more of those guys with a big hat, wearing khaki trousers that you don't want to bother with? I'll take any you want to send. I don't mind telling you that was the fastest cash deal that ever came my way."

From that time on, however, Anthony bought his Cadillacs in Worcester. He just was not vindictive, and he was a firm believer in buying locally.

The Success

When Anthony was just starting his business, he frequently reminded his friends that he was "going to be a millionaire someday." He would,

in fact, emphasize it often, making this announcement periodically as if to convince himself.

I remember him stopping in one day on his daily visit to Mother. After his hello and his routine question—"Do you need anything, Ma?"—the talk as usual turned to the store. Enthusiastically, he recounted the day's activity. "Business was pooping along," he said, "I'm seeing new faces and also faces of people who have been in before. Ya know, Ma," he added, pointing his finger at her, "I'm going to be a millionaire someday. I'm going to make a million dollars, and when I do, you're going to be the first one to know it."

Mother nodded in acknowledgment. "Good, Anthony. I know you will have a big business. But, remember," she said softly, "money isn't everything. Take time to have fun as you go along the way. Make sure you take vacations with your family. Time has a way of passing. Years go by."

For Anthony, it did take time and hard work. Then after several years of determination, imagination, and thousands of loyal customers, that day did arrive.

The scene is vivid in my mind. One day in the spring of 1954, we heard his whistle as he came down the path, which ran from the back door of his house to our parents' back door. His daily visits brought sunshine to Mother's face, no matter how cloudy the day. Then we heard his footsteps as he crossed the porch and entered. After his cheery "Hello," he asked Mother if she needed anything. Then in a pleased but casual tone, he said, "Ma, I came over to tell you that I found out today that I am a millionaire."

Returning his pleased look, Mother replied: "That's wonderful, Anthony." She paused a moment, and then added, "And now that you are a millionaire, tell me, Anthony, what is it you have learned?"

Anthony looked intently into her eyes and said in all humility, "Ma, I already found out that I don't have to have a million dollars to be happy. All that is necessary is to have enough for what you need and a little more to do what you might want to do. And beyond that, money doesn't mean a thing."

Then Mother, in her serenity, answered, "Good Anthony. I see you have learned your lesson well."

And indeed, he had learned his lesson well. He knew what was important, as reporter Nancy Sheehan pointed out when she quoted

Anthony's friend, Ernie Tosi, in an article:

> He could have had a castle. He could have had a
> yacht. He could have had homes in various places. But
> he lived very commonly. There is a swimming pool
> there. That was his only concession to wealth… [2]

But "wealth," as far as Anthony was concerned, had nothing to do with material things. His wealth lay in having family, friends—and the opportunities to help others.

The Isaiah Thomas Award

Throughout his lifetime, Anthony received many awards from various organizations; each time he was singled out for a special honor, he accepted it graciously. Underneath, however, he was deeply moved— sometimes almost to tears. One such time occurred when he received the Isaiah Thomas Award[3], which the Worcester Area Advertising Club bestowed upon him in 1975. The Evening Gazette published an account of the ceremony, from which I gleaned the following:

In his welcoming speech, Robert C. Ballantine, then president of the club, spoke about Anthony as one "who symbolizes the ultimate in distinguished and unselfish service to his community." He was followed by the evening's main speaker, Joseph T. Benedict, president of First Federal Savings & Loan Association. Mr. Benedict called Anthony "imaginative and self-disciplined," then added, "When these traits are controlled by standards of integrity, which marked all of Spag's dealings, and are guided by compassion for others, life becomes a true instrument for good. For such a life, we honor Spag tonight…"

After receiving the miniature printing press that symbolized the award, Anthony addressed the 800 guests: "You people overwhelm me. I don't know what I did to deserve this…" He finished by saying, "I'm prouder than hell to have you people as my friends. My heart's just bursting. I can't say too much more because it's getting to me." He sat down to a thundering ovation.

Anthony may have had his rough edges, but to those who knew him well, he was a gem.

---

[2] Nancy Sheehan, *Telegram and Gazette*, February 25, 1996.
[3] Isaiah Thomas (1749–1831) was the publisher of *The Spy*, founder of the Worcester Antiquarian Society (where his printing press is on exhibit), and renowned for his generosity.

Robert Ballantine presenting the Isaiah Thomas Award to Anthony.

Olive and Anthony.

The Final Years

I have no regrets.
—Anthony

When Christmas of 1983 rolled around, employees received the following note with their bonus checks:

> Dear Friends:
>
> Congratulations! You did it again. Teamwork, understanding, and your cooperation made it all possible. The year 1984 is going to be extra exciting. SPAG'S Supply will be celebrating 50 years in business, serving our many friends in the community, as well as those nationwide. We are planning on many Super Spagtacular Sales and celebrations. With your help, it will be a fun-filled and eventful year for all to remember.
>
> Again, thank you for making it possible for us all to share with you.
>
> Merry Christmas to you all and your families. May the New Year bring you and your families good health, happiness and God's blessings.
>
> Sincerely,
> Olive and Spag

The year 1984 would bring blessings for Anthony and Olive, too. To celebrate the store's 50th anniversary, Anthony made plans for daily give-aways throughout the year as a way of expressing his appreciation to his customers. He also planned to give $100 every week to the lucky person whose name was drawn from the entry boxes placed in several sections of the store, as well as a grand give-away prize of $1,000 to be awarded at the end of the year.

While Anthony was making his plans, two of his suppliers, Arthur Dobson of the Charlie Cheddar Cheese Company and Bob Kinchla of Decatur Hopkins Company, decided to take advantage of this opportunity to show their appreciation for all the support they had received from Anthony and Olive through the years. Receiving an enthusiastic response to their idea from other suppliers, Arthur and Bob planned an "appreciation night." Before proceeding, however, Arthur talked over the plan with the two honorees. Olive and Anthony agreed to go along with it as long as the proceeds were donated to the Worcester Chapter of the American Heart Association.

When news of a dinner to honor Anthony and Olive spread, Arthur received an avalanche of requests from other suppliers and friends who wanted to be included. He and Bob soon realized that they would need to rent the Centrum, a large convention hall in Worcester, to accommodate everyone. Aware of the fact that they had no initial funds for a rental fee, they went ahead and booked the side and main hall of the Centrum for September 20, 1984. Three days later, Ed Maher, Chairman of the Centrum Board of Directors, called Arthur with delightful news: "The City of Worcester is donating the use of the Centrum for the Spag testimonial." Mr. Maher went on to explain that this was "in appreciation for Spag's history of service, generosity, and good will to the community (and beyond) for fifty years." When Olive and Anthony learned about this warm gesture, they were overwhelmed.

Arthur and Bob hired the Rogal Company of Newton, MA, a convention service company, to book the orchestra, make arrangements for food service, decorate the Centrum, do the mailings, and manage the records of expenses and collections.

On January 1, 1984, Anthony began his give-aways and the weekly $100 drawings. On July 11, however, he suffered a heart attack and underwent surgery, a quadruple bypass, at Massachusetts General Hospital in Boston. Upon learning about Anthony's operation and some complications that followed it, Arthur and Bob were faced with a decision regarding the dinner. But as Arthur noted, "We both agreed that the good Lord would not dare take our dear friend. We decided to carry on with our plans." True to their prediction, Anthony recovered from the operation and was back on his feet in time for the celebration.

The anniversary party was a memorable one. Jim and I enjoyed the festivities, along with family members and close to 1500 friends who were there to pay tribute to Anthony and Olive. The Master of Ceremonies was Robert C. Achorn, then president and publisher of the *Worcester Telegram and Gazette*. He introduced Bishop Timothy Harrington, who shared an amusing (but no doubt a fictitious) tale about Pope John Paul's arrival in Boston on his North American tour. According to the Bishop, "After kissing the ground at Logan Airport, Pope John Paul rose and whispered to Cardinal Madeiros, 'Where is SPAG'S?'"

After Bishop Harrington's invocation, numerous local dignitaries extended their greetings to Olive and Anthony, including: Joseph Tinsley, Mayor of Worcester; Richard Carney, Shrewsbury Town Manager; Robert Moroney, Chairman of the Shrewsbury Board of Selectman; John D. Hunt, Chairman of the Worcester Chamber of Commerce; and Francis McGrath, City Manager. Mr. McGrath noted that "After awhile, we sometimes take success for granted. SPAG'S is the epitome of American opportunity. It shows what can be done if someone has talent, courage, and just plain goes out there and does it."

Speakers at the dinner included: Alfina "Fi-Fi" Lundgren, a friend; Louis M. Caplan, President of the Central Massachusetts Division of the American Heart Association; Richard C. Steele, retired president and publisher of the *Worcester Telegram* and the *Gazette*; Father Bernard Gilgun; and Joseph E. Sullivan, former president of Swift and Company and retired chairman of Vigoro Corporation. In his remarks, Mr. Sullivan commented upon "Spag's honesty, brilliance, work ethic, straightforwardness, and commitment to family, friends, and employees." After the testimonials, Mr. Achorn presented a check for $45,000—the proceeds from the dinner—to Mr. Caplan, who said, "This is the largest single donation ever received by the Central Massachusetts Division of the American Heart Association."

Mr. Achorn then read messages from Congressman Joseph E. Early, Senator Edward M. Kennedy, and Malcom Baldrige, Secretary of Commerce, and also a scroll from Pope John Paul. After Reverend

Leslie H. Johnson gave the benediction, Arthur Dobson showed a 15-minute videotape depicting the history of SPAG's—a video that he and Bob Kinchla had especially created for the occasion.

When Mr. Achorn eventually introduced Anthony and Olive, the guests greeted them with a tumultuous ovation.

"I'm overwhelmed," said Anthony. He thanked everyone for coming, and added, "I'm alive and well, only because of your prayers, your understanding, and your help." He looked around as he continued, "Old friends, new friends, not everybody is lucky to have so many friends. Life is made up of people. It is they who make everything possible. I am grateful and thankful to always have had the warm hand of a friend."

Anthony concluded his brief comments with a flourish of his arms, saying, "Let's dance! We're here to have fun!" And with that, the Winiker orchestra began to play.

Arthur Dobson later said, "It went just as Bob and I planned. Everyone seemed happy to be there and to be part of the joyful celebration."

1990-1991

Six years after the store's 50th anniversary, Anthony and Olive were looking forward to celebrating the 50th year of their marriage. A party to mark the event was planned for November, 1990. However, their plans became complicated when, in May of that year, Olive underwent surgery for the removal of a malignancy. Unfortunately, the cancer recurred. Despite this, Olive continued her daily activities, and flew the Citation as her energies permitted.

By August, she had accepted the fact that her illness was terminal, and from that day on, Anthony was by her side constantly. Astutely, Olive encouraged Carol, Jean, and Sandy to take their places at the helm of SPAG'S while she was there to share her knowledge of the business with them.

Without any qualms, she also urged her daughters to go ahead with the anniversary celebration, as planned for November 24. On the morning of the party, Olive made an emergency trip to the hospital. In spite of this, she somehow mustered the strength to join her family and friends that evening, even to the point of asking for the microphone so that she could welcome the guests and thank them all for coming. Like the others who were present, I admired her spunk and determination to be there.

The next day, Olive joined the family at Carol and John's home for Thanksgiving dinner. One month later, on December 28, 1990, she passed on. Anthony was grief-stricken.

All during those last few months, in addition to our concern for Olive's deteriorating health, the family had been also deeply concerned about Anthony because he was not well himself; he was facing bladder surgery, which was scheduled for January 6, 1991 at Massachusetts General Hospital in Boston.

On Sunday, the day before his surgery, Jim and I went to Anthony's home to wish him well. He was just hanging up the phone as we entered. He looked up at us and said with a look of satisfaction, "There, I did it!"

—Pat O'Connor

Carol, Anthony, Sandy, and Jean.

"What was that?" I asked.

"I called the girls [Carol, Jean, and Sandy] and told them that early in July they, their husbands, and the children are going to Alaska with me. I told them they were to plan accordingly because I wasn't taking no for an answer. I want them to see the last frontier as it is now, before it changes. I just called Evelyn Rooney [his travel agent friend] and told her my plans and what I wanted to cover."

I marveled to myself, thinking, "That's Anthony, ever positive." With major surgery scheduled for the next day, he was busy focusing on a trip six months down the road.

The operation the next day went well. Anthony's bladder was removed and a urostomy tube was inserted, to which a pouch was attached. He made a remarkable recovery. Jim and I witnessed this for ourselves when we went to visit him in the hospital on Thursday. We arrived at his room just as Dr. Pablo Gomery was coming out. When we asked the doctor how my brother was doing, he shook his head in total disbelief and told us that Anthony had insisted on trying to walk the day before—his second day after the operation. He had not just tried to walk, in fact, he had succeeded, with the help of a nurse on either side and one in back following with a chair. Dr. Gomery added, "He walked again today, shortly before you arrived." He went on to explain that "Ordinarily, following this operation, it takes a patient two days before he is able to turn over in bed with assistance."

At that point, Anthony's nurse told him that we were there; then she came to tell us that we could go in. When we entered the room, Anthony appeared to be sleeping, so we sat quietly beside his bed. We were waiting for him to wake up when, without opening his eyes, he spoke to us. In a weak voice, he called to Jim.

"Jim, what's the forecast? They said something about snow earlier."

"We're supposed to have a storm," Jim answered.

"Get me Vinnie at the store. I want to remind him that there's a pile of shovels in the trailer and to put them out now. Where he's busy, he might not think of it."

That was the way he was! Anthony recuperated fully and did take the family on the trip to Alaska the following summer, as planned. Jim and I also took several trips with Anthony and one of his nurses, Dana Brown. The four of us attended magnificent flower shows in London and in Cincinnati. We also fondly recall a trip to Florida, where we visited with his dear friends, George and Janetta Harvey. Anthony loved to hop into a cart and drive into the grove, where he plucked oranges and sampled to his heart's content.

Our trips became shorter as Anthony's health slowly and steadily declined. Nevertheless, still another challenge lay ahead for my brother.

The Expansion Proposal

Even though Anthony had always experienced good relations with the town of Shrewsbury, not everyone was happy in 1991 when he offered

Anthony in Alaska with three grandchildren: Jeremy and Joshua Travinski, and Cecily Morrison, 1991.

to purchase a small plot of land from the town for the appraisal value of $270,000 and to give an additional gift of $450,000. He had made this offer when he learned that the Worcester Foundation of Biology in Shrewsbury had given the town the first option of buying 19 1/2 acres of prime land on Maple Avenue near the center of town for the sum of $720,000.

During the previous years, the Foundation had allowed the land, which fronted the main thoroughfare in Shrewsbury, to be used as a soccer field and for other recreational purposes. In need of funds to meet their current budget crisis, they offered to sell the land to the town for $720,000. If the land were not purchased by May 31, 1992, the Foundation would make it available to the public. As one might expect, developers were waiting in the wings to purchase this prime property; the 40 houses they could build would bring a tidy profit. The citizens of Shrewsbury were in favor of purchasing the land, but the town coffers had no money for such a purpose, and taxes could not be raised without obtaining an override of Proposition 2 1/2.[1]

When Anthony learned about the Foundation's offer, he saw an opportunity to help the town to purchase the land on Maple Avenue and, at the same time, purchase space for expanding the store. Adjacent to SPAG'S was a parcel of land, 1.3 acres, which encompassed the Harrington Avenue fire station and a small ball field. The ball field, which at one time served as the playground for the children of the Artemus Ward School, was under the jurisdiction of the School Department. Less than an acre in size, it was located on the corner of two busy streets. The fire station bordered one side, and the store property abutted the fourth side. The ball field was used occasionally by young people playing basketball. Because of the heavy traffic at that corner, however, crossing the street to the playground was dangerous for children.

Anthony felt that the basketball players and the children could use a safer location. He also figured that he could use that small parcel of land, the playground, to expand the store and minimize traffic congestion around the store. He believed that his solution would benefit both the store and the town.

The town fathers were talking about moving the fire station to a more central location, so Anthony included the fire station in his initial offer, with the understanding that the town could continue to use it until the new station was ready. He offered $270,000 for 1.3 acres of

[1] A law passed in 1981, Proposition 2 1/2 restricts Massachusetts towns from raising their budgets by more than two and a half percent, unless approved by a majority vote.

335 • The Final Years

land that included both the ball field and fire station property. He later withdrew his bid to buy the fire station, but continued to offer the same amount for the ball field alone. His additional gift of $450,000 was the remainder of the amount the town would need to purchase the land on Maple Avenue. Along with his proposal, Anthony included a request for a zoning variance for an expansion of the store.

Anthony saw his proposal as a win-win situation. However, some of the neighbors in the area thought differently and balked. They expressed their concern about the loss of the recreational land in their neighborhood and the increase in traffic that the expansion of the store might bring. Anthony understood and tried to address their concerns. He added a $50,000 gift to the town for the purchase of land for a playground in a safer area nearby and offered to furnish the necessary equipment. He also explained that the traffic in the area would be reduced because the land he wanted to purchase would provide room for trucking docks on an upper level, away from the pedestrian traffic. Thus, his trucks and trailers would no longer have to enter Baker Avenue. With all the trucking on the upper level it would be safer for pedestrians.

But the neighbors continued to look unfavorably on the proposal, and organized the Committee to Preserve Open Space. When Anthony's proposal was placed on the warrant for a special town meeting on November 9, 1991, his opponents obtained a preliminary injunction in Land Court to prevent the town from holding the meeting. When the injunction expired, the meeting was rescheduled for December 9, 1991. The Committee to Preserve Open Space continued to protest. At the same time, a group of people who were in favor of Anthony's proposal organized the Pro-Land Committee, which cited the benefit of obtaining the Maple Avenue land at "no cost to the taxpayer."[2]

When some people who supported the proposal started to criticize those who were against it, Anthony stopped them, saying, "They have their reasons for doing what they are doing, and they have the right to disagree." He did not bear any ill will toward his opponents. Nevertheless, although he never said so, I think that the opposition to his proposal was a hard pill for him to swallow. He expressed his disappointment by saying, "The hell with it! We've lived 57 years without it. We'll keep going the way we are."

[2] Ellen L. Weingart, "Spag's Plan Tops Agenda." *Telegram and Gazette*, December 6, 1991.

On December 9, the special town meeting came to order. After two hours of debate, the town council members voted 186 to 22 to accept the articles relating to the purchase and the expansion plans as proposed by SPAG'S Supply, Inc. Then the town formally accepted the $450,000 as a gift, added it to the $270,000, and exercised their option to purchased the acreage on Maple Avenue. Without raising taxes, the town of Shrewsbury had acquired 19 1/2 acres of prime land for an athletic field. Anthony's additional gift of $50,000 was turned over to the Parks Department, which subsequently used the money to purchase land on Greylock Avenue and to build a playground.

After the purchase went through, Anthony expanded the store, built loading docks on Harrington Avenue, and thereby reduced traffic in the pedestrian area. The addition was completed in 1993 and the formal opening took place the following year.

The Portrait

Shortly after the satisfactory conclusion to his expansion proposal, Anthony came down with a severe case of shingles. He suffered through the excruciating pain without complaining, believing, as Mother did, that "God doesn't give us any burden we can't carry."

After the shingles subsided and after much persuasion, Anthony agreed to sit for a portrait by Leon Hovsepian, a world-renowned Worcester artist. Anthony was reluctant to spend the time for such an endeavor, but he finally agreed to the request for at least four two-hour sittings in Leon's studio.

For his first sitting, Anthony, wore a dark, navy-blue business suit. Leon, who had known Anthony since he was a teenager, was surprised.

"What's the matter?" Anthony asked.

"It's not you," Leon replied. "People will expect to see you wearing your khakis and hat."

Anthony, who had gone out of his way to please Leon by wearing the suit, was happy to oblige. At the next sitting, he wore his usual garb, including his badge #100, his spiral pad, and colorful, stubby pencils.

"I chose his rusty-colored leather jacket with the thick fleece lining, to provide color contrast and textural differences. I wanted Anthony's clothing to symbolize his earthiness and humility."

During the sittings, Anthony and Leon chatted off and on. In their conversations, they covered many subjects, ranging from sports to moral issues.

"When I asked his opinion on a current controversial subject, euthanasia," recalled Leon, "his response was, 'Oh, no! That's not God's way.' Anthony had a deep, innate gift, the gift of unquestionable faith. He believed that there was one Single Power, and he knew that to be God. All his actions, his sharing, helping, and his self-effacing attitude, reflected his spiritual core, the center of his being. These are the concepts I have epitomized in his portrait."

No Regrets

I was glad that I had persisted in getting Anthony to sit for the portrait, because just a few months later, in 1995, a routine medical checkup revealed that one of his kidneys had failed, and only 40% of

—Jim Tivnan

The portrait, the artist, Leon Hovsepian, and Anthony.

the remaining one was functioning. The prognosis was not good. I saw Anthony wince when he heard the word "dialysis," but when it became necessary, he gracefully accepted the challenge before him and rose to the occasion, saying "You gotta keep going and do what you have to do." He fought hard to live, even when the fight became increasingly difficult.

As Anthony's health declined, he required more staff to care for him. In addition, Jim and I stayed with Anthony in his home during his last two years to keep him company. We were available and wanted to be there with him. I sensed that Anthony derived comfort and a feeling of security from our presence; even more when Jim was there. We knew that he was suffering and in great pain, yet his cheerful manner, although subdued, remained constantly pleasant. We were truly inspired by his patience and extraordinary tolerance of pain.

As usual, Anthony loved to have people drop in to visit him. When anyone called to ask when would it be convenient, he appreciatively responded, "Anytime!" Many came.

One afternoon as I was sitting alone with him, he closed his eyes. I thought he had dozed off, but evidently he was just in a pensive mood. He began to speak.

"You know, Elsa, I have no regrets. I have done everything I intended and planned to do. I had a good partner and a good family. I have many good friends. I have had good health. I have traveled, and I have been able to share my good fortune with others, those who made it all possible. I am content with my life." At the end, as throughout his life, Anthony was at peace with himself and the world.

With his life ebbing away on February 23, 1996, the family and a few close friends gathered around Anthony in the family room. Jim asked Libby, who was busy in the kitchen, to join us. Libby, a devout person, led us in prayer and in singing a hymn.

Then, surrounding Anthony even more closely, we joined hands and recited the Lord's prayer. Just as we concluded with the "Amen," Anthony drew a quick audible breath—his last.

"I have no regrets. I am content with my life"—Anthony.

Tributes to a Legend

...the goodness of man in its purest form.
—Roscoe Blunt

If I could print all the letters I received and the conversations I have had with others about Anthony, they would alone fill an entire book. As it is, I have had to omit more than I wanted to. But I cannot end this book without including just a few more tributes that represent how so many felt about my brother Anthony.

Many people who wrote to me had wonderful things to say about his character:

> What can you say about Spag? He was one of a kind and I do mean "kind" in all concepts of the word. He was always there when you needed him. If I had a real bad day, after talking with Spag even for a few minutes, I felt the world was a wonderful place. Even though I am now retired, I so often think of the "good old days" when all I had to do was to make a call on him and know all would be O.K.
> — Roderick McDonah

> He is and always has been my ideal of the finest, most honorable, most considerate, and most caring individual that I ever met. He was not just a

customer; he was my friend. Please know that as we have these too few years still to go, one thinks of those who have meant so much in this life. For me, it has always been Spag. He is to be admired and truly cared for as epitomizing the best in man.

—Al Gross

More often than not, I thought about Spag and tried to model my company to his. When I had problems, I always said, "Maybe I should call Spag; he will know what to do." Just his phone calls over the years have been a great inspiration. I hope I can turn out to be half the man he was.

—John Creedon

In all the years that I knew him, I never heard him say a bad word about anyone. He was a priceless gem of a man.

—Steve Tankinow

Spag is a real phenomenon. He has been deservedly honored not only in New England trade circles, but nationally as well. On a personal level, he is beloved, admired, and respected for the fair and considerate manner in which he conducts business and treats his employees. His humane and charitable interests bespeak of his character.

—Arthur Reid

He had the courage to be himself in business; that was pretty daring.

— Florence Pickens

He had all the elements of success—himself, Olive, his family, his friends, and his thousands and thousands of customers who appreciated his honesty, his values, his personality, his philanthropies, etc. I feel privileged to have known him.
—Lee Adams

In a brittle business environment, Spag and Olive have not been afraid to be human, nor afraid to trust people.
—Joseph E. Sullivan

Spag always had a smile and a good word for everyone. We are thankful for all the nice things he has done for us and for being our friend.
—Bill and Marion Marsten

The bottom line is that when God created Spag, he threw the mold away. I have never met a person who is so generous, but yet so quiet about his generosity; a person who has such a wonderful sense of humor, but also is a very sensitive man.
—James Coghlin, Sr.

Too bad there are not more people like Spag— what a wonderful world it would be!
—Audrey Furst Dugmore

I called Roscoe Blunt, a retired reporter for the *Telegram and Gazette*, to obtain his permission to include a letter he wrote to Anthony in January 1978. In our conversation, Mr. Blunt said, "I knew Tony [Anthony] when I was an investigative reporter, but I had- n't seen him for many years. In 1978, my home burned down to the ground. I don't know how he did it, but he tracked me down at the Days Lodge in Worcester and said, 'I have a gift certificate for you. I want you to come and get what you need to get going again.' The gift certificate was for several hundred dollars. I bought clothes, saws, hammers, nails, and so on. Elsa, if there is anything I can do to help you to tell the world about this good man, please let me know. I want the world to know how I feel about him."

Here is the letter Roscoe wrote to Anthony in January 1978:

Anthony A. Borgatti Jr.
5 Beverly Road
Shrewsbury, Mass. 01545
Sir:

It is difficult to express the deep gratitude we feel for you, a man of such huge social conscience. You are obviously a man who still believes in the basic elements of life, the basic emotions, the basic needs. It is so refreshing to find someone who has not been carried along by the tides of this modern and complex world with its often plastic moral values.

You seek out people who have suffered the misfortunes that seem to be part of every life. Then you, without fanfare and wanting only the reward of Christian spirit, offer the helping hand that in times of suffering is almost like being touched by the hand of a saint.

When a fire victim is left literally with nothing, your basic instinct is first to offer clothing, warmth, or shelter. If someone was hungry, I am sure you would offer food.

Beyond the clothing to cover us, you offer the materials to take the first step back to normalcy. You pave the way, you smooth out some of the bumps. You literally make a smile wipe away the tears.

To be able to so unselfishly give of yourself is, without a doubt, the goodness of man in its purest form.

Bless you for being the friend to us all that you are.

Roscoe C. Blunt Jr. and Beatrice S. Blunt

After Anthony died, an article written by Dianne Williamson, a newspaper columnist, appeared at the top of the front page of the *Worcester Sunday Telegram* with the title, "Spag's generous spirit touched the lives of many." The article, one of many that were written in Anthony's memory, read:

> It was cold and rainy and I was standing outside, selling roses in front of the big store on Route 9. I was 16, or maybe 17. On weekends, my friends and I worked for a flower guy who would pick us up in the morning at Newton Square, then plant us and his flowers at various locations.
>
> The job was great in the summer, when you could sit in the sun and work on your tan. In the winter, it was miserable. The money was good, though, which is why I found myself freezing to death one December Sunday afternoon in front of the big store on Route 9.
>
> I had been there a couple of hours when a station wagon pulled into the empty parking lot. A man holding two big dogs on a leash got out, said hello, and walked toward the store's entrance.
>
> "It's closed," I told him.
>
> "I know," he said with a smile. He produced a key and disappeared inside with his dogs.
>
> I had pretty much forgotten about the man when he emerged an hour later. In one hand he held the leash; in the other he balanced a cardboard box that he placed hastily on my table as he walked back to his wagon.
>
> "Enjoy," was all he said, tipping the brim of his Stetson in my direction.
>
> Inside the box was a treasure trove of goodies: Pepperidge Farm cookies (Mint Milanos and chocolate chip); two bags of jelly beans; a jar of cashews; a box of crackers, and a wedge of cheddar cheese.
>
> I spent the afternoon selling flowers and snacking. When my boss picked me up, I told him about

the nice guy in the Stetson hat.

"You idiot," he said. "That was Spag."

It was indeed. Every weekend after that, whenever I worked outside his store on a Sunday, Spag would drive up with his dogs and deposit a box of treats on my table. Once, when it was especially cold, he came out with a pair of brand new gloves. We never exchanged more than the most perfunctory small talk, but I always looked forward to his visits.

Years later, when I was a reporter for this newspaper, I covered one of the countless community tributes to his generosity. After the dinner, I introduced myself and told him that I was the flower girl he brought cookies to 10 years before. He smiled and said he remembered me. He didn't, of course.

Stories of his kindness and generosity are legion.... Like when the wife of one of his employees died of cancer. Faced with a big hospital bill, the man was stunned to learn it had been paid by an anonymous source, later discovered to be Spag....

Clearly, the man was a dinosaur. His heart was bigger than his business, his generosity as seamless as the aisles that snaked through his store, his manner as unpretentious as the signature Stetson and trousers he wore throughout his remarkable life.

"It's the end of an era is what it is," Ron Dufault, an employee, said. "The man was part of history. Everyone here is asking themselves, 'What do we do now?'"

Rest in peace, Spag. And thanks for the cookies.

Roasting the Legend

In April, 1979, five years before SPAG'S 50th anniversary celebration, Jim and I received an invitation that read: "Join us when we roast the Legend!" The Worcester Lion's Club, whose motto is "Love, compassion, spirit in action," had chosen Anthony as the "Celebrity Roast" of the year. Irving "Jimmy" Donahue, a long-time friend, was to be the chief roaster. The program booklet, which I found later in Anthony's files, contained a photograph of Anthony and a copy of the "roast." I think it says it all:

Badge #100

Every roaster here tonight in one way or another has expressed the problem: "How can I say anything bad about Spag?" (this roastee). The answer is, of course, one cannot in truth say negative things about tonight's roastee. (He's the one in the ten-gallon hat.) At best, we can only pretend, scratch, and dig for something... anything... to use for a laugh. Talk with some of Mr. Borgatti's friends (and he seems to have more genuine friends than any of us can expect to have), and one comes to one conclusion: tonight we roast a saint. And it's a tricky business.

Roasting Spag is like walking through a minefield. You have to step carefully. Over there are some of the numerous awards he's received: Isaiah Thomas, the Most Prestigious in Central Massachusetts for Community Service...the Worcester Area Association for Retarded Children's 1970 Man of the Year Award... his membership in the select Jimmy Fund Hall of Fame...to name but a few.

Walk further and discover the respect and love held for him by his employees. That's pretty rare today.

Over there, Spag, the humanitarian, the man who shares what he has with scores of worthy causes.

Go on and see his imaginative self-discipline...the integrity that marks all of his dealings (even to the point that Spag is probably one of the few men to whom suppliers have awarded special honors for integrity!).

Continue on and notice everywhere his compassion for others.

And no one deserves more points for humility: "Good fortune, good luck, and good friends have a lot to do with my success. With my family and good luck, I made it." His praise for his good wife, Olive, is boundless.

But as we continue the journey, we manage to find some material for humor: the famous "Cadillac" story...Spag's shoot-from-the-hip language...$35 worth of firecrackers that launched the legend...the free tomato plants...no bags, no checks, no Master Charge, no smoking...and Spag's merchandising philosophy: "I like to see merchandise piled everywhere. It makes people buy. Others watch, and they start to buy. Before long, you've moved a carload!" And one writer's description of his store: "If you see something that interests you, grab it, throw it in the box you've brought along, you may not get the chance to go down the same aisle twice!" The description matches the way Spag deals with others. Knowing he won't be this way again, he's doing a "Spagtacular" job the first time.

Later that evening, as I thought about the "roast" to Anthony, Mother's words came to mind. I could hear her saying, "Anthony is going to accomplish great things, and always his purity is going to radiate from within. You will be proud of him."

And I was.

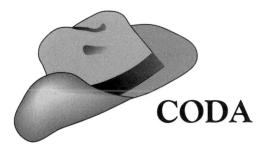

CODA

To this day, people still flock to SPAG'S at 193 Boston Turnpike (Route 9), Shrewsbury. Anthony's daughters—Carol Cullen, Jean Borgatti, and Sandy Travinski—are now the store's owners, and, respectively, president, executive vice president, and treasurer. They continue to follow their father's tradition of "quality merchandise at affordable prices."

Ample parking near the large entrance at the rear of the store provides easy access to the main building, the Tent (in season), Ye Olde School House, the Garden Shop, and the Sport Shop. Bowing to demand, the store now opens on Sunday afternoons and accepts credit cards. Some customers like the changes that have taken place, saying, "It's better than ever!" Others would like the store to stay the way it was forever, but time marches on and changes are inevitable.

Some of these changes have included a SPAG'S website, which, in addition to advertising products, also provides customers with yet another way to share their enthusiasm for shopping at SPAG'S. One self-described "Spagaholic," Mark C. Gargiulo of Goshen, NY, recently e-mailed the following to the store:

> My wife is originally from the Worcester area. SPAG'S is my absolute favorite store. I always must go to SPAG'S as part of my routine when I go to Massachusetts with my wife to visit her family.
>
> I truly am a Spagaholic! I wish we lived closer! Is it true that there is going to be another SPAG'S opening in Springfield, MA? If so, when? I wouldn't want to miss the big opening of such an historic event!

If my wife dies before I do, she wants me to sprinkle her ashes in the parking lots at SPAG'S so she can rest knowing I'd always come to visit her. Thanks for all the great bargains! See you soon.

If Anthony had heard that story, he would have smiled and said, "All customers are welcome at SPAG'S!"